BREAKING THE GAME
WIDE OPEN

BREAKING THE

with Bill Libby

GAME WIDE OPEN

GARY DAVIDSON

NEW YORK   1974   ATHENEUM

Portions of Chapter 14, "Tomorrow the World," first appeared in *The Chicagoan*.

To my wife, BARBARA, *and my children,* ERIC, PETER, JANA, *and* KATIE, *who have had many of the hardships and few of the satisfactions of a father who has been busy in business in recent years.*

GARY DAVIDSON

The authors wish to thank Matt Merola and Paul Goetz of Mattgo Enterprises and Marvin Brown of Atheneum Publishers, who made this project a reality; Don Regan and Dennis Murphy, who were so fundamental a part of the subject's sporting ventures; and all the presidents, commissioners, franchise owners, coaches, players, publicists, lawyers, and agents who contributed to this book in one way or another, as well as all the writers who wrote about the leagues and thus contributed to the fund of information that went into this book.

Finally, the authors wish to thank all the photographers represented in the volume.

BILL LIBBY AND GARY DAVIDSON

CONTENTS

ILLUSTRATIONS

follow page 140

BREAKING THE GAME
WIDE OPEN

CHAPTER 1

A Life of High Stakes and High Risks

He looks like a surfer. He is close to forty, but he looks ten years younger. He is short and husky and his skin is sun-tanned and his hair is sun-bleached blond and it falls loosely across his forehead. Hs is a good-looking young man, southern California style, short of being Hollywood handsome. He has good features and blue eyes that move over you fast, sizing you up. Everything about him is fast. He moves in and out of his office fast. Friends and associates are always popping in and out of the office fast. Sometimes on business. Sometimes to arrange a tennis match or a basketball game. It seems like someone is always coming in to arrange a match or a game. He tried golf, but he didn't like it because it was too slow. So he plays tennis, which is faster. And basketball, which is faster and rougher. He likes to sweat and stay in shape. He weighs 165 pounds and worries if he takes on five pounds more. He makes a religion of keeping in shape.

He gets hurt a lot, but it doesn't bother him. He broke an arm playing basketball and had his arm in a cast when he was spotlighted in ceremonies and meetings in which the formation of the American Basketball Association was announced. He wore his cast as if it was a medal of honor and now remembers it affectionately, as if it was a funny thing that typified him, which, in a way, it did. He has sponsored and played on a team in an amateur league in Orange County, California, for many years, and he laughs and says they'll take on any team of lawyers in the country. Only the biggest of his business deals interferes with his basketball schedule. Only major meetings take him away from a tennis match in the evening after work or on weekends. When he takes vacations with his wife Barbie and his four kids, he likes to go skiing or takes tennis vacations. But he doesn't take as much time off for vacations anymore. He wants to work.

His work is sports, and it has become his life. It has taken him away from his wife and his kids and hurt his family life and threatened his marriage. He is sorry about that, but that is the way it is. His wife says, "I love him and he loves us, but his work comes first, before us. It works a hardship on our marriage. I think our marriage will survive. We both want it to work. But he wants his work more than anything, and he is willing to risk everything else for it. At first, he used to take me along on business trips. Now there are too many trips and he doesn't have time to fit me in. He is just moving too fast now, spread too thin. I worry about him and I worry about us."

Gary Davidson sits restlessly in his swivel chair in his office and he smiles and he says, "I worry too, but not too often because I just don't have the time anymore." He speaks with a nasal twang and a slight lisp. It used to be worse, but he has worked hard to overcome it. He is not as articulate as you might expect him to be, considering what he has accomplished, and he knows it. It is one of the things that worries him, because he knows he is intelligent and sharp and has good ideas and can make ideas work and is good at finding solutions to problems. It concerns him that he may not be able to communicate this properly. But he just works at improving himself—he is always working at improving himself —and he tries not to think about it too much.

Gary hates to lose. He is very competitive. The challenge is what counts with him. He is always getting involved in one new project or another and making it work and hopefully making money out of it and then moving on to another new project. He could stand pat and reap rich rewards from some of his ventures, but once they are working, he wants to move on to new ventures. He wants to make more money, but in something else. "The money matters, but the challenge counts the most," he says. "Every project I make work, it's like winning." He grins.

He has been winning lately. He has been winning, and everything he touches has been turning to gold. He was the first president of the American Basketball Association and the World Hockey Association, and now he is the first president of the World Football League, which he formed. Dennis Murphy and some others dreamed up the basketball league, but Gary got in on it at the beginning and they became buddies. Dennis dreamed up the hockey league, but Gary formed it with him and made it work. And the football league was Gary's baby from the first. These were all rebel leagues, coming along in competition with established, powerful, and almost monopolistic circuits, and bucking them was a daring idea and surviving the bitter and costly wars a triumph of imagination and determination. He started with nothing, and he made a little bit out of the basketball and a lot out of the hockey, and he hopes to make much more out of football. "It would mean a great deal to make a million," he says with a grin, "but now that I know I may make more it doesn't mean that much to me. It's coming through that counts. It's winning, almost any way you can, that means the most. It's going into the jungle and surviving."

At this time he had just got the hockey league going. The football league was yet in front of him. His office was starting to fill up with framed photos of himself with hockey players and the owners of hockey teams and plaques reproducing newspaper headlines and stories about him and his WHA. There was an enormous picture blow-up of the one-million-dollar check given Bobby Hull as a bonus that brought the sport's most explosive scorer and most exciting personality from the old, established league into Gary's new, rebel league, which, as much as any single thing, made the new league believable to the players and the public and hoisted it over the hump. On a counter is a framed check for $10,000. Gary picks it up and smiles. "It's from the Miami Screaming Eagles for a franchise in the World Hockey Association. It bounced," he beams, proud of the problems he has overcome. In one corner is a red, white, and blue basketball, symbolic of the ABA, which people laughed at in the beginning but which worked to give the circuit an identity.

In the beginning, Gary didn't like the idea of the red, white, and blue basketball, but now he says he was wrong because it worked for the league. He has made mistakes and is not afraid to admit to them. He is an honest sort, incredibly candid for a person in his position of power.

He doesn't pretend to be one of nature's noblemen, an altruistic sort whose sole aim in life is to enrich the lives of others. Forming his leagues and making them work has provided jobs and increased salaries for players, coaches, managers, referees, executives, and team and arena personnel, and has brought an imitation of big-time sports to some fans in some cities that could not enjoy them before, but he smiles and shrugs and confesses that these were just things which happened because the leagues happened, they were not the reasons he wanted his happenings to take place. "I went into these ventures because I saw them as good business opportunities," he says. "Others see them the same way and have been willing to participate with me. Many people didn't want to go into them, so they didn't. Enough did to make them work. And there are always more ready to move in for those who move out. I can't speak for the motives of all these men. I was motivated by the chance to do something for myself. I could see the advantages. If the league worked, fine, that was a plus, but it wasn't what drove me."

What does drive him? What makes Gary run? He considers this a moment, tilting back in his chair, his eyes on the ceiling, as if he could see through it to the stars. "I wanted to succeed, I guess. Just making it, that's the thing. I come from a broken family. I had little. At times, I ran with tough gangs, and I could have come to a bad end. But I had brains and a sort of desire to make something of myself, and I was willing to work. It's all out there for anyone who wants to go after it. Maybe because I had less, I wanted more than the next guy. I studied hard to give myself the tools to build a good future.

"I went into something that was dull and didn't have a future. So I looked around to see what people did that was the most interesting and made the most money and decided they were stockbrokers or lawyers. I decided to be a lawyer, so I became a lawyer. But it wasn't enough. Much of law is dull. Chance put me into sports, and when I found out it was anything but dull I fell in love with it. I was in one sport, then another. After I get this one going, I'll go into another one. I won't stay in sports forever. Eventually, I'll try something else.

"I've thought a lot about politics. I'm a liberal Republican.

7

At one time I thought I should get into politics on the local level. Now, it's too late for that. I can't settle for that now. Maybe some day I'll run for Congress. Perhaps the Senate. Maybe in 1976. I'm not good at detailed administrative duties. But I'm good at seeing the overall picture, at seeing how things should fit together, at recognizing problems and finding solutions and making things work. Probably I'm best at organizing.

"Right now I'm tied up in sports. I'm a lawyer, but I don't practice law anymore except as it assists me with the leagues. My firm represents the leagues. My partner, Don Regan, is involved with the leagues. He supervises most of the legal work for our leagues. He's in the background and I'm up front, but he's part of everything. We work together. We're very close. The firm does other legal work and does it well, but sports has become our biggest business. I have other businesses. I'm co-chairman of General Residential Corporation, which builds retirement homes. I'm president of Mammoth Sports, Incorporated, which is a leisure-land recreational development company. I'm chairman of SIS Temporary Services, Incorporated, which provides part-time help. I'm president and a trustee of California Real Estate Trust. I'm spread pretty thin, which drives some of my hockey men up a wall. They want to get me out so they can get in." He laughs.

The phone keeps ringing. Secretaries keep moving in and out with this paper to sign or that question to be answered. Associates keep dropping in and out with this bit of business or that bit to discuss. He answers questions quickly. He makes fast decisions. He signs swiftly. He is for this or against that. He doesn't waste time. At first you wonder how he can make it all work. He seems too young. He's dressed too casually. You figure it's a freak. But soon you see it. You see he's a man with ideas. They pour from him. His mind doesn't stop. He's a man who can make up his mind.

"Oh, hell, a lot of it's luck," he says. "But a lot of it's being tough, too. The stakes are high. The risks are high. Men invest millions in sports. Why do they do it? They want to own teams. It's a tremendous attraction to men who are attracted to sports. They get hooked on it. Some guys go for gals. Some go for dough. And some men want to own sports teams. It puts you in a position of power. Power's a tremendous narcotic. I want it, too. It's one of the things I enjoy. I'm a leader. I'm out front. It's one of the things I enjoy in life. I'd be a liar if I didn't admit it.

"I don't talk people into going into my leagues. I attempt to lay it all out for them, the great risks and the potential profits, the pleasure and excitement, the headaches and heartbreaks they may get. I don't candy-coat my product. I don't sweet-talk people. I tell them what the opportunities are. I tell them what it'll cost them. If they can't afford it, they shouldn't go into it. It's a roll of the dice. It's a gamble. A good gamble, but a gamble. If they want to play, fine. They put up their money and roll the dice.

"As a business, it's a questionable investment. Most of these men could go into a thousand other things that would bring them a good return without the risk. But they wouldn't have half the enjoyment. And the thing is, the history of professional sports for some years now is that no matter how much money you lose operating a team, you can usually get it back and turn a profit selling the team later. You can't do that with losers in other businesses. It's not guaranteed, but most franchises appreciate. I don't know why. In recent years, rising television money has accounted for a lot of it. But it seems to come down to the fact that there's almost always someone else who wants to own a team badly enough to meet the increase in price. Some are frustrated jocks. Some merely want to be a part of the scene, to be in charge of a club and associate with superstars. I can understand that most people want to be where there is action.

"They want to make money, but if that was the main motivation they'd go into something else. But at the base of it, these guys are businessmen. They made a bundle doing something, and they all think they can make a team work better than the next guy. They don't all understand that sports is a very special business and what works in some other business may not work in sports. Good business methods will work. But if your team doesn't work, the business will go bust. You can try, but you can't always buy the best players or the smartest coach. And some teams lose with good players. The chemistry that makes a team succeed is elusive. If anyone knew what it was, he'd bottle it and make a fortune. And if the league doesn't work, the teams don't work.

"To a great extent, when owners take a team and roll the dice, they're gambling on me, because I'm the person that has to make the league work. And it's tough. They make it tougher. Everyone wants something else from you. They won't let you do your job. Individuals I've counted on have betrayed me and bailed out. Not everyone has the guts to go the distance. They say they do, but they don't. So I find someone else."

He shakes his head wistfully and says, "I found out early what money means. Money men respect money, and they respect men with money. They'll listen to guys with money, and they won't listen to guys without money. They can hire the best brains in the world to work for them, and they won't listen to them because they're working for them. You have to be able to deal with owners as an equal. As a partner, not an employee. Money gives you clout. Money makes you seem smart. I guess they figure if you made it for yourself you must know how to make it for them.

10

"I didn't make much from the basketball, so I didn't move any mountains. But I'm making it in hockey, and I'm beginning to make things move. It's corny, but I thrive on challenges. I like competition. It took guts to go up against the powerful professional leagues, and it's been tremendously satisfying to succeed where most people felt we had no chance. It hasn't been smooth sailing. It's been rough out there. A lot of it has been laughable. Silly things have happened. I've made mistakes. Others have made more mistakes. It takes a lot of guts and a lot of luck.

"My life has become a series of adventures," he says. "It's exciting. I'm not doing anything someone else couldn't do. But I'm doing it. Others could have formed leagues, but they didn't. Some did, but couldn't make them work. We have established a formula. It's not that hard if you're willing to work hard. If you've got ideas and the guts to go all the way with them. I've learned some lessons the hard way. I've become a specialist at starting sports leagues. I know where to find most of the pieces. I know how to fit them together and with a little luck the leagues will succeed.

I think there was a lot in my background that drove me down the road I've taken, though, as I've said, it was sheer chance that got me into professional sports.

I was born Gary Lynn Davidson in Missoula, Montana, on August 13, 1934. My parents separated and divorced when I was a few months old. My father's name was Truman Ross Davidson. He was called "Cutty." He had been a good baseball pitcher. He was offered a tryout by the New York Yankees, but he cut off the tips of his pitching fingers in a canning factory accident before the tryout. That was that. He was a foreman in a sugar-beet cannery when I was born. Later, he was a farmer in southern Idaho. But I didn't meet him until about the time I was starting high school, and I really didn't get to know him until I left college.

I never did know him well. I never got close to him. It was too late. He could see that. But he was proud of me, I know that. I remember when I bought a fairly nice house and had him out, he said, "I wish I had more friends, so I could brag about your house." He was lonely by then. However, he had remarried and his new wife had children. He had a son by a wife before my mother. My half-brother's name is Truman Davidson, and I hardly know him. One of my father's stepsons is going to college at Brigham Young University. He's a good student and I've helped him some financially.

My father was a very nice person. I liked him, as much as I knew him. He died in his sixties in 1972, oddly enough on the day the World Hockey Association opened play in Quebec City. I received a telephone call at the airport there telling me of his death. It shocked me and left me sad that we'd had so little time together. I'm sorry he never was a father to me.

My mother, Estella, was married to a number of men. She was married to a man named Barney Glennon when I was growing up, and for a while I went by his last name, but he never adopted me, and when I went into the sixth grade I began to go by my original name, Davidson. I don't really remember why. Maybe I just wanted to go back to my own identity. Maybe I didn't feel that close to him. He treated me all right. She's married again now, and she works for me. She wants to work. Her husband would support her, I'm sure. If she wasn't married to him, I would. But she's always been an independent woman who wants to go her own way.

I have another half-brother, Bob Littell, on my mother's side, and I was more or less raised with him. He was born in

July of 1931, and is three years older than I am. We fought a lot, but we were close at times, especially after Mom broke up wtih Glennon and there were just the three of us. However, Bob and I had different friends and different interests and wound up going our different ways. He did help me in many ways over the years. He's an engineer here in southern California now, but we don't see each other a lot.

My mom treated me well, but we moved too often. She moved to be with the men she married and to get new jobs. We moved from Missoula, Montana, to Long Beach and Compton in California, to Gold Hill, Oregon, and back to Compton, Corona, Garden Grove, and Santa Ana here in southern California, around the Los Angeles area. Mom always worked, and after I was old enough I always worked.

After I was graduated from grammar school, Mom promised I could stay in one school all the way through high school. We knew we were moving to Garden Grove, so I started to go to Garden Grove High School when I was living 38 miles away in Corona. She'd drive me in every morning and drive me home every night. She was working in a grocery store which was a few blocks from my first law office in Santa Ana. The store has been torn down, but I can see the spot from my office window. Nothing was too good for me within the limits of what she had. She didn't have a whole lot, but she tried to spoil me. I didn't want that much from her. I wanted to get things for myself. For a while there, I went about it in the wrong way.

I went wrong in Compton, which is a tough town just outside of L.A. There were a lot of fights among the gangs there and I was in some of them. I didn't have much of a life at home, and I was running wild on the streets. We used to shoplift, though I never got caught. I guess I just didn't have any sense of responsibility at the time. I was on my own, making out as best I could.

One time some of the guys wanted to break into a school. I had figured out how to do it and I told them to go down before dawn on Thanksgiving morning, when no one would be around, unscrew the back door off the hinges, take some sports stuff from the storeroom, and screw the door back on and get away. I figured no one would know anything was gone for a while and no one would even know anyone had broken in until they took inventory. Well, they went down at ten in the morning on a Saturday. They just broke the door down, and they were caught.

Fortunately, I wasn't with them. I did what I had to do to get along with the guys. But the guys blew the whistle on me. School officials and police couldn't do anything to me because I wasn't with the others and they couldn't prove I'd been the brains of the deal they loused up. But we were in junior high school at the time, and the principal told everyone in the school no one should associate with me because I was a bad influence. That brought me up short and made me take a hard look at myself and the way I was headed. When I was in high school we had a gang that shoplifted stores all over Santa Ana, stealing things right and left, but I began to hear rumors about it, word got around who was involved, and I decided to drop out of the gang before I got caught.

I was smart enough to see I was headed down a rough road and better reverse directions before I messed up my life. I knew I had enough on the ball to do something decent. I'm basically an honest person. Today, I wouldn't cheat anyone of a dime. I behave honorably. I believe in treating people fairly. I have to hustle in business. I'm competitive in business. I make enemies. But I don't think anyone I've done business with would say I'm not honest or honorable. It was just that I was growing up with kids who didn't have much, much less a code of honor, and I wanted to be well liked, so I sometimes went along with the gang. I think most of us do things as kids we regret doing and wouldn't do as adults.

I was lucky. I saw my chance and took it. I had noticed that the way to be recognized in school was through studies or sports, so I began to bear down on both. I was really hungry for recognition. I wanted to be someone special. I concentrated on my studies and I got good grades. I had to work at it. Some guys could float. I couldn't.

I liked to read, and I was willing to spend time at my studies. I saw that the best people were in the scholarship society, and I wanted to be with the best. I made it. I went out for all the teams and I did well. I ran the quarter-mile in track, played second base on the baseball team, played guard on the basketball team, and quarterbacked the football team. I was not a fast runner, but I had fast hands. I could field and had pretty good timing at bat. I could handle the ball and was a good shooter and led the basketball team in scoring. I could pass pretty well in football. I had a sixth sense for where the action was. I didn't have the talent to be a star at a top college. I probably could have made the team at UCLA, but I'd have been, say, third string. But I really loved sports, and once I got into them they kept me out of trouble.

I wasn't a natural anything, but I worked at developing myself until I got good at everything I went into. I've had a lot of arguments with my wife about this because she doesn't buy my self-improvement program. She's super at a lot of things, but she's content to do a lot of things poorly. She plays tennis, but she's not so hung up on it she wants to work eight hours a day at it until she's the player she could be. It's just fun for her. Well, that's fine, but I can't stand it. I keep bugging her to go at it harder, and she gets annoyed about it. I'm always wanting her to work at this thing or that thing until she masters it, and she just doesn't care that much about some things. We're just different in this way, and our life would be a lot more laughs if I could just do things my way and let her do things her way, but it goes against my grain, it rubs me wrong, and I keep irritating her about it.

I'm by nature an organizer. I'm always getting into something, and I always have to be the leader. That's not the best way to be, but it's my way and it's paid off for me. I used to sell programs at Compton College sports events, and I organized it until it was really a paying proposition. I'd organize teams to play other teams. Then I'd get teams together and organize leagues. I was doing that in high school and college, which I guess was a sign of things to come for me.

Some guys are natural leaders. They have a personality and a chemistry that causes other guys to look up to them and believe in them. They're always president of this and captain of that. Later on, they often become successful at something, say coaching. Maybe they're not as smart as other coaches, but they are able to sell themselves and their system to their players better than other coaches. Well, I didn't start with this type of personality and this chemistry, but I wanted to be a leader and I was willing to work at it so hard that I became one.

I talk so fast that I slur my words. I remember when I was in Garden Grove High School and I was supposed to represent my school at some function but the advisors wouldn't send me because I didn't speak well enough. That hurt. I think I lost a couple of elections because my image wasn't better and I've never forgotten it. But I didn't let it discourage me. It only increased my determination.

After high school, I went to Redlands College on a scholarship. However, I stayed there only one semester and then gave up the scholarship. It was a small school and I didn't know anyone there and I was unhappy. It was good for me in one way. I roomed with a fellow named Hal Himmelbauer, who, despite that name, spoke well and was able to help me start to speak better. He was interested enough to want to help and I wanted help enough to take it.

Later on, my wife took over. She helped me and she still corrects me when she hears me start to slur or pronounce a word incorrectly. I want her to and I work at it. For a while I used a tape recorder and I'd record myself talking or giving speeches and I'd play it back and listen to it and correct myself and try again and again until I felt I had it right. I'm not there yet, but I'm getting there. I'm not so self-conscious about it now, because I've got something behind me. I have a track record of success, and I know now people are inclined to listen to what I say.

I was turned off by Redlands, not by college. I went to Orange Coast Junior College in Costa Mesa the next semester. I wanted to play baseball, but I thought I was a second baseman and they had the best second baseman in the state playing first team for them, so I quit the school after that semester. I could have played another position, but I was stubborn. I was a good student, but I didn't know what I wanted to study. I didn't know what I wanted to do with my life.

The next year I enrolled at Long Beach City College and tried out for baseball. But I hurt my leg, which ended any dreams I had of making something of myself as a baseball player. By this time I was supporting myself.

I worked as soon as I was old enough. I was a box boy in a grocery market in high school. Then I went to work on a construction gang for $110 a month. I laid pipe and dug ditches. For awhile, I helped a plumber. My job was to lie on my back and chip cement off the bottom of foundations. You might say I started at the bottom. Later, I did sheet-metal work. I helped a pattern-maker. We made molds. I remember, he said, "Gary, if you stop screwing around and quit

17

school and come into this full time, it'd be a good job for you." It wasn't what I wanted, but maybe I was wrong. Those guys make good dough.

One day I went to pick up a girl who was going to school at UCLA. I walked across the campus at twilight. It was really beautiful. I was impressed. I applied there the next day and was accepted. And here I was happy. Here I finally settled in. I met the girl I would marry here. And I made a lot of friends.

I joined the Beta Theta Pi fraternity house at UCLA, and it was a great house which had a great influence on me. The Betas had some super athletes and some young men of great wealth and social standing. I could say, "Hey, I'm a Beta," and I felt it gave me stature. I felt accepted. It was important to me. More then than it would be now. Now I'd rather be admired for accomplishments than for my social standing and influential friends, but then I was a poor kid from a broken home, who had never lived in nice homes or had nice clothes or much money, whose working mother made maybe at most $400 a month, and who had supported himself with common labor, and it was something to be a Beta.

I majored in political science. It was at UCLA that I began to broaden and meet people from all kinds of cultures and backgrounds. I earned good grades there and graduated easily enough, in 1958, but I really didn't know how to use what I'd learned.

I tried to go into the Army, figuring I had to go in sooner or later, but they wouldn't take me because I had a deviated septum. It's funny, but I went down with a fraternity brother who'd been working as a lifeguard. It seemed to us we were the only two guys in the group really in good physical condition, and we wound up the only two guys they classified as 4-F and wouldn't take.

I went to work for Pacific Mutual Life Insurance Company, but when I found out the guy ahead of me was making $9,000 a year after working there twelve years I figured this wasn't for me. I pulled myself up short. I looked around trying to figure out who was making the most money, doing the most interesting things in their work, and having the most fun in their lives, and I felt they were the stockbrokers and lawyers. The law interested me. So I made a decision and applied for admission to UCLA's law school and was accepted.

I worked part time at the Armstrong Mortuary in Downtown L.A. to support myself. It may sound funny, but it was a fine job. I went to school by day and worked by night and slept in-between. I sat in an office and studied, and when I got a call I went out and picked up dead bodies. It got me through the year. The second year I got married and went to work in a law office as a clerk. It wasn't so much that it was a better job, but it was another way of learning law. I worked there two years. After I graduated from law school in 1961 I was twenty-six. I tried again to get in the Army, in the judge advocate's office, but they wouldn't take me until I passed my bar exam, so I said screw them, and I went on my way and never went into service. I passed the bar exam that year.

I had a few offers. Mainly, I had to decide whether I wanted to practice in L.A. or Orange County. I knew I wanted to stay in southern California. This was home to me and to my wife and as far as we knew the finest way of life we could find, so why not? I decided opportunities were more open in Orange County and it was my home, so I went that way. As far as I could see it wasn't as important to come from a wealthy family or make a mark in a large firm as it was in L.A., and a young guy was pretty much able to make a name for himself based on what he accomplished in Orange County, which was growing fast.

First, I joined the Schlegel and Friedemann firm. They had just left the district attorney's office and had a lot of trial experience, but they were going into real estate and wanted someone interested in business and tax law, so I said, fine, I'll do corporate and tax work and that sort of thing, which most young guys usually aren't that interested in, but which interested me.

I practiced with them two to three years, and I became especially interested in the business side of things. I didn't want to just be an attorney representing different companies, but I wanted to participate in them and in new projects which were being developed. I decided to form my own firm. I had wanted to, all along. At UCLA I had become especially close to Don Regan. We played fraternity ball and intramural ball against and with each other. It's amazing how many future associates I met this way. After school, he suggested we get together, but I had just joined my first firm and didn't think it would be wise to leave right off. Then he had just joined a firm and thought he shouldn't leave, so I formed Fairbairn, Davidson and Fenton with two other fellows in the city of Orange, but it wasn't with them the way I felt it would be with Don. When he became available we went in with Pat Nagel and formed Nagel, Regan and Davidson in Santa Ana.

I ought to say right now that it would be difficult for two men to be closer than Don and I. We work together and we play together. We share everything except our wives and kids, and our families are close. Don and I complement each other perfectly. He has qualities I don't have and I have qualities he doesn't have. He's a detail man, for example, which I'm not. He's fantastically efficient. His mind is very quick. Yet he doesn't hold up deals because this little thing isn't just the way it might be or that thing isn't just right, the way some lawyers do. He is a doer. But he doesn't like being out front. Oh, he may envy me some of the spotlight. We kid each other about these things. We don't agree on everything. We argue about a lot of things. But we reach decisions between us and we go into everything together and we share everything equally, and it's been that way from the first day we got together.

Our firm does other business. We have a number of associates with us. And Pat Nagel takes care of other business, especially in the labor field. He's an outstanding attorney in the field of labor negotiations, and he has supervised our negotiations with players' groups and such in our sports leagues, but otherwise he has been our partner in our law office, not in our sports business. Our firm represented the American Basketball Association and still represents the World Hockey Association, and it now represents the World Football League, the International Track Association, and World Team Tennis. Don Regan has been chief counsel for each of these as well as my partner in every way and a participant right down the line in my sports ventures.

We were buddies in law school, both married and both broke with kids coming. I'm more of a gambler than he is. I can see the long-range perspective better. I happened to see an ad that offered an opportunity to get into the commodities market and he wasn't so sure of it, but I was all for it and talked him into it. We borrowed $125 each from friends and I invested the $250 and we ran it into $15,000, which was enough to live on and move into homes in Orange County until we were through with school, and it left us with $3,000 over. We reinvested that and we lost it in about a week, and we never went back into that market.

We were so broke in those days we couldn't afford the dollar a night it cost to get into the Santa Ana YMCA to play basketball, so one of us would sneak over the back fence and into the building and open a side door to let the other guy in. We owe the Y a few bucks, but we're still playing basketball one place or another or tennis together when we're not putting together business deals.

Our first business venture after we got together in 1965 was a Mexican restaurant we bought in Santa Ana. It had super food and still does. But the day we opened as owners we found out the previous owner hadn't paid his taxes and we had to pay them. We wound up broke again and had to sell the place.

We got together and backed a subcontractor in the painting industry. He went broke. So did we. And we were 0-fortwo. We finally got a hit with the American Basketball Association, and we've been batting over .500 percent ever since. And Don is as much responsible as I am. This book is about me, not Don, but let it be understood from the first that he has been behind me—with me, really—in all the leagues and all the ventures ever since, and we divide the profits and losses equally.

Another person who has been behind me and with me in everything for a long time now is my wife, Barbie. She was Barbara Jane Dapper when I met her at UCLA. She was a cheerleader—a pompom girl—and she became head cheerleader. She was and still is a very pretty, bouncy gal. And very bright. She majored in education and taught grammar school for two years after graduation. We met when I was being rushed by the Beta house. She was interested in one of the guys in the group. I got her interested in me. We went out together for four years. I pinned her, got engaged to her, and finally married her on August 29, 1960, after my first year in law school. Our first child, Eric Kenneth, was born in September of 1961. After him came Peter James in May of 1963, Jane Ann, whom we call Jana, in October of 1964, and Katherine, whom we call Katie, in September of 1969.

Our first home was in San Clemente. Then we bought the

house we're now living in, in 1967, on Emerald Bay in Laguna Beach. I guess it doesn't matter where you live, so long as you are happy. And Barbie and I have been happy in Laguna Beach. It's a quiet, peaceful, pretty place. We like it there— we're just not together often enough.

We've been able to enjoy our money some. We don't have expensive tastes. I don't have to have my own jet or a boat. I like sports cars. I like nice clothes. I like fine wine. But I don't dress up much; I'm more a casual sort of character. I don't drink much, and I'm not much for parties. Barbie likes nice clothes and she likes parties, and it's not much fun for her to go to get-togethers without me, and ever since I began in basketball she's been without me a lot. I'm just always on the go.

I used to get a kick out of traveling to the big cities, going first class, staying in top hotels, eating at the best restaurants, dealing with important people, and I used to take Barbie with me. But I go too often now and she can't be away from the kids as much now that they're growing up, and so she stays home a lot and it's not as much fun for either of us. I fly in fast and fly out fast. I've been there before— I've done it all and seen most of it.

I find it hard to relax now. I find it hard to sleep now. I always have some business deal turning over in my mind, or problems I have to figure a way out of. These deals don't put themselves together. There's always a thousand loose ends to be pulled into place.

I like to get away when I can. There are tennis resorts we go to in Palm Springs, Mexico, and Hawaii. And I like to go skiing in the mountains in Colorado. We've taken the kids a lot, but lately Barbie and I have been going sometimes by ourselves to try to pull ourselves together. I have to admit my business life has pulled Barbie and me apart, and there were times when our marriage appeared to be going down the drain. She wants friends and a social life. She wants to be a part of my life. But it's changing too often, moving too fast, and I can't bring her into my business that much.

It's the same with my kids. I love them and want to be with them whenever they want me or need me, but I just can't be with them as much as I should. I'm not really cut out to be a suburban-type father. I could say I'm doing what I do for them. And to some extent, I am. I want to be a success in the eyes of my family, and I want to be able to give my family the best possible life. But I do what I do for myself, because it's what I want to do. And what I do has worked a real hardship on my marriage and my family life, and I've been hanging on to them with both hands and, the last year or two, hoping to hold everything together.

I'm not asking for sympathy. I've got a lot more out of life already than most guys will all their lives. If I've risked things that are important to me for it, well, no one pushed me down the path I've taken. It was the way I wanted to go.

BASKETBALL

CHAPTER 2

As Gary Davidson Sees It, I

I didn't exactly choose it. It chose me. I didn't dream up the idea of bouncing into basketball. Dennis Murphy did. The smiling Irishman is another important part of my story. He's another guy who's become close to me and with whom I've become partners in various ventures. The little round guy has a big imagination, and he's a dreamer. But he's needed someone like me to make dreams come true, to turn visions into reality. Murph can start a helluva deal and I can close a deal. That's my strength. He's a personality guy. He can gather prospective owners. He can get them interested in a dream. I can get their signatures on contracts and get them to take each other's hands and form a partnership. I turn a group of guys into a project. I'm a dreamer, too. But I'm also a closer. That's my true strength.

Dennis dreamed up the basketball, and I helped him turn his dream into a real league. He dreamed up the hockey, and I turned that into a real league, with his help and the help of others. Football is my dream, and I'm turning that into a reality, with the help of others.

Dennis brought John McShane into his basketball venture. John McShane brought Roland Speth into it. Roland brought me into it. Roland was working for McShane in public relations. Roland had an office in the same Orange City building that Don and I did. He was putting out a golf magazine at the the time. I got to know him. He knew I liked sports. He figured me for a sharp attorney. He figured me for a guy who might go for a gamble to make some money. One day he walked across the hall and told me he was throwing in with a group who were going to start a new professional basketball league and he wondered if I would be interested. I said right off I thought I might be. I didn't even give it that much thought. If I had, I might not have gone into it. If I'd investigated it as thoroughly as I should have, I might have passed. If I knew what sort of idiocy I was getting involved in, I'd have said thanks, but no thanks. But I liked the idea right off. And it worked, which is a wonder. And while it didn't pay off that much for me, personally, it led to things which have paid off and will pay off.

So, a guy I hardly knew decided on a whim to stroll across the corridor and invite me into a wild idea, and it turned my life topsy-turvy, brought me recognition, and brought me some wealth. It was just that casual, just that simple.

There usually has been a key man in the formation of every major venture. I was not the key man in the formation of the American Basketball Association, but I was a key man in the formation of the World Hockey Association and the World Football League. I was the first president of each of the three new leagues.

There were many persons involved with the formation of each league, and if I forget one here and there I'm sorry, but I'll try to give credit where it is due.

28

Dennis Murphy was seeking an American Football League franchise for Anaheim Stadium, home of baseball's California Angels and a key Orange County community. When the AFL merged with the National Football League in 1966, the idea suddenly went down the drain. The Los Angeles Rams of the NFL were ready to exercise their territorial rights to keep out of any team within its area, which included Anaheim.

Disappointed, Dennis decided to set his sights elsewhere. He figured it would be a waste to have gone through the experience and then just disband. He was excited at the prospect of getting into sports, and he looked around for another avenue. The success of the AFL in forcing a merger with the NFL in just six seasons made him think of starting a new basketball league. The Los Angeles Lakers had territorial rights in the National Basketball Association, so he couldn't hope to get an NBA team into Anaheim, but he could try to start a new league with a team in Anaheim which could force a merger with the NBA.

People call new leagues "rebel leagues" and term their leaders "invaders" who are trying to tap into a good thing an established league has going for it, but this is normal business practice. No one is entitled to a monopoly in business, and major-league sports is big business. Once one oil company went into business to offer fuel to the motoring public, others came into competition. If there is a gas station profiting on a busy corner, a rival opens up across the street. If a department store does big business in one shopping center, another moves into another center nearby.

As soon as I was invited into the new basketball project, I realized professional sports had a history of competition between new and old leagues.

Baseball's National League was formed in the late 1800s with several franchises which were to become members of the American League. Some teams withdrew and formed the

American Association, which folded fast, with some of its teams absorbed back into the National League. The Western Association, a minor league, was reorganized, renamed the American League, and went into competition with the National League as a major league in 1901. Two years later, it achieved a merger with the National League. Later, the Federal League moved up from minor to major status and competed with the National and American League, but it failed, though some of its members went into the established league at the time.

In the 1950s, men who had been unable to obtain major-league franchises formed the Continental League. It never got off the ground, but the threat of it forced expansion which brought some of the Continental League members into baseball's major leagues. Bill Shea, Shea Stadium, and the New York Mets are among those who became part of baseball's major leagues as a result of the formation of the Continental League. Jack Kent Cooke, who became a member of the establishment in the National Basketball Association, the National Hockey League, and the National Football League, may resent intrusions onto his territory by the ABA, WHA, and WFL, but he never has been abusive about it, no doubt because he was a member of the Continental League group, proprietor of the prospective Toronto franchise.

It would be difficult for representatives of the Cleveland Browns and San Francisco 49ers to complain about the formation of the WFL, since they were members of the All-American Football Conference, which came into existence to compete with the NFL in 1946 and were brought into the NFL in 1950, when the AAC folded. The Baltimore Colts and New York Jets really are outgrowths of AAC teams in Baltimore and New York, too, although those franchises folded. Baltimore did play a season in the NFL after the AAC folded. And then, of course, most of the teams in the

American Conference of the NFL now are from the American Football League, which merged with the NFL in 1966 and lost its identity in 1967. It might be remembered that Miami, now the dominant team in the NFL, had a franchise in the old AAC, as did Buffalo.

In pro basketball, the American Basketball League operated from the mid-1920s until the Basketball Association of America was formed in 1946. The National Basketball League had been operating since 1937 and was drawn into a war. In 1948 the BAA badly hurt the NBL by stealing away four of its franchises, including the Minneapolis team, which had the sport's greatest star, George Mikan. The others were Rochester, Indianapolis, and Fort Wayne. Rochester was the NBL champion. A year later, the two leagues merged into the National Basketball Association. It is not really fair for the franchise holders in New York, Boston, Philadelphia, and such cities to scream bloody murder about any ruthless invasion of their private domain by the ABA when their teams were founded in a rebel league which made war with the established professional circuit in its sport and won.

Nor it is fair for members of the establishment in the professional football, hockey, and basketball leagues to complain that the formation of rival major leagues spreads the available talent among too many teams in too many towns and thus dilutes the quality of play at the top. Since the NFL and the AFL merged, the NFL has expanded by putting new teams in Cincinnati, Miami, New Orleans, and Atlanta, and it is about to add Tampa and another new city now. Seattle is a strong possibility, as well as the Memphis and Honolulu territories which have been claimed by my new WFL. Since the WHA began in business, the NHL has expanded by putting new teams in Atlanta, Long Island, Washington, and Kansas City, and it plans to add more. Since the ABA began, the NBA has expanded by putting new teams in Buffalo,

31

Phoenix, Portland, Seattle, New Orleans, and San Diego, which went to Houston, and transferring the old St. Louis and Cincinnati teams into Atlanta and Kansas City–Omaha.

If there are not enough good players to go around, why have these leagues done this? A benevolent desire to see major-league sport in deserving communities which had been denied previously? Maybe. But more likely to gain a toehold in towns about to be invaded by new rivals in an effort to cut down the competition. And most of all to make money, because the millions of dollars in entrance fees into the established leagues obtained from new franchise holders were divided up among the members of the establishment.

The last NFL franchises cost the incoming clubs $8.5 million each, and the new ones probably will cost in the neighborhood of $18 million. It probably would cost from $20 million to $25 million to buy an existing team, depending on the quality of the team and the territory it occupies. The original NHL expansion franchises cost $2 million. The more recent ones cost $6 million. In the case of the Long Island franchise it cost another $6 million to get the Rangers to accept the invasion of its New York territorial rights. Recent entries into the NBA have paid close to $3 million apiece on the average. The last seven new teams have paid a total of $19.6 million in admission fees. And NBA commissioner Walter Kennedy concedes that newcomers now will have to pay $5 million or more each. The value of the Boston Celtics, as measured by purchase prices, went from $2.8 million in 1965 to $6.2 million in 1969. The value of the San Diego Rockets went from $1.7 million in 1967 to $5.7 million in 1971 when they became the Houston Rockets.

Every man is in business to make money, in sports just as in everything else. Maybe there are better businesses than sports, and maybe many men go into the sports business because it is a spotlighted activity and so much more exciting than, say, selling shoes or insurance policies, but they remain businessmen who want to make as much money as they can from their venture and they do things which are destructive to their league and their sport in the interests of pure profits. And they seek to cut down their competition to protect their profits and the value of their property. They're not wrong for doing this. There is nothing wrong with trying to make as much money as you can from a venture and from trying to beat your competition as long as you operate fairly.

People cut corners in sports, but I'd guess no more and probably less than in other businesses. It's more competitive than most businesses.

It is possible to turn out the best possible product in most businesses if you spend the money and hire the best men to do it, although few really try to do so, but it is not that easy in sports because even if you could get the six best hockey players or the five best basketball players or whatever you need, you still might not have the best team. And if you had the best players you'd have to pay more for them than for other players, so you'd have to charge more for your tickets in order to make any money, and a lesser team that didn't have your payroll might be able to draw more fans at lower prices and make more money. I guarantee you the players are in this to make money. Some might play for nothing if no one is being paid, but almost all seek as much money as they can get and many will not play if they feel they are underpaid.

As I've said, I'm motivated by more than money. I like challenges and coming through against them. I like overcoming obstacles. I like winning. I like the prestige and the power that comes from being where the action is. I am warned by the spotlight. I probably could make more money in other businesses besides sports. I've found sports more interesting. I'm not a big spender who likes to live high. But I do like good things, and it takes a good deal of money to buy them.

And making money is part of my motivation. I like to think that's the good old American way.

One of the things that attracted me to the new basketball league was that I could get into a venture which might make money without having to invest much. I wasn't sought as an "angel," but as an energetic young attorney who liked sports who might be able to help put the project over. It was strictly speculative, and if it had been something else, a fling in some other field, I'd have skipped it, but the fact that it was sports interested me.

I talked to Don Regan about it and met with Dennis Murphy, John McShane, and Roland Speth. They were all basically public relations people and promoting hell out of their idea. It smacked something of pie in the sky, but I still was attracted to it. They had laid a lot of groundwork and were ready to roll. They had thrown in with a rival group headed by Connie Serudan and John Murther, which had been developing a similar league idea in the East. Gabe Rubin also had thrown in with them. They had some prospective franchise owners lined up and some attractive cities to go into.

One worry was that another new pro basketball league, the American Basketball League, had folded only a few years earlier. It had started up in the 1961–1962 season and folded midway in its second season with losses estimated at $2 million. It had franchises in Los Angeles, San Francisco, Kansas City, Chicago, Cleveland, Pittsburgh, Washington, and even Honolulu. The Los Angeles franchise wound up in Long Beach before it folded. The Washington franchise wound up in Long Island before it and the league folded on the last day of 1962. It had some good players, too, including Bill Spivey, Connie Hawkins, Ken Sears, Mike Farmer, and Dick Barnett.

However, Dennis Murphy had checked wtih Bill Sharman, who had been a championship coach in that league. Bill emphasized the point that Abe Saperstein, who owned the Harlem Globetrotters, had bankrolled the new league and had owned many of the teams with fellows fronting for him and he simply was not in a position to handle all the losses himself. Bill made the point that any new league has to expect losses for a while as it builds up, but if each franchise had an owner or owners with sufficient money and determination to ride out the early years they could eventually turn the corner to profits.

Also, a lot more money was being poured into sports through television, and this represented an increasing source of potential revenue. And professional basketball was getting bigger all the time. Sharman was convinced there were more than enough players and there was plenty of room for more pro basketball and a new league could work. Finally, we had the example set for us in football, where the AAC had not made it, but a few years later the AFL had come along and to the surprise of almost everyone had made it big.

So Don and I decided to go into it. And we almost went in over our heads. It turned out that for all the groundwork they had laid, the founding fathers remained on rough ground. They were so disorganized it was almost beyond belief. They knew nothing whatsoever about starting a league or running one, and, of course, neither did we.

Our firm became the legal counsel for the league, which was a plus, since that was strictly business for which we would be paid, provided the members could afford to pay us, which was doubtful for a while. They weren't charging anything for franchises. There was no way the founding fathers could make any money or the league could accumulate funds to operate with or support any shaky franchises. Each group that came in had to ante up five grand for expenses, but that was barely enough for travel expenses for the leaders, who were trying to pull this thing together. I went out of my pocket for my expenses.

All anyone had to do to get a franchise was to say he had money, to appear to have money, and to say he wanted a franchise and was prepared to support one until it succeeded. There were promoters who said they wanted franchises who didn't want them at all. Sam Schulman said he wanted a Seattle franchise, Dick Bloch said he wanted a Phoenix franchise, and Bob Breitbard said he wanted a San Diego franchise, but before long Dennis became convinced that they were running with the new league just to scare the NBA into granting them a franchise. As it happened they soon dropped out of the new league and all wound up with franchises for their cities in the old league. Gene Klein, owner of the NFL's San Diego Chargers, also was in and out.

A group from Cleveland said they wanted an ABA franchise and by midnight, when the meeting broke up, were raring to go. Then everyone retired to their beds. In the middle of the night the Cleveland guys packed their bags, caught a 3 A.M. flight home, and were never heard from again. Some were scared away when they saw how disorganized we were, and if we'd have been smart we would have been scared away, too. It was just blind luck that the league survived.

Dennis Murphy didn't even get the Anaheim franchise for himself. His partners had promised that to Art Kim without Murphy's knowledge. Understandably, that upset him. But that was the way they were going when we got into it. The founding fathers were running around in a hundred different directions at once, meeting with prospective backers all over the country and making deals with them without the others' knowing about it.

We were from Orange County. It was probably the fastest-growing area in the country, and we recognized the potential there for professional sports in competition wtih the Los Angeles market, but the coveted Anaheim territory was given to an outsider. Kim was supposedly a good basketball man, but I'm not sure he was a good businessman. Letting him have southern California was a waste of a terrific territory.

Murphy staked out the Kansas City territory, but he had to get backing from the engineering company that employed him. He wound up selling the franchise to Denver interests.

I looked at a map and located my "floating franchise" in Dallas. I didn't have any better basis for this than the fact that Dallas seemed to be the best city without a pro basketball franchise. It was strictly a shot in the dark, and it missed the target as it turned out.

Every new league has "floating franchises." The founding fathers usually each take one for themselves and locate it and back it or find financing for it or sell it to an outside group which will sponsor it somewhere. It's one way of trying to make money out of your position as a founding father.

I wasn't exactly a founding father, but I jumped into bed with these guys close enough to conception to qualify for favored status. I was more of a midwife, brought in to help bring the baby into the world. Dennis Murphy had got himself pregnant with an idea, but he needed help to get the baby born and breathing. I took one of the franchises because they were there to be taken. I was making less than $30,000 a year, had less than $30,000 in the bank, and was looking to make some money, but it was the wildest sort of flyer. My partner, Don Regan, also took a floating franchise, which landed in Louisville eventually.

Don and I went to the New York Public Library, looked up what we needed to know, and drew up the articles of incorporation. Don did most of the legal work. Dennis and I did a lot of closing work, running around trying to get the signatures of agreement to operate franchises from fellows who'd said they'd do so but hadn't put their names on the dotted line yet. Fortunately, we didn't ask them for money, too. We just wanted partners to share the responsibility for the league with us.

Arthur Brown agreed to take the New York franchise. Sean Downey, who was the son of Morton Downey, the Irish tenor, agreed to take the New Orleans franchise. Ken Davidson, whose partner was Pat Boone, the singer, took the Oakland franchise. Dennis Murphy was supposed to be Davidson's partner, but Dennis didn't have any money and Boone did, so Boone became the partner. T. C. Morrow took a Houston franchise. Larry Shields from Anaheim took a Minneapolis franchise. Gabe Rubin took the Pittsburgh franchise. John McShane, Roland Speth, and Connie Serudan took aspirin.

We met at the St. Regis Hotel in New York City the first part of 1967. After two days of meetings, we scheduled the official announcement of the formation of the American Basketball Association for February 2, 1967, at the Hotel Carlyle in Manhattan. Right up to the last minute we were frantically trying to pull ourselves together. We argued about everything. We were supposed to be partners, but everyone was pulling his oar in a different direction. I told them so. I stood up and let them have it. By then I knew enough to see that the only way a league like this would work was if the members worked together to obtain talent and promote their product. I said we were in competition with the NBA, not with each other. I said when we were on our feet and walking it would be time to become competitive for leadership within our league, but if there was no league there could be no leaders.

I was so angry that I started to storm out. I saw little chance for success for a group of guys who were worried more about their individual interests than the group interest. I was ready to give up on the gamble as a bum bet. I'd invested a lot of time and a little money and I'd lost, that was all.

But Dennis Murphy grabbed me and got me back into my seat. He begged me to hold off for a little while. Then he started to make the rounds among the members. He wanted me to become the president of the league. Maybe he should have become president because it was his idea to begin with, but he felt he wasn't cut out for it. Don Regan has called him a wandering minstrel. It wasn't a bad description of Dennis. He amused people. More than that, he got them to like him. And he was more than that because he was an imaginative man. But he wasn't a tough guy. Or wasn't at that time. He's changed a lot. Adversity has toughened him.

Mark Bimstein had been named acting president, but the members felt he wasn't the front man they wanted. He was a show-business type. Dennis said later he saw that many of the members had been impressed by the way I handled myself and the direction I suggested the ABA take. He and the others felt it would be a good image and helpful for a lawyer to be their leader, especially one with an interest in business. He and the others felt I was young and would project a favorable image, even if I was inexperienced. Dennis and Roland Speth staged a whirlwind campaign for me, and I was elected president. It was the first election I'd ever won.

It caused me to stay in. I had enough of an ego to feel I could lead them out of the wilderness they'd wandered into. I had a one-year contract for $30,000, and I felt that was enough time to get things going right. I was right in a way because I honestly believe the ABA would not have got off the ground if it had not been for me. But I was wrong if I thought getting elected president guaranteed me the right to run things.

From the moment they named me president, they fought me at every turn. They never stopped fighting among themselves. They never stopped pulling in different directions, and there never was a time they were not pulling themselves apart.

I know I was not right in everything I wanted them to do. I don't have so much ego that I think I'm always right. But I did try to do the right things for the league as a whole, unselfishly, because if the league did not make it, I would not. I believe that every league needs a dictator. Without one there is no way to get a group such as these guys to agree on anything. Characters become owners of sports teams and they become barracudas. They'll eat one another alive.

If the dictator is wise and benevolent, the league will prosper. Pete Rozelle is a dictator, but smart enough and tough enough and endowed with enough authority to have brought the National Football League to a status of success unsurpassed in professional sports. When Judge Landis was dictator, baseball got through its most difficult times to become the national pastime. But he was hated for the way he exerted his dictatorial authority, and since he passed from the scene, the owners have been unwilling to endow another leader with similar status. Baseball has suffered as a result.

I am not saying Rozelle and Landis are or were always right in their rulings, but it is better to have someone make the best decisions he can than not to have decisions made. Problems demand solutions, and someone has to decide the single best solution he can see to every problem and have the power to put it into effect or the problems will linger destructively. It has been my experience that in sports leagues you are fortunate to get two or three men to agree on any course of action and you are unfortunate if you have to get more because you won't get it.

The National Hockey League and the National Basketball Association, like baseball, have been unwilling to delegate a dictator to lead them, and it has hurt them immeasurably. Clarence Campbell and Walter Kennedy are good men, but they were hired by the owners, who limited their authority and tried to reach their own decisions in committee.

As the owners were unable to agree for many months on what to do about the floundering San Diego franchise in baseball, so, too, were the owners unable to agree on a solution to the floundering Oakland franchise in hockey. And the NBA has spread its franchises into some unproductive territories. Both the NHL and NBA have lost precious players because the owners could not agree on a course of action to keep them. Also, they have suffered from the competition from the WHA and ABA because they could not agree on the best ways to meet it, and so frequently did not do anything at all.

If you get a bad man, you're beat, of course. You have to get a good man. Whether I am a good man to be a dictator to a league is for others to decide, but I did not get a chance to show it in the American Basketball Association. I did not have sufficient clout, in the form of cash and prestige, to meet and deal with the owners on equal terms. The owners did not give me the authority I needed. Instead, they named a commissioner, George Mikan, to divide leadership of the league with me. It is unlikely that co-leaders can conduct a league's business properly, but it was for sure George and I could not, because we could not agree on many things. We quickly became like the rest of the league, feuding and fighting.

I was against Mikan's being named commissioner in the first place. He had been proposed originally because he was a big name in basketball, a big man who made an impressive appearance, a lawyer, and an attractive personality. This was all to the good. And he agreed early in the going that the league was a good thing and he was interested in becoming an important part of it. What was bad was that he refused to throw in with us when we needed him most. He wanted to wait until he was sure we were for real. He didn't want to disgrace his name among the powers of the NBA unless he was sure it would pay off for him. So when we needed a front man, an image, a star of stature to bring us a sympathetic press and bring important investors into our ranks, he was safe in the shadows. We anted up, but he didn't. We crawled out on a limb, but he didn't.

An hour before we held our press conference to announce we had a league, big George finally agreed to accept the position of commissioner the owners insisted he be offered over my objections. I would not have objected so much if he had been put strictly in charge of basketball affairs, while I was clearly the overall leader in charge of league affairs, but I did not like the divided authority his appointment brought. The owners felt they needed a basketball man atop their basketball league. I felt they did not. I felt they needed a businessman. After my experiences with big George as a businessman, I felt that more than ever. Any league needs a businessman to run its league business. The sport itself is like a tube of toothpaste. You want the best toothpaste you can get to sell. But financing, manufacturing, distribution, and selling of it are strictly business. The toothpaste can't run the business. The business has to sell the toothpaste.

The press conference announcing the ABA was hysterical. We wanted to make an impression on the press. Gabe Rubin and Connie Serudan set it up. Strictly show biz. The buffet was loaded with delicacies of every description. The whiskey flowed like water. A free ABA basketball was given to every writer and broadcaster in the place. Naked dancing girls circulated everywhere—well, they weren't really naked and they weren't really dancing girls, but you get the idea. I don't know what they were or what they were doing there. I guess Rubin and Serudan figured you needed pretty girls to jazz up any show. We spent $35,000 and we got a circus for our money. Everyone had fun, but no one took us seriously. It was a joke, and it made us look ridiculous. Well, we didn't know what we were doing. We were novices. We tried to keep the newspaper reporters and the radio and TV people separate and do interviews with everyone individually. Everyone waited endlessly, and it turned them off. We were trying to turn people on, and we turned them off. It's amazing we survived it. It's proof there was a place for the league. With all the mistakes we made, the league still survived.

CHAPTER 3

As Gary Davidson Sees It, II

I don't think anything typified George Mikan better than the time in the ABA's second season when it was catching on in Oakland and George went to represent the league in the playoff finals and he stood up in front of almost a full house in the Oakland arena and he said, "I am happy to be here in Oklahoma."

Not that George did not do many good things for the ABA. He was at first the image we wanted up front for the league. No one knew me. Everyone knew George. Even now, I am not all that well known. Everyone knew Bobby Hull, who became in a way the image of the WHA.

George not only was a big name, but he was a big man. When he walked into a room, his physical presence was dominating. He was smart and he could be charming. And he contributed many things to the ABA, most notably the red, white, and blue basketball. I was against it, and I was wrong.

The red, white, and blue basketball was George's idea. I

guess he's a patriot at heart. He thought it would lend color to the league. A lot of us thought it would make us look like a bush league. I thought those colored panels on that basketball would make us look like we were playing with the Harlem Globetrotters.

Mikan made it a mission in life to get it accepted, and because he wanted it and the owners wanted him he got his way. And as small a thing as it may seem to be, it may have made the league. It gave the ABA an identity apart from the other league. It attracted attention. It became an image for us.

I'm sure some are still against it. Some still think it's bush. But it was good business. It worked. They must sell half a million of the ABA balls a year in this country now. Go to any sporting-goods store and you'll see our model or imitations on sale. Go to any playground and most of the time you'll see as many kids playing with a red, white, and blue basketball as with the old brown one. That's the ABA, represented repeatedly all across the country.

It did not come without its problems. The dye ran at first, and players ran around with red, white, and blue hands after they started to sweat. Their uniforms got stained. But that was a problem which could easily be solved. Some felt it produced an optical illusion as if it wobbled when it spun through the air. Some felt the dye made it slick. But most of those who use it are used to it now.

I wish we had pressed for a colored puck in hockey. We wanted one. A blue one. Every test we took showed the fluorescent-colored pucks showed up twice as well as the black pucks customarily used, and seeing the puck is a problem in hockey, especially for fans in the distant seats and for television viewers. But the die-hard hockey men in our circuit, especially the Canadians, were against it. They won, and it was their loss.

45

I guarantee you the footballs used in my World Football League will have a special color scheme, one which will make the ball instantly identifiable with the league.

Art Kim came up from the old ABL with the 30-second shooting clock and the three-point "home run" basket from beyond a ring extending approximately 25 feet from the basket. Both were helpful to us, improving play and adding identifying features to our league. The NBA already had a 24-second clock. Our 30-second clock is not necessarily better. But it serves the same purpose. It's a nice round figure fans can remember. It gives teams a little more time to set up a shot, while still speeding up play and destroying the stall, which is the most deadly feature of college basketball. The three-point basket promotes the little man and the long shot, which is what the game needs, and encourages comeback efforts, which add excitement to the game.

I am not for a whole lot of gimmicky rules, but over a period of time the way a sport is played alters, and rules must be altered to keep up with the times. I am against change for change's sake, but the old leagues tend to be against change, period. They are wrong, and it restricts their growth. Starting fresh, a new league can put into play modern rules.

The NBA should have gone to the three-point long-shot basket long ago, but they haven't, only because we have it. We should have made more changes in our WHA. We should have removed either the red line or the blue lines to speed up play and open up breakaways. The offside rule as it is now is too confining and stops play too often. We should have promoted penalty-shot calls to discourage flagrant interference from defenders on breakaways. We did restore sudden-death overtimes to eliminate a lot of ties, which are dissatisfying to all concerned. The NHL should have returned to overtimes long ago. It has been one of the most exciting features of our games. Our teams don't coast through the last minutes of games to settle for ties.

There was a lot that was exciting in the ABA that first year, on and off the court. There were some wild scenes. When the league had its ceremonial meeting to announce its formation, I had my arm in a cast, having broken it in a basketball game. George tried to have me removed as president. I avoided open warfare with him because I thought it was best for the league. I went along with him on things I felt were wrong to keep things moving smoothly. But I should have gone to the mat with him. It might have made George more responsive to the needs of the league. Mikan wasn't tough enough. The owners were always fighting among themselves, sometimes physically. Arthur Brown and Gabe Rubin were after each other physically at one meeting and Rubin and Art Kim went at each other at another. Brown ran the New York team, Rubin ran the Pittsburgh team and Kim ran the Anaheim team. They ran them right into the ground. Rubin went after his own coach, Jim Harding, at a banquet when the all-star game was played in Louisville one season. They just couldn't get along. Kim stormed into the official's dressing room after one game and went after one of the officials. George Mikan's brother Ed, who was head of the officials and a big man, broke them up.

It was not surprising that George's brother was head of the officials. George's offices were in Minneapolis, so that's where they put the league offices. Not in New York or Los Angeles or some other major city, but Minneapolis. George's offices housed his Viking Travel Agency, so he handled some of the travel arrangements for the teams in the league. We didn't bargain for the best deal we could get; we just let George do it. At first, outside his offices on top was a big sign: Viking Travel Agency. Beneath it was a smaller sign:

47

American Basketball League. We were small and second, even with George.

Every time Mikan and I got together we wound up fighting with each other. We exchanged some letters so nasty the U.S. Postal Service should have arrested us. The old ABL did business in a bush way. If one owner got mad at another he saw to it that when the other guy's team came to his town there was no hot water or towels in the shower room, for example. We had the idea we could operate more professionally than that, but we didn't always do it. We opened the season on Friday the thirteenth, which should have been a tipoff. We closed the season in Teaneck, New Jersey. That's where the New York franchise had been located. Of course.

The New Jersey team and the Kentucky Colonels had tied for fourth and last playoff position in their division. New Jersey's Americans had a seasonal edge in play between the two teams, but Mikan decided on a playoff game between the two teams. New Jersey merited the home court advantage, but a circus was using its home court, so they were permitted to take the game to Commack, Long Island. When the teams arrived to play, they found the court unfit for play. So Mikan forfeited the game to Kentucky. And the Colonels went into the playoffs. The Americans went into shock. And the next season moved to Commack, Long Island. Naturally.

Pittsburgh and New Orleans won the pennants, and Pittsburgh won the playoffs that first season. Whereupon when the Minneapolis franchise gave up on Minneapolis and moved to Miami, the Pittsburgh franchise gave up on Pittsburgh and moved to Minneapolis. And the next season the Pittsburgh team that had moved to Minneapolis moved right back to Pittsburgh. Oakland and Indiana won the pennants the next season, and Oakland won the playoffs. So Oakland moved to Washington, D.C. Naturally. It is very important to move your champion to another city every season, it seems.

I do not put all the blame on Mikan. Certainly, I deserve a lot of it. Divided authority will not work. But as it turned out, Mikan had more authority than I, so I'm giving him more of the blame. He wasn't tough enough on the owners. The one thing guaranteed to happen when you start a new league is that everyone is sweetness and smiles until the first shot is fired. Then all hell breaks loose and everything starts to turn sour and sad and it takes a strong hand to keep control.

Ideally, you accept only the wealthiest, most businesslike, and most dedicated men to own the teams in the league. Realistically, you take what you can get. And it is very difficult to judge what you're going to get in advance. Money alone won't make men good owners of sports teams. Nor will past success in business. They have to know how to spend their money in the unique business that is sports. If we had run a credit check on the men who took over the Indianapolis franchise we might not have let them in the league. They were not wealthy. But they turned out to be the best owners in the league and to this day are the only ones of the original owners who still have their team in the league. Men who seemed much more qualified did not do nearly as good a job.

You have to keep on top of owners, but you can't control them completely. Once you give them a franchise, it is theirs, and short of their not paying the bills or not showing up for games or refusing to provide uniforms for the players and sending them out naked, you are at the mercy of how they operate. They all promise to spend sufficient money to put out an attractive product and promote it properly, they all say they understand they are not apt to make money for a few years, and they all agree they are in it long enough to give it a chance to go. But once some red ink starts to run some of them start to run for the hills.

In professional sports, you have to spend money to make money, but some men come in saying they know this when they really don't know it at all, when down deep they dream of some miracle that will make them millionaires overnight. They think if they put five bodies on a basketball court they will be blessed by a miracle that will make them the best team in the world. And when it doesn't happen they fire coaches and criticize fans. A lot of owners think they're better coaches than the coaches. Even winning is not enough for them, if they're not winning the way the owners think they should.

Gene Rhodes was on a winning streak when Kentucky's owners fired him. Gene Rhodes is now the general manager in Kentucky under new owners. A black star, Spencer Haywood, was lured to Denver partly because it had a black coach, John McLendon. As soon as the owners got their black star, they fired their black coach. The new coach, Joe Belmont, took the team to a pennant and was voted "coach of the year." When Haywood left the team and it got harder for the team to win, the "coach of the year" was fired. In Miami the owner called his coach, Hal Blitman, "the best coach in the league" one month and fired him the next.

We got some good coaches in the ABA at the start, which is important, though some owners went for names. Former pro stars Cliff Hagen, Max Zaslofsky, and Slater Martin were among our first coaches. Later, Bones McKinney, Alex Groza, and Frank Ramsey coached in the league. Bill Sharman and Lou Carnasecca loaned the league a lot of class for three seasons. Bobby Leonard, Alex Hannum, Joe Mullaney, and Al Bianchi came in and stayed awhile and they are among the best in the business. Babe McCarthy came in at the beginning and coached in Kentucky in 1974. He is a southern gentleman who was hired by another southern gentleman, Charlie Smithers, to coach the club in New Orleans originally. Both were funny fellows and good company, which was important in the early days when parties were a major part of our operation. But McCarthy and Hannum now have been fired.

Smithers had the gout, but he always had a cigar in one hand and a shot glass full of bourbon in the other. He always wore a white suit and looked like a Democrat from Dixie. He was a good guy and fun to be with. The only time in my life I ever stayed up all night was in New Orleans. It was after a bitter battle settling Mikan's contract with his lawyer, with whom it was almost impossible to settle anything. I had to get away and started down Bourbon Street. The next thing I knew it was seven in the morning and I was sitting in a bar discussing philosophy with a model, a dancer, and a stripper. Unfortunately Charlie Smithers' New Orleans franchise didn't go and we had to move the team. Further trips to that town might have been interesting.

When owners start up a sports team in a town you can't tell them whether to set their prices high or low, whether to discount tickets or give them away a while. There is a school of thought that once you give your product away it is hard to sell it later, and another that says you get people in your place any way you can and you have a chance of getting them to come back. Every situation is different.

Southern California is thick with attractive sports teams, and the Anaheim Amigos needed to get people to their games to sell them on the new team in town. Roland Speth

51

promoted some superdeals to discount blocks of tickets to major groups in the area that could be the backbone of future support. Art Kim told him to tell these customers to take their business elsewhere. He wouldn't honor the deals because he was a first-class man with a first-class club and people would pay first-class prices or they could stay home. They stayed home.

When owners operate a team, you can't audit their books. When the Oakland franchise turned up with almost a million bucks missing after two seasons and you can't finger the culprit, you forget it. What's a million, more or less?

All the owners in our league agreed to go after the best talent available. They knew it would be expensive, but they agreed it would be worth it. Only they didn't do it. The owners in Oakland did when they went after Rick Barry and Nate Thurmond and others, but most didn't. The owners in Oakland did a lot for us. When they signed Rick Barry for $75,000 a season for three seasons it gave us a big-league image. What hurt was that Barry couldn't play the first season.

The NBA had a clause in its contract requiring players to play for a team for a year beyond the expiration of his contract. This was the "option clause." They had an option on his rights for another year, whether or not he signed with them for another season. We figured this was unfair and felt we could break such contractual restrictions in court. We lost in court. I still think it's unfair. A mechanic can go to work for the gas station across the street if he wants for whatever reason to change jobs. A sportswriter can go to work for another newspaper. Only an athlete is deprived of such freedom of opportunity.

I can see where a common draft has merit. Competitive bidding drives salaries beyond reason for unproven players out of college or amateur ranks. This practice can drive teams and leagues out of business. But once a player has proved himself in a professional sport for a reasonable period of time, he should be free to make the best deal for his services possible. After his option year expired, an NBA player was free to sign with another team, only the teams would not take players from another team in their family, so the freedom was worthless. Until we came along, the player had no choice. We gave players a choice.

By first bringing Bruce Hale into the Oakland franchise, the ABA laid the groundwork to bring in his son-in-law, Rick Barry. Rick's marriage was going bad, he wanted to save it, and so he made the move, moving with his wife and children to her father's side in Oakland. However, he had to wait out a year. By the time he got on the team, his father-in-law had been kicked upstairs. That was the way they operated in the ABA.

Few other franchises went after a Rick Barry that first season, and none landed any stars. The only NBA player the ABA got that first season was Wayne Hightower, and he was no bargain. A fringe player, he was more temperamental than talented. We had a lot of no-names. Our record-setting three-point shooter went by the name of Wes Bialosuknia, and no one has heard from him since.

Owners went into operation so poorly prepared that many had no managers, coaches, or scouts, and they drafted their first players from sheets of statistics. At our first draft meeting, one guy used a stack of press brochures from which he made his choices. He drafted a D. Smith, who had impressive scoring and rebounding statistics. She turned out to be Doris Smith or something like that, who had led the school's girls' basketball team. He didn't sign her.

We did have some talented players. Connie Hawkins and Roger Brown were available to us because they had been damned by association with a fix scandal of the past. They never were convicted of any crimes, and when Hawkins later pressed a suit against the NBA for having blackballed him, the NBA bought him off with a fat contract and took him in. He was the star of our first championship Pittsburgh team, was Most Valuable Player our first season, and stayed with the ABA three seasons before leaving to join the NBA. Brown could have followed the same route, too, but has stayed in the ABA.

Mel Daniels, Larry Jones, Jimmy Jones, and Louis Dampier were good players overlooked or rejected by the NBA, and they starred in the ABA. Mel Daniels was the only college star signed from the NBA by the ABA. Daniels was the star of the Minnesota franchise. Short of money, the Muskies sold the all-league center to Indianapolis, where he became the backbone of a club which has won three pennants and three playoff championships in the seven seasons of the league. He has twice been named MVP in the league, and selling him sold the Minnesota franchise down the river. Moved to Miami without talent, it expired. The sale was a disservice to the league.

It set a pattern which is still sometimes followed, much to the detriment of the league. The Oakland franchise could have been successful. Taken to Washington and then shifted to Virginia by Earl Foreman, it has been stripped of such a superstar as Julius Erving and such promising stars as Sven Nater and George Gervin in cash transactions. This has turned the state against the team, destroyed its value, and leaves it destined to die. A league is only as strong as its weakest owners.

It was clear that the only way the ABA could be competitive with the NBA and force a merger was to be competitive in the bidding for talent and become sufficiently competitive on the court to capture fan interest. It had to live down its image as a minor league. It took a long time doing it. The ABA did finally begin to go after name players and landed some and lost some of them.

It has been forgotten that Lou Hudson, Dave Bing, Bob Love, Clyde Lee, Leroy Ellis, and other NBA stars signed with ABA clubs but backed out because their NBA contracts had not expired. Billy Cunningham signed with an ABA club after his NBA contract expired, tried to back out, was not allowed to do so, and became the MVP in the ABA in 1973. He may be free to return to the NBA in 1974 or 1975. Zelmo Beaty and Joe Caldwell jumped the NBA to sign with the ABA and have been solid stars in the younger league.

It was through signing college stars that the ABA finally made the NBA think merger, but before that the ABA missed many good bets in this area. Mikan bragged about being willing to spend $2 million for Lew Alcindor. If the ABA owners had gone in on this and put Alcindor on a team in prime territory it would have brought the NBA to its knees, begging for a merger. But Mikan and the men around him didn't put their money where their mouths were.

Alcindor said he wanted to play in New York. The ABA assigned him to the New York Nets. The NBA draft put him in Milwaukee, not New York. Alcindor didn't want to go to Milwaukee. He was ready to go to the ABA. Owners and officials of the ABA had promised him a big bonus to go with them. He was ready to go. But when Arthur Brown, the owner of the New York Nets, and Mikan met with Alcindor and his advisers Sam Gilbert and Ralph Shapiro at Brown's Manhattan town house, the ABA representatives tried to bargain for a cheaper deal. They offered a contract full of so many ifs, and, and buts that most of the money hinged on the stock market investments. When Alcindor and his advisers asked about the promised bonus, they were told it was incorporated into the package. When Alcindor and his advisers asked if this was the final offer, Mikan said it was. Alcindor did not want to cheapen himself by bargaining. Insulted, he and his advisers went to the NBA and accepted an offer of $1.4 million to play for five years for Milwaukee.

That night, a couple of the ABA owners approached Gilbert and told him they were ready to offer a better deal. Gilbert said they'd been told they already had been given the league's final offer. Gilbert was told that Mikan, the league commissioner, had no power to declare any offer final. Gilbert, Shapiro, and Alcindor agreed the honorable thing was to stick to their NBA agreement and to refuse any further bids by the ABA. Alcindor admitted later he had preferred the ABA to the NBA, and the Nets to any other team. If they had even matched the Bucks' bid with real money, the Nets would have had him in the ABA, ensuring the league's future and additional jobs for players. In Alcindor's own words, the ABA had "blown it."

Mikan went around with other owners screaming bloody murder that they'd been double-crossed by Alcindor and his advisers and never had a real chance to bid for him. It made them look bad. More than anything else, it cost George his job. Alcindor became Kareem Abdul-Jabbar, one of the dominating performers in the sport. Elvin Hayes, Pete Maravich, and other potential superstars were lost the same way.

Mikan was gone when the ABA finally made its move. It started when Steve Arnold, a very active and imaginative agent who since has been associated with me in the WHA and WFL, brought Spencer Haywood to Denver. He had been the star of the United States' championship Olympic team in Mexico City in 1968. He had just completed his sophomore season at Detroit University as the leading rebounder in the NCAA ranks. However, he had been made unhappy at Detroit and had heard bad things about Jim Harding, who, fired by Pittsburgh of the ABA, was coming in to coach the college club.

Haywood wanted to quit college and turn pro, but the NBA had a rule against signing undergraduates. Haywood had no money, and his mother was struggling to raise a large family working as a cleaning lady. Arnold reasoned that the hungry new league might go for him, shopped around, and found the Ringsbys in Denver interested. Will Robinson, who had coached Haywood in high school, but been denied the chance to coach him in college, was courted. He encouraged Haywood to make the move. Establishing a new "hardship" rule by which needy undergraduate collegians can be signed, the ABA accepted Haywood when he was signed by Denver.

Frankly, I have mixed emotions about signing undergraduate collegians. The hardship rule is a joke which is applied indiscriminately. And in sports such as basketball and football the colleges serve as a farm system for professional leagues. Players prove themselves to some extent in college and come into the pro ranks with well-known names. But colleges also take advantage of players. They reap returns from players who are not paid. It is true that they provide players with college educations, but many potential pros could not care less. Many young men who are not qualified for college study accept scholarships as the only avenue they have to pro ranks. Many young men go to work instead of going on to college at the age of eighteen or nineteen, so why not athletes? Many athletes lose several seasons of big money because they are compelled to attend college first. It seems to me that it is something a young man must decide for himself.

If a professional team is willing to sign a player, he

should be free to sign. Which the courts have ruled he is. A most significant aspect of the court ruling is that once a player has been signed by a professional team to a valid contract, other teams in that league cannot claim rights to him through any subsequent draft. After Haywood jumped to the NBA and signed with Seattle, the NBA's Buffalo team drafted him and sued to obtain his services. They lost the suit.

The draft is an agreement between partners in a business operation and has no legal standing. Any team in any professional league today can sign any player out of college ranks to a valid contract which cannot be broken by another team which takes the player in that league's draft. The NBA fined Sam Schulman, the owner of the Seattle franchise, but so lightly he accepted it rather than take it to court. The NBA's only alternative was for the other league members to disband and form the same league all over again without Schulman. They chose not to take such a drastic step. But there is no way you can guarantee partners in a league will abide by the majority vote.

The problem of signing undergraduates is one every league has to deal with. The original owners of the World Football League have voted not to sign undergraduates. We wish to cooperate with the colleges, who develop stars for professional football. Further, we want to maintain the integrity of our draft, which is the only way yet found to distribute new talent among members equitably.

A draft system which gives the highest choices to the lowest finishers is not really fair. It penalizes the teams which operate more successfully. But the success of leagues usually is in proportion to the balance of power among the teams. The more teams that are competing for the title, the more interesting the league is. The draft places the best players with the teams that need them most.

Unfortunately, the draft does not give players a choice of places to play or organizations to join. Competing leagues with separate drafts at least give the players two choices each. Unfortunately, these wars produce competitive bidding which boosts salaries beyond reason. Frankly, however, the economic pressure a dollar war works on a rival is a weapon a new league must use to win acceptance.

They used to tell the Redcoats to stand up straight to show the Indians how proud and unafraid they were. Well, that's baloney. All that shows the Indians is how easily a man can commit suicide. In a war with the Indians or anyone else you sneak around in the woods and shoot from behind the rocks. You are as cunning as you can be, and even deceitful, if necessary, to survive. If you survive, then you can adopt different standards. Once you are on equal terms with the enemy you can stand up and look him in the eye and take him on out in the open and go by the rules. Until then, you pick 'em off, one by one.

The Haywood signing opened the floodgates. The ABA soon signed such undergraduate and graduating college stars as Dan Issel, Julius Erving, Ralph Simpson, Charlie Scott, Rick Mount, Johnny Roche, Johnny Neumann, Artis Gilmore, George McGinnis, Jim McDaniels, Jim Chones, Brian Taylor, and others who were coveted by the NBA. To sign them, the ABA had to go high. Barry's annual $75,000 paycheck, which seemed so sensational when first signed, soon seemed small by comparison. Most of these players were signed for $150,000 to $350,000 a year, depending on the team's need and ability to pay, the star's attractiveness, and the persuasiveness of his agent. And they were signed for five or six years apiece.

The NBA had to raise its salary levels to meet the competition. The NBA signed Elmore Smith, Sidney Wicks, Austin Carr, Ken Durrett, Howard Porter, and others for similar sums. When veterans protested such sums being paid to unproven stars, their salaries had to be raised. Today there are around sixty-five players in professional basketball earning $100,000 or more annually. There are 20 or more earning $200,000 or more. A Jerry West is making $300,000. To lure Wilt Chamberlain into the ABA to attract voters to secure a new arena, Lenny Bloom is paying him $600,000 a year. To lure jumpers such as Barry and Cunningham back to the NBA, their franchise owners had to offer them more than they really could afford. To lure Scott, McDaniels, and others into the fold, NBA owners had to top their ABA pay.

There is a method to what seems madness. You may never get your money's worth from any player priced so high, unless he produces a championship for you, but you are making an investment in the future of your team and your league, which will pay dividends in the long run. NBA owners were vulnerable to such pressure because they were not paying players what they were worth.

About 35 percent of any professional team's gross income should go to player salaries. Until we came along they were not close to this. In basketball, about a third of the gross income goes to the players; in hockey, about a fourth; in football, about a fifth; and in baseball, less than a fifth.

When we went to war in basketball, the average salary for a rookie was $12,000. Even a college superstar such as Rick Barry received only $15,000 to start with. Today, it is around $45,000. Maybe the superstar collegians get too much, but the average rookies still get a lot less. The average player used to earn about $25,000 a season. Today, he gets around $65,000. Maybe it is too much and maybe not. He is entitled to a fair share of the profits. The average player's career is short by comparison with other professions. On the other hand most teams in basketball are losing money.

Some teams are turning profits. Only a few are turning profits on gate receipts alone. And few include returns from parking and concessions in their statements, which may account for half of their income. The New York Knicks gross more than the Mets, between $6 million and $7 million annually, and their player payroll does not amount to much more than a million. The Los Angeles Lakers gross between $3 million and $4 million, and with Wilt gone their player payroll may be below a million. The Milwaukee Bucks and Boston Celtics gross around $3 million each. There have been teams which lost $1 million in recent years. But even the biggest losers are sitting on potential profits. The Cincinnati franchise never made a nickel—until it was sold to Kansas City–Omaha for more than $5 million. The owners walked away with a profit.

You must remember that most owners have businesses. Any losses they suffer in sports usually can be written off against their other profits. If they are in the 50 percent tax bracket, the government absorbs half their losses. In many states, state taxes take another 10 percent. Some owners are paying only 40 cents on the dollar for their losses. In a successful league they have a property that is appreciating in value that they can sell at some future date for capital gains. The better the players on that property, the higher the sale.

One reason it is not hard to find buyers for a team is that when a man buys a team with players, he can depreciate that portion of the purchase price which is allocated to players immediately. He charges away most of his investment to the players, and their value can be depreciated annually, as if they were worn merchandise. The original franchise holder wasn't able to do this, but he has the

61

advantage of using this as a sales pitch to a potential buyer.

Not a team in the ABA made money the first season. These losses ranged from a couple hundred thousand dollars in Indianapolis to maybe a million dollars in New York–New Jersey. And few are making money today. The Indiana team is. New York would be, except for its high payroll. It could be in another year or so. Kentucky has a high payroll, but could turn the corner to profits in another year or so. Utah, too. But these franchises are worth small fortunes today. There are only a few that could not be sold for much more than the owner has invested.

The press and public have been brainwashed and fed a bill of goods by the established leagues and teams. They have been close to the established teams they cover or follow and are led to believe the team really belongs to the people and any action an owner takes is for the public good. The owners want to enjoy a monopoly, like the telephone company, without the controls that go along with it. The owners did not amass their fortunes by using stupid practices. No one is holding a gun to their heads when they pay premium prices for players. They pay it because it pays off for them. They expand because it pays off. And they fight the formation and success of a rival league to protect their vested interests.

They call players who jump leagues traitors. But who calls Carroll Rosenbloom a traitor when he trades his Baltimore football team for the Los Angeles team? Or calls him or any other owner or manager or coach disloyal when they trade one player in mid-season for another player they think will help them more? Who squawked when Bill Sharman left a championship team in Utah to become coach of the Lakers in L.A.? Professional sports is a business, and with few exceptions everyone is out for what he can get.

The ABA almost broke the back of NBA resistance with

their signings and an antitrust suit that had everyone in the NBA scared. Representatives of the league met and worked out a merger agreement, subject to approval by congress, in 1971, just four years after the ABA began. The ABA was to pay $12.5 million for admission of its franchises to the NBA and they would be members in good standing. There would be a common draft. And the antitrust suit was dropped. As it turned out, the NBA got what it wanted without giving up a thing.

A complete merger with a common draft would seem to be in violation of antitrust laws, but Congress had granted an exemption to the NFL and AFL when they merged, and basketball might have been granted the same status. However, the NBA Players Association, headed by Larry Fleisher, had become powerful with the passing years and lobbied bitterly against the loss of bargaining ability. And many NBA owners were not happy with the thought of taking in the ABA's weaker members. They stuck to the thought that the ABA would fold and the stronger members would become available to the NBA. They stalled. The ABA did not press for the merger. A time limit had been set on it, and the agreement ran out in January of 1974.

I had resigned when my year ended. I had only a one-year term, and Mikan had a three-year contract. When we disagreed, he threatened to suspend me. I threatened to suspend him. But I was without power. I had no real money invested in the league, and it was pointless to pursue it. So I said goodbye and went on my way.

I am not irreplaceable. There are many men able to do what I do. There are powerful men who could have been put into the presidency who would have given the league shape, a sense of direction, and stable, consistent supervision. But the owners did not want to replace me with a powerful man. From the outside I watched as they went through man after man, replacing me as president and, eventually, Mikan as commissioner, picking men they felt they could control.

The league has lacked direction and still seems to lack it. There was no one to get behind the merger agreement and make it move. There seems to be no one to arrange a new agreement now and get it going. Early in 1974, Indianapolis attorney Dick Tinkham, trustee for the Indiana franchise and secretary of the ABA, said a new $35 million antitrust suit would be filed against the NBA and the league would expand into such key NBA territories as Chicago and Los Angeles, as well as into Toronto and Mexico City. He said the ABA no longer wanted a merger and was about to renew warfare. Swiftly, Mike Storen, ABA commissioner now, denied that there definitely would be such a new suit or that moves would be made into new cities, though he did not say it was impossible. As it happened, it was filed. Clearly, even the leaders of the ABA cannot agree on what to do. They make announcements and retract them. They correct and criticize one another. They are pulling their oars in different directions, and there is no one with the power to get them to pull together in a single, purposeful direction.

The ABA has missed many good bets. They should have kept their franchises in Southern California. Properly financed and promoted, ABA teams would work in L.A. and in Chicago, where a new building is going up and WHA franchise owner Jordan Kaiser wants an ABA franchise. Sam Schulman wanted to put Alcindor, Walt Hazzard, Gail Goodrich, and other former UCLA stars in the Los Angeles Sports Arena as the L.A. Bruins. If he had, he might well have wound up with Sidney Wicks, Curtis Rowe, and Bill Walton. If he had, the Lakers and the NBA might be in trouble. But no one from the ABA encouraged him. The

64

ABA went after Walton, the most precious prize in years, but let him slip through its fingers.

The ABA has let one star after another slip away. Spoiled by increasing salaries, stars are difficult to satisfy these days, but they are precious properties and must be protected. We did not draw up the ABA contracts. Mikan's lawyers did. They were full of loopholes that served as escape hatches for a smart attorney like Al Ross.

Barry wanted to stay in California. He contended he had been promised that when he signed with Oakland. It is believable that he was. Courting the handsome youngster on the golf courses, Pat Boone apparently promised him a shot at the movies as a cowboy star and everything else he could think of that Rick wanted. But when Rick did not want to go to Washington with his team, no one in the league went to bat for him in an effort to keep him. He'd have to honor his ABA contract, they said. So he signed with San Francisco to return to the NBA. Oh, he had to honor his contract in the ABA, all right. For a couple of years. No sooner was the big guy booming business in the ABA shop in New York than the courts ruled he had to return to the NBA to honor his new contract in San Francisco. He didn't have a Ross representing him. Poor Rick paved the path for a whole series of guys who went wherever they wanted for as much money as they wanted, but he never got to go where he wanted to go and he never made as much money as others did. He was one guy who never won a court case. But he's well ahead of where he would have been if the ABA had never existed.

Ross took the Haywood case to court and won. Spencer signed three contracts in Denver, each for more money. Twice he wanted more than he had been getting, and twice the Ringsbys gave it to him. The third time they got so disgusted they tried to give him the shaft. But they didn't have a case. They had advertised their contract with him as worth $1.9 million for six seasons. But they were only required to put out a half-million dollars. This included $10,000 a year for ten years invested in something called the Dolgoff plan, devised by Ralph Dolgoff in New York. Many ABA contracts were pegged on this plan. This was an investment in mutual funds which was supposed to generate the additional $1.4 million to be paid Haywood in his declining years. There was no way such monies promised the player were protected or guaranteed, and there was no way the contract could be considered binding. Others saw this. But the Ringsbys refused to face it.

Carolina offered Denver $1 million for him. Kentucky offered Denver a package of players for him. Clubs were willing to pay Haywood what Ross wanted for him. The ABA offered $2 million to Denver for him. He was prepared to stay in the league and play for another team. But the Ringsbys refused to sell him to others in their league. They went around bad-mouthing Haywood and Ross until Ross angrily put Haywood's services up for sale to the highest bidder in the NBA. Most would not touch him, but Seattle's Schulman signed him for $1.5 million in cash for six seasons.

The Haywood case was full of cloak-and-dagger histrionics that would have been funny if it hadn't been so serious a situation for the leagues. While the ABA was hunting him, Haywood was hiding out in Ross's home. Haywood was supposed to stay under cover, but he wanted to stay in shape, so he ran at a public park. Suddenly everyone knew where he was. Kids followed him up to Ross's office, seeking his autograph. Ross couldn't figure out how anyone knew who Spencer was, until he realized that the black giant had been running in a sweatsuit boldly lettered on the back: HAYWOOD—DENVER ROCKETS. But it wasn't funny to the ABA when it lost Spencer, who had been its MVP the previous season, and its brightest star. The Dolgoff Plan made contracts like his a sieve.

Through such loopholes, stars fled the ABA coop. Ross promptly peddled McDaniels and John Brisker to Schulman in Seattle and Scott to Dick Bloch in Phoenix. When the Carolina club missed a payment due Scott, he had his out. The league should have stood behind all payments promised all players. It did not. Many of these stars have left Ross, including Haywood. It's a case of, "What have you done for me lately?"

The ABA still has such stars as Erving, Gilmore, Cunningham, McGinnis, Issel, Caldwell, and Beaty, but it is in danger of losing some of them to the NBA.

In this bloody dollar war, some men have been wounded. The opportunity to operate a professional sports team does not bring with it built-in wisdom. Schulman overrated the worth of McDaniels and Brisker. He paid a lot to get them, and they have not been worth much to him. By the time he got a good basketball man to run his team on the court and tell him how much his players were worth, he was out a bundle of dough. Bill Russell told him McDaniels and Brisker were not worth keeping. The Sonics tried to trade them, but no one would take them with their salaries. Schulman may have to pick up part of the tab to get another team to take either of them. McDaniels passed waivers. Released, he still would be entitled to his $300,000 a year. On loan to the minor Eastern League, Brisker still is entitled to his $250,000.

Ross is a smart man, but he may have outsmarted himself. He sold Schulman a bill of goods and Schulman bought it, but he will hesitate to buy from Ross's store next time. So may others. It is a battle of wits, and Schulman is not the only wise businessman who made a bad investment in basketball players.

The NBA's Philadelphia team went for Dana Lewis, Phoenix went for Greg Howard, San Francisco went for Cyril Baptiste, and Chicago went for Jimmy Collins for fat pacts. Who are they? Where are they? Well, they flopped, but all had to be paid. In the ABA, the L.A. Stars spent a bundle for Simmie Hill and he never made it. New York was badly disappointed by Jimmy Chones and let him go.

The only guarantees that accompany players go to the players. Well, it is a players' market these days. If many have been overpaid in recent years, many were underpaid in previous years. However, the owners must start receiving more for their money or their problems will mount rapidly.

With a dictator directing a united effort, the ABA could be booming today. It exists only because there was a need for it which was greater than all the goofs it has made. I have stood on the sidelines and watched while franchises were passed from owner to owner and moved from town to town like used cars, declining instead of increasing in value, and while the owners have gone from leader to leader, like a vain and attractive girl going from boyfriend to boyfriend depending on who looks best to her at a given time and whom she can push around the easiest. It has been an education in itself.

CHAPTER 4

As Gary Davidson Sees It, III

The original officers of the American Basketball Association were myself as president, Gabe Rubin as vice-president, Sean Downey as secretary, and a friend, Jim Ackerman of Anaheim, as treasurer. You do not see Dennis Murphy, John McShane, or Roland Speth in there, do you? It was only their idea, originally. Nor do you see Connie Serudan or Barry Murtha in there, who merged their proposed league with the Murphy group's. It is a simple proposition, steeped in the tactics of business. If you have an idea but don't have the money to put the idea over, you must bring in money to help you. Soon, the money men move you out. They say it is their money, so they have the say over how it is spent. Unless you have protected yourself with some sort of strong contract and extracted percentage points from the operation or guarantee of royalties, you are soon on the outside looking in.

The men with money control teams and leagues, either

up front or with fronts. Politics plays a part, but as in all politics, the men with money call the shots. The more money, the more powerful the player. Most of the men in the ABA originally did not have massive amounts of money, but the men with the most money were more influential than those with the least.

Dennis Murphy was devoured. I don't think he received a dime, except some salaries he got working for some clubs. Connie Serudan received $35,000 after he threatened to sue. John McShane was offered the same payoff, but felt he merited more and took it to court. It was never settled. He died a few years ago. Roland Speth did not get anything. Nor did Barry Murtha get anything, I don't believe. He was assistant general manager of the New York franchise for a while.

Since I resigned, the league has had a number of presidents, including Jim Gardner, H. Wendell Cherry, Bill Daniels, J. W. Ringsby, and Tedd Munchak. It is not always easy to name the right man. Even though I didn't like Bill Ringsby, I thought that he would do a good job and I pushed him as my successor until he had the votes to be elected the new president. Well, I was wrong. He did a terrible job. He got himself disliked by many people who could have helped him. Finally, the league had to turn elsewhere. By then, I had no say in any selections.

After two years, George Mikan resigned as commissioner under pressure. The league has had three others since, starting with Gardner, who controlled the Carolina franchise. A television executive, Jack Dolph, was made president primarily to produce a lucrative national television contract with CBS. That network went for the NBA instead, luring it away from ABC. After two years, Dolph dropped out and was replaced by Robert Carlson, a Wall Street lawyer. After another year Carlson was replaced by Mike Storen, originally a partner in the Indiana franchise and later general manager in Kentucky. Thurlo McCrady, who was the assistant to Joe Foss, the original commissioner in the old AFL and the assistant to Mikan, the first commissioner in the new ABA, became executive director of the ABA when Mikan resigned. He remains in that role now as the only link to the first family in the formation of the circuit as it finished its seventh season in 1974.

Obviously, the league has had little continuity at the top and less stability. The commissioner is out front, but he is controlled by strings pulled by the president, who is one of the franchise owners who sit on the executive committee.

Originally, the ABA announced ten franchises in the New York–New Jersey, Los Angeles–Anaheim, San Francisco–Oakland, Minneapolis–St. Paul, Indianapolis, Pittsburgh, New Orleans, Dallas, Houston, and Kansas City territories. The New York franchise settled in Long Island, the Los Angeles franchise in Anaheim, the San Francisco–Oakland franchise in Oakland, and the Minneapolis–St. Paul franchise in Minneapolis. The Minneapolis and Indianapolis franchises adopted their respective state names of Minnesota and Indiana in an effort to lure statewide support.

The original announcement of franchises supposedly set in a new league usually are subject to sudden and swift shifts. Often, ownership and financing for such franchises are still unsettled at the time of such announcements, but you have to name cities in which you plan to play if people are going to believe you are really going to open play. You announce the franchises with as much conviction as you can muster, you provide as few details of ownership and financing as possible, you hope no one will ask too many questions about such minor details, you shove up front those owners of franchises who are firm, and you set about privately trying to tie up the loose ends of the packages that are not set.

Often, men who are considering sponsoring a franchise come and sit in on announcement affairs and accept being passed off as set owners when in fact they are far from ready to commit themselves. Often, they want to see how the press and public accept the announcement of a new league, they want to see what sort of men do commit themselves to the new league, and they want to see what sort of offers they might get from the old league. Often, they use the threat of putting teams in their towns into a rebel league to pressure the old league into taking them. And often the old league strings them along until it is too late for them to join the original league at its inception, then dumps them and their hopes.

It is a selling job the founding fathers have to do to convince prospective sponsors to make their move. Joe is waiting for John and John is waiting for Joe and you have to get one to make his move to get the other to move. In the leagues I have been associated with, some men did make it into the established league through an association with the rebel league; some did not. Some wound up paying up to ten times as much as they would have paid originally to get into the new league. The gamble may be greater to get in at the beginning, but the costs are less. Once you wait to see if a league can establish itself, franchises within a newly established league will usually have multiplied in cost.

Indiana was not committed to the ABA when we announced it as one of the first ten franchises, but we felt it would make its move and it did. Indianapolis previously had a successful NBA franchise which featured the University of Kentucky's national championship and Olympic players. Revelations of the involvement of some of these players, such as Alex Groza and Ralph Beard, in collegiate "fix" activities of the past destroyed faith in the franchise and caused it to fold in 1953. As a hotbed of basketball, with two old but big buildings available to it, Indianapolis should have been brought back before, but the NBA never did it.

When it became obvious that the NBA was not going to go for Indianapolis, a group of young businessmen from that city led by Richard Tinkham, John DeVoe, and Mike Storen agreed to go with us, to be called by the Indiana state name. At the same time, a group headed by Joe and Mamie Gregory, of Hope Diamond fame, H. Wendell Cherry, and Bill Boone agreed to go with us with a franchise in Louisville, to be called by the Kentucky state name. This also was a hotbed of basketball with old but big arenas available. Kentucky became the eleventh franchise. Cleveland should have been the twelfth, but blew town.

The odd number did not disturb us. However, I remember all too well that when we proposed acceptance of the Indiana and Kentucky packages, Gabe Rubin ranted and raved in opposition to it, claiming that these were minor-league towns. He insisted that including them in our league would destroy our major-league image. He stood up at a meeting of our executives and owners and threatened to bolt if we brought in these "bush leaguers." Well, he was outvoted, but he stayed, which wasn't anything wonderful. Indiana and Kentucky became two of the best franchises in the league the first few years, while Pittsburgh was worthless. At least the way Rubin ran it.

I had the Dallas franchise, but I did not want to operate it. I should have sold it, but I wanted to keep an interest in it. At the time it was attractive to me to be an owner of a sports team. I felt it would flourish and prove profitable. Now I'm more interested in operating a league than a team within a league. When I take a franchise as a founding father's right, I sell it to produce part of the profit I'm entitled to as a man who put a league together and got it going. At that time, I did not have the money to sponsor a franchise and I was unable to find an individual with money to back it and me. I was too busy trying to get the league going to pursue it. First I sent Roland Speth to run it. Then I sent Mike O'Hara down to find ownership for me.

Mike, who later became the founding father and president of the professional track and field project, went to Dallas and somehow was able to pull together thirty-three businessmen to back the franchise. They had a net worth of more than $350 million. They had the money, but there were too many of them to operate effectively.

Despite its size, Dallas does not have a decent indoor facility. The team played mainly at SMU's Moody Coliseum, which seated less than 10,000 spectators. I invested $4,000 for 3 percent of the package, but as more men moved into the operation, it was divided more ways and my points became less and less valuable. I had no clout in the conduct of the operation and was far removed from it. Finally, I sold my shares for one dollar to establish my tax loss. In a sense, I broke even. My firm received some legal fees from the franchise. However, for a similar effort I probably could have put together two or three successful companies.

Dallas lost money every season, and in its seventh season the franchise was shifted to San Antonio, which is a smaller city but has a bigger arena and seems to have greater enthusiasm. The franchise averaged only around 2,000 fans a game in Dallas, but averaged 6,200 fans a game in San Antonio. And Red McCombs and his partners who now run the club apparently are willing to spend money. I understand they spent $300,000 to acquire a strong rookie center, Sven Nater, from the financially plagued Virginia franchise.

However, San Antonio is rated only the fiftieth-best market in the country, and it does not have a major-league image. For example, when Ernie DiGregorio was much sought by both leagues as the most colorful performer coming out of college ranks in 1973, he asked, "Where do you think I'd rather play, Madison Square Garden or San Antonio?" McCombs, himself, may have put the kiss of death on the operation when he strolled in, shrugged, and said, "Well, we'll give it a couple of years and if it doesn't go, we'll go on our way."

My partner, Don Regan, spent a lot of time trying to place his floating franchise in towns from Philadelphia to Phoenix. Finally, he parked it in Louisville. He paid $6,000 for it and sold it for $30,000, plus a 5 percent interest in it, which was sold for $35,000 when John Brown bought the club. I shared in all of this, as did Mike O'Hara, and it was the most money we made out of the ABA.

Dennis Murphy's partners dealt him out of the Anaheim deal by promising it to Art Kim. Dennis was then supposed to become a partner of Ken Davidson in Oakland. Dennis brought Davidson into the league. But Davidson then dealt Dennis out by pairing up with Pat Boone. With the backing of his boss, Jim Trindle, Dennis then tried to cut it in Kansas City but was unable to obtain satisfactory dates at the arena there. The franchise was shifted to Denver. Dennis, who is a Californian and had desperately wanted to stay in California, went to Denver to try to get the franchise off the ground.

Vince Boryla, former Notre Dame and New York Knick star, was hired, then promptly fired, as general manager. He subsequently sued and collected on a three-year contract and collected before the first season was completed. A one-

75

third partner was sought and a two-thirds partner was found, J. W. (Bill) Ringsby, who put up $170,000 to gain control of the infant franchise, then another $85,000 to take it over completely. Dennis was just trying to bail his company out of the financial bind he'd drawn them into and he did not profit from this, nor did they. The money went to pay back bills.

Dennis drifted back to work for his firm in southern California, then responded to a call for help from a friend, Larry Shields, who was getting into trouble running the Minneapolis franchise. Dennis went there. When the franchise was transferred to Miami the second season, he went with it as general manager on salary. However, he stayed with it only one season, then dropped out of the ABA and headed home. Dennis's dream had become a nightmare. He had become a gypsy. And he had little to show for it.

McShane went to Hawaii, where he died. He had sued for money from the ABA, but did not get any. Now, his widow is suing John's lawyer for failure to pursue the suit. Speth remains in public relations and pursues some projects for me. If he did not make any money, it did not make him bitter. Life is fun for him, and he writes off the ABA as an interesting experience.

After the first season, the Anaheim Amigos became the Los Angeles Stars. Against my advice, they transferred from the Anaheim Convention Center to the Los Angeles Sports Arena. Art Kim sold the club to Jim Kirst. Bill Sharman had left San Francisco and the NBA to come in to coach this club in the ABA and it was becoming a good team, but it had not yet caught on at the box office after three seasons. Kirst was suffering financial losses in his construction business and needed money so started to seek a buyer for the franchise. He announced that if he hadn't sold it by season's end, he'd have to give it away. This destroyed any chance he might have had to sell at a profit. Potential buyers just stood off and waited. Attendance started to pick up in the playoffs as the team went all the way to the finals, but by then it was too late. I'm convinced an ABA franchise could have succeeded in southern California if properly and patiently financed.

Kirst blew a bundle. He wound up all but giving the team away to Bill Daniels, who put it in Salt Lake City as the Utah Stars. Zelmo Beaty became eligible to play the first season there and Bill Sharman coached the club to the league championship. An expansion team or an existing team locating in a smaller community should have been located here. However, the franchise has only scratched the surface of the potential. The splendid Salt Palace, which seats 12,200, seldom has been half full. It was not sold out once during the 1973–74 season, although the club was a championship contender. The average attendance was only 6,800. And Daniels was seeking to sell it so he could concentrate on his campaign to become governor of his home state of Colorado.

The Oakland franchise lasted in Oakland only two seasons. It brought in Bruce Hale from Miami as coach as a way to bring in his son-in-law, Rick Barry. It worked, but Barry didn't. The courts ruled he could not play for the Oakland ABA franchise until the option season in his San Francisco NBA contract expired. Barry sat out the season. The next season, Hale was kicked upstairs, Alex Hannum became coach, and Barry became eligible to play, though he was injured before season's end. Oakland did win the championship. However, the Oaks had got off to such a terrible start their first season, losing seventeen in a row at the end of the season, that by the time attendance started to rise, the second season, the bank account was in ruins.

It turned out Ken Davidson didn't have much money. He used most of what Boone could borrow. It also turned out that about a million dollars were spent that no one could account for, which depressed everyone no end. When Earl Foreman arrived, waving money, Davidson and Boone welcomed him with open arms. He bought the club at bargain rates and transferred it to his city. Washington, D.C. Mikan didn't care. He thought Oakland was Oklahoma, anyway.

Barry cared. He signed again with San Francisco, saying he had an agreement with the original owners that he wouldn't have to move from his beloved Bay area if the club moved. The court didn't agree, saying he had to play two more years in the ABA. So he played in an ancient arena in our nation's capital that no one would go to. The Carolina club was showing promise with a regional operation that played in three North Carolina cities. Impressed, Foreman made his franchise a regional operation in Virginia that played in Richmond, Norfolk, and Hampton Roads.

Barry was sent a Virginia uniform so he could pose for a *Sports Illustrated* cover story. Foreman was so pleased that he ordered 500 copies. However, when he opened a copy he found that Barry had blasted Virginia and the South as the last place on earth he wanted to live. Among other things, Rick observed he didn't want his son coming home from nursery school and drawling "How y'all, Daaaad." It was Rick's way of saying he didn't want to play there. Foreman got the message.

Backed by San Francisco owner Franklin Mieuli, Rick offered Foreman $220,000 for his contract, but Foreman refused and instead sold him to the New York Nets for what I believe to be $250,000. Roy Boe, the new owner in New York, got Rick to sign a contract for $800,000 for five years, provided he was able to stay with the team that long. He was not. After his original ABA contract expired after two seasons in New York, the courts required Rick to return to the San Francisco NBA contract he had signed when the Oakland franchise shifted. Now he is back in the NBA with San Francisco, which, by the way, is now playing in Oakland.

Foreman has not made it in Virginia. The franchise seems headed for the poorhouse or some other place, but Foreman has a way with money and will not go with it. He got the Oakland Oaks simply by taking over a $1.2 million note from the Bank of America, which was set to foreclose on the previous owners. All he had to do was agree to repay the sum without interest from his profits when he sells the franchise. I've heard Virginia interests paid him $500,000 to get him to take his team there. He got the $250,000 for Barry. He signed Charlie Scott, who became a superstar, out of college, and when Scott defected to Dick Bloch in Phoenix in the NBA, Foreman received a settlement perhaps as much as another $500,000. He signed Julius Erving out of college, and when Erving tried to defect to Atlanta of the NBA, Foreman sold Erving to his old buddy, Boe, in New York, for a cool million. He drafted Sven Nater out of college and sold him to San Antonio for $300,000. Nater, Bill Walton's understudy at UCLA, shows signs of becoming a superstar. Foreman had put up another star, George Gervin, as security for a loan of $250,000 from San Antonio, and when he could not come up with the cash, he was compelled by the courts to come across with Gervin. By my mathematics, Foreman has received between $2 million and $3 million on his maneuvers. He now may sell or fold his franchise, which attracted an average of only 3,100 fans per game in the 1973–74 season.

The regional concept for sporting franchises seems to

have failed. After a disastrous start, the Houston franchise was sold to Jim Gardner in North Carolina, but after it showed promise for two seasons playing in Charlotte, Greensboro, and Raleigh, interested started to sag. Gardner sold out to Todd Munchak, who now wants to sell out. The team payroll shot through the ceiling with the acquisition of such name stars as Billy Cunningham, Joe Caldwell, and Jim Chones, and it has not paid off at the box office or on the court. Attendance averaged less than 6,000 fans per game in the 1973–74 campaign. Munchak cut Chones, sold star Ted McClain to Kentucky, and announced he wanted to move the team, sell it, or fold it.

Minnesota moved the second season to Miami, where Ned Doyle took over the club. However, after three seasons there, the Floridians folded. Pittsburgh moved to Minnesota when the Muskies moved out the second season, then the Pipers moved back to Pittsburgh for the third season. After the fourth season, they folded. After three seasons, New Orleans moved to Memphis, where Charles O. Finley bought the team. But Charlie O., the controversial owner of the Oakland A's and Seals, has shown no interest in either the Seals or the Tams. He has had skeleton staffs struggling on their own to survive and has been seeking to sell the franchises somewhere before they fold or are returned to the leagues. Attendance averaged only 2,300 last season.

A San Diego dentist, Lenny Bloom, came into the ABA with an expansion franchise for his city the sixth season, bringing with him a dream of getting his own building built in suburban Chula Vista. San Diego has a perfectly fine arena, but it has an arena boss, Peter Graham, who seems impossible to live with. Dr. Bloom went so far as to buy one of our WHA franchises, the Los Angeles Sharks, as a prospective tenant for his new San Diego building to make the arena proposal more attractive to the residents who had to vote on the bond deal. He even enticed Wilt Chamberlain away from the Los Angeles Lakers as player-coach of his basketball team, the Conquistadores, at $600,-000 a season to encourage interest. But the courts ruled Wilt had to sit out the season before he could play.

Wilt didn't even get up off his duff to charm the voters. Then the voters turned the proposition down, by a mere 300 votes out of 19,000 cast. Nor did many fans get off their duff to go sit in the seats to watch Wilt sit in his seat coaching, when he showed up for games, that is. The Cons played in the 3,200-seat Community Concourse, and I don't think they've filled it yet. Attendance last season averaged 1,800. Bloom hasn't even been around to see his team lately. General manager Alex Groza is getting lonely. Soon they will be the ex-Cons. Having been rejected by his hometown, the good doctor may move to Los Angeles to take on Jack Kent Cooke's Lakers.

Only three teams have stayed put from the first—Denver, Indiana, and Kentucky. The original New York–New Jersey franchise remains in operation, too, but it started as the New Jersey Americans and only moved to Long Island to become the New York Nets after that. And Denver was supposed to be Kansas City. Denver was booming when it acquired Spencer Haywood and won a divisional pennant a few years ago, but the Ringsbys let him get away and it hurt the franchise and it hurt the league. Disappointed by the experience, they sold out to Frank Goldberg and Bud Fischer, but the Rockets have been unable to recapture the magic. Alex Hannum was fired after his efforts to rebuild the team were frustrated. The ancient arena holds only 6,800 fans and attendance averaged only 4,100 this past season. But with a big building and competitive teams, Denver can become a boom town in both basketball and hockey.

The Kentucky franchise has an arena that seats almost 17,000 in Louisville and an area that loves basketball, but there has been talk of moving this franchise to Providence or Cincinnati in recent seasons. I have to feel that if you can't make a go of pro basketball in Kentucky, you can't make it anywhere. Actually, Kentucky averaged an attendance of 8,100 last season, second best in the ABA, and lost money only because players such as Artis Gilmore and Dan Issel cost them so much in salaries. The new Kentucky Colonel, John Brown, bought Colonel Sanders' Kentucky Fried Chicken franchise operation. He made $30 million and spent $1 million of it for 52 percent of the basketball team. He was going to move it until his ten-year-old son wept. Instead, he turned the team over to his wife, Ellie, as a sort of playtoy. She promptly brought in an all-gal board of directors and surprised everyone by how well she hustled tickets. However, one wonders about the stability of an operation which can fire a coach who carried his club to the best record in the league. Babe McCarthy was bounced after his side lost the playoff finals.

Dick Tinkham, Charles DeVoe, and John Weissert have run a stable operation in neighboring Indiana. Of course, Indianapolis is in the heart of the best basketball country, but the old arena the Pacers have been playing in seats only about 10,000 fans and it has required productive methods to turn a profit. They have kept an exceptional coach in Bobby Leonard, have kept adding new stars to a solid nucleus of veterans, and have won three pennants and three playoff championships. Their attendance average of 7,500 fans per game was only third-best in the ABA during the 1974–75 season, but should soar with a move into a new downtown arena, which seats some 18,000 fans. The same operators will run the new World Hockey Association team here and should do well with it, too.

Under the ownership of Roy Boe, the New York Nets have been building brilliantly. Once the new Nassau Coliseum opened, he had a large and lavish building to attract fans from a prime population center and he has spent extensively to bring in business. He brought in Barry and did everything he could to keep him. Then he bought Julius Erving, who led the team to the title in 1974. Attendance of around 9,000 was the best in the ABA and the 16,000-seat arena was sold out at times during the playoffs. The New York Nets should be the cornerstone for the building of a basketball league which could last forever, but there are too many weak spots remaining in the construction of the circuit, too many problems for which satisfactory solutions have not been found.

The first season, the ABA drew 1,200,000 fans to its regular-season games and averaged 2,800 fans per game. Last season, the ABA pulled 2,300,000 fans and averaged 5,500 a game. It has been averaging around 5,000 fans a game for several seasons now and shows no signs of moving up. Only three of the ten teams increased attendance in the 1974–75 season—the New York, Kentucky, and Texas clubs. The first season's playoffs pulled an average of 3,900 fans a game. Last season's average reached 9,300 fans a game. Clearly, there is some potential there the league has not yet reached.

The ABA has resumed efforts to force the NBA's hand with a new $600 million anti-trust suit filed in 1974. But it has not applied adequate pressure to the NBA. It has lingered too long in small towns. It has permitted too many good players to get away from it. It has failed to land the superstars. It has only a couple of players comparable to the best in the other league. It missed its best bet when it let Lew Alcindor get away. He wanted to go with them. It missed again with Bill Walton.

The ABA tried hard to get Walton. It was willing to shift its San Diego franchise with Wilt Chamberlain to L.A. as his team. It offered to set up a new team for him or move an existing team with his UCLA teammates as his pro partners and tried to get Jerry West as coach, but when West decided to remain with the Lakers, Walton decided to join him in the NBA. I believe the ABA offered Walton a better contract than he accepted from the NBA, but he preferred to accept the challenge of the NBA.

Philadelphia and Portland of the NBA had to toss a coin for draft rights to Walton. Philadelphia did not offer the life style preferred by Walton, but Portland did. Philadelphia lost the coin flip to Portland and I wonder if that was a two-headed coin the NBA used. The NBA was not as willing to work out what Walton wanted as the ABA was, but the NBA won out, anyway. The ABA lost more than just another player. It had not built up the prestige needed to attract a player of Walton's type and may have forfeited its future.

As this is written, the ABA badly needs a merger, but so does the NBA. The two leagues need a common draft to arrest the salary spiral before it spins away any opportunities for profitable operations. They could set one up with contractual provisions which would free the players from slavery. They could keep their separate identities by operating in two divisions under the same banner. Interleague competition bringing the top stars of both circuits into all the cities on the tour and a sort of Super Bowl of basketball as a playoff finale would be a bonanza for the sport.

Mike Storen still was insisting at this writing that the ABA will operate as an entity with ten teams in 1974 and 1975. He speaks of relocating old franchises or locating new franchises in Los Angeles, Chicago, Tampa, and Albany.

I sympathize with the school of thought that to succeed the ABA had to buck the NBA in the big cities, such as New York, Los Angeles, and Chicago. But I also would have been tempted to seek to establish franchises in such large and glamorous cities as Toronto, Honolulu, and Mexico City, which have been denied big league basketball up to now. To me, this would make much more sense than trying to make it in small cities in Virginia or North Carolina.

I do not believe the ABA will make it, but it is fighting hard. A merger may be inevitable. Tedd Munchak sold the Carolina club for a half-million down to New York interests who have relocated the club in St. Louis and hit a home run by signing one of the college stars most sought by the NBA, Marvin Barnes, for $2.5 million over six years. Other ABA teams signed other top stars. However, the Carolina club already had been stripped of its stars, as had the Memphis and Virginia teams. The ABA finally put together a group to buy Memphis from Finley and Mike Storen resigned as commissioner in order to take over the team. Munchak replaced him as commissioner. Musical chairs. Foreman finally sold the Virginia franchise to a Norfolk group for more than a million.

It should be becoming apparent that if troubled owners hold out long enough they can unload their teams for more money than they put into them almost every time. It discourages sportsmen from buying teams, unfortunately, but big businessmen can benefit from buying teams by applying most of their purchase price to the depreciation of the players over five-year periods, and can apply these and other losses incurred in running the team against any profits from other business, providing themselves with tax shelters that are so attractive as to minimize the actual cost of purchasing a franchise. The sale of players becomes capital gains.

All these are selling points salesmen such as myself use in offering franchises around. One job I wish I'd held in my younger days was that of used-car salesman. I'd probably have learned something I could apply successfully today. But I really don't try to con anyone into coming into one of my operations. I lay out the good possibilities and the bad possibilities. It's just that the possibilities for businessmen are better than the press and public realize.

The ABA has players who are attractive to the NBA. Julius Erving of New York is the top all-around player and most attractive performer in basketball today. George McGinnis of Indiana may be the next-best forward in basketball. Artis Gilmore is the sort of center who could make a winner of one of the NBA's losers. And there are others who could contribute a lot to NBA teams. The ABA also has franchises which are attractive to the NBA. The New York, Indiana, and Kentucky, franchises, of course. Salt Lake City, San Antonio, and Denver operations have potential, too, but may not all make it.

It's a shame, but pro basketball has problems. The NBA has been in business more than a quarter-century and the ABA has been in business the last seven years, yet the two together still are grossing only about $55 million a year, which is the least in major league sports. The NHL is supposed to have a far more limited market, but its gross business has been $50 million and the first two years of the WHA has pushed the combined total for the two past $65 million. The major league baseball business grosses $130 million a year. And the National Football League $140 million. It's no wonder I went into football.

Competitive bidding between the two basketball leagues has pushed payrolls past reason. I suppose we who started the ABA are responsible for this, but the players are responsible for prolonging it. By refusing to accept a common draft they have boosted salaries, but they may wind up eliminating paychecks for all the players and other personnel who will be out of work when ABA teams go out of business. In the long run, more players will be harmed than helped.

It is not as if professional basketball has a strong hold on the public. The ABA was hurt by its failure to land a good television package, but NBA telecasts are dying. The NBA has almost as many sore spots as the ABA. Many of its franchises have never turned a profit. The owners shore up their bank accounts by charging for franchises in new territories, such as New Orleans, where the ABA failed.

By its nature, basketball is a badly constructed game. It was conceived as a stylish, non-contact sport, but the large size of the players, the small size of the playing surface and the aggressive style of play that has developed have turned it into a different, rougher game than originally intended. The tall men are too close to the ten-foot baskets, and it is too easy for them to dominate the game. The fastest and most spectacular players, the smaller men, are overshadowed by giants, only a handful of whom are attractive players.

Fans may support their hometown teams, but in most cities hockey and football are more popular. This is why basketball on television does not draw as wide an audience and so attract nearly as much money as football does now and as hockey will when most of those who are strangers to it in the United States are exposed to it extensively.

To be brutally blunt, basketball has become a black man's game, and that limits its potential popularity. I don't believe blacks are necessarily physically superior, but there are more good black players than white players. Most of the blacks still hail from harsher backgrounds which produce tougher and hungrier athletes. Basketball is the least expensive game to play and is the game most played in black neighborhoods. Blacks had won thirteen consecutive Most Valuable Player awards in the NBA until Dave Cowens won in 1973 and the first five MVP awards in the ABA until Billy Cunningham won in 1973. Blacks have become the best basketball players, and there is only a handful of white superstars such as Cowens, Cunningham, Dan Issel, Rick Barry, and Jerry West. Yet, whites make the most money and can most afford to attend professional sporting events. Whites control most of the companies that buy blocks of season tickets to sports. And I do not believe the average white can identify as well with the blacks who are the dominant superstars of professional basketball as they can with the stars in baseball, football, and hockey, where the balance is better.

Boxing people will tell you their sport sagged when blacks and other minority groups became the best in the business and the white customers could not identify as well with the men in the ring. It sounds like a prejudiced point of view, but it is true that boxing promoters and managers hunger for "white hopes" to attract white audiences. It is business.

I would have liked to have had as many black stars as possible in my hockey league. I would have liked to have attracted business from blacks. But there are few black hockey players, so there are few black hockey fans. That is a fact which limits hockey's possible popularity. But it is not as limiting as the lack of whites is in basketball. There are tremendous black stars in baseball and football, but there also are tremendous white stars. Thus, both blacks and whites are attracted to the sports. These sports appeal to a varied audience, and their popularity is thus unlimited, which is ideal.

I do not feel I have to apologize for having played a

part in starting the American Basketball Association, whether or not it survives. It could have prospered. As it is, it has developed some marvelous players, given employment to many more, and provided a better way of life for many people connected with the league. It has developed some profitable or promising franchises and provided enormous entertainment for many fans in many cities, many of which did not have big league basketball before. The mere fact that it has endured seven years despite tremendous problems is proof there was room for it and a place for it in sports. The fact that the established league has survived is proof the rebel league was not the monster it has been portrayed to be. I do not believe the death of the ABA would pump fresh life into the NBA. Professional basketball and the NBA are better off with competition.

CHAPTER 5

As Others See It, I

SPENCER HAYWOOD

He lay in bed all day, watching cartoons and soap operas on television and thinking about the game he had to play that night. He took time out only long enough to eat enough to keep him. His mind was on the game, not on food. By the time he got dressed to go to the arena, in what he calls his Chicago gangster suit, he was worked up high.

The closet was packed with fancy clothes. The suit was raspberry shaded, striped, and double-breasted. He hummed a jazz tune as he pulled it on over silk underwear. He was a black man, 6 foot 9 and 215 pounds, and he seemed imposing in the gaudy gangster garb. He knotted the laces of shiny black shoes, pulled a large, feathered hat down over one eye, admired himself briefly in the mirror, and cut out of his large, lavish apartment.

He went downstairs and got into his shiny new Cadillac and drove the big car through downtown streets to the

Denver Auditorium. He got out and was surrounded by kids, hailed as a hero. He was only nineteen years old, a rookie in professional basketball who should have been just a junior in college, but he had left to turn pro and he was the top player in the young American Basketball Association his first season.

"I'm good and I'm getting better. I'm going to be the best." He smiled, looking a lot like the comic Bill Cosby. But he was not joking. He was enthusiastic and confident beyond his years. He was good and he knew it. The crowd that night went wild as he led his Denver team to a triumph over the best team in the league, Indiana. He had the size and strength of a big man and the moves and touch of a little man. He was a complete player with fancy skills developed on ghetto playgrounds.

Born into a big family locked in a grip of poverty in Mississippi, he endured incidents of racial oppression and lack of opportunity until as a teenager he left to live with brothers and sisters who had escaped to the big cities of Chicago and Detroit up north. He figured, as they had figured, that anything would be better than what they'd known, but it wasn't much better for poor, poorly educated blacks in these rat-infested ghettos, surrounded by hard people hustling to make it with prostitution, narcotics, or crime.

He was saved by a brother who brought him to Detroit and turned him over to Will Robinson, a high school coach who turned out great basketball players. Spencer had the ability to become great, and Robinson got him going. Sought by college basketball factories, but lacking educational polish, Spencer was prepped at a junior college in Colorado. Detroit University landed him with the hint that Robinson would be hired to replace its departing coach.

When more mature blacks boycotted the Olympics, Spencer was one of the youngsters recruited to fill the gap, and he became famous as he led the U.S. team to the gold medal in Mexico City. In his first season at Detroit, he led the nation in rebounding. But he was unhappy with college life and disenchanted with university officials when another coach, Jim Harding, who had the reputation of being a hard task master, was hired to coach the club, not Robinson. The ABA was desperate for talent, and an agent, Steve Arnold, got to Robinson and told him there was no reason an undergraduate could not jump to the pros. He sent Robinson and Haywood to Denver, and Robinson encouraged Haywood to sign with the owner there, Bill Ringsby. Haywood did.

The ABA invented a "hardship rule" by which college players in need could sign with professional teams if they were in need. Haywood's mother still was washing floors and clothes for whites back in Mississippi. He and his brothers and sisters had little. The need was real. It didn't matter. There really was no reason a player who was not interested in college could not pass up college to play for pay. Why should he waste what might be the most financially productive years of his life?

The NBA, which had courted Haywood, was outraged. Their rule, presumably to protect youngsters from forgoing an education, required players to wait until they graduated and were drafted by an NBA team. The ABA destroyed the strength of that rule. There was no reason for Haywood to wait. The fattest part of his life lay in becoming a basketball star, not a scientist or teacher or scholar of some sort. He was ready, as he proved that first year as he led his team to a divisional pennant and was voted Most Valuable Player in the league.

He had signed at first for a contract that promised to pay him $450,000 for three years of service. He was to be paid $50,000 a year for three years, then receive an annuity of $15,000 a year for twenty years from age forty. A New Yorker, Ralph Dolgoff, devised for the ABA a plan for the investment of contracted monies which promised greater returns in the future for lesser expenditures in the present. The Ringsbys, father and son, who operated the Denver team, proposed to Spencer that he sign one of these new contracts, which would cost them less but bring him more under this plan. He signed a new contract for another $450,000 for three years, but one which had a chance to be worth even more in his later life if the investments paid off.

Haywood had been happy in Denver. He had money in his pockets, a fancy car, a fancy apartment. A bachelor, he loved the ladies and was popular with them. "Hey, life can be beautiful," he beamed. But then, NBA scouts began pressing him, promising him fortunes if he would jump to their side when his college class graduated. The Ringsbys responded by offering Haywood a far richer contract, calling for $1.9 million for six seasons' service. He was to receive $50,000 a year for the two years remaining on his contract, $75,000 a year for four additional years, and $1.5 million between the ages of forty and sixty. He signed it.

During the summer, he traveled across the country. On his tour, he visited with many pro basketball players. They questioned the quality of his contract. They said there was no way he could be sure he would get what he had been promised and that, anyway, a lot of cats were receiving more. Troubled, Haywood took the contract to Al Ross, a Los Angeles attorney recommended to him as a manager of professional athletes. Ross reviewed the contract and said it was worthless. Ross said the contract revolved around the Dolgoff Plan and there was no way it guaranteed the payments Haywood had been promised.

Ross demanded that the Ringsbys provide a new contract guaranteeing that his client receive the announced sum. The Ringsbys, by now feeling nothing would satisfy their star, refused. In the fall of 1970, Haywood left the Denver team during the preseason and hid out at Ross's house while Ross and the Ringsbys negotiated bitterly, threatening to take each other to court.

Finally, Ross put a price on Haywood and made him available to others. ABA interests fought to keep him in their league, but could not pry him from the Ringsbys. Although his college class still had not graduated, Haywood was signed by an NBA maverick, Sam Schulman, owner of the Seattle franchise, for $1.5 million in cash for six seasons' play, spread over ten seasons. And the Ringsbys, Ross, Schulman, and Haywood went to court.

The NBA threatened to expel Schulman for violating their bylaws, but Sam insisted he was within his rights. He defied his partners, and the courts upheld him, ruling there was nothing illegal about a professional team's signing a college player, nor anything that gave a team in a league which drafted that player later rights to him over a sister team which already had signed him. The court case between Seattle and Denver dragged on through much of the 1970–1971 season with Haywood playing for Seattle under great pressure, commuting to court appearances.

He sat in a Seattle hotel room, stripped to the waist, too disturbed to finish getting dressed, too restless to call down for food. He wasn't hungry, anyway. He sat for a long time, his head down, staring at the carpet. He lay back on the bed. It was mussed and uncomfortable, but he didn't bother to straighten it out. He wasn't looking for comfort. After a while he stood up and went to the big picture window and stared out at Seattle and the fog-shrouded bay beyond. It was a gloomy day, and he was gloomy.

He had been speaking and then he had grown silent for a long time and now he had begun to talk again, slowly and with effort. "All I want is what's coming to me," he said. "I want to tell you there are so many lawsuits and court cases flying around me I can't even begin to keep them straight."

He sighed, dispirited. His face was somber. He had lost weight and seemed thin. He said, "I am tired, man. I am tired and I am scared. All I want to do is earn a living, playing basketball. I don't know how much I'm worth. All I know is what they tell me I'm worth, and then they won't give it to me. So I have fought for it, and I am being made to look like the worst man since Hitler for it. A man on the street told me a long time ago, 'If you don't stand up for something, you'll fall for anything.' Well, I'm standing up for Spencer Haywood.

"I am not playing well. Man, I am playing poor. But I'm tired and I can't keep my mind on the game. The Ringsbys treat me like a nigger. The ABA commissioner, Jack Dolph, he just laughs. And the NBA commissioner, Walter Kennedy, wants to throw me out on my ear. My own teammates resent me. Who'm I, Superman, come to save their souls? Who've I got? Al Ross, yes. My lawyers, yes. I hope to hell I can trust them. My family. I can trust them. But Will Robinson, he's like family . . . and he's turned on me. He's with the Ringsbys. They must be paying him off. With promises. Poor black man getting paid off with promises ain't never gonna come true."

Ross and Schulman were winning their case. The Ringsbys were losing. They settled out of court with Schulman. Haywood was freed to play with Seattle. He said it was as if a giant weight had been lifted from his shoulders. But the memory of it stuck to him like some stain. He had been scarred by it. He felt he had been put through hell. He felt he had been manipulated like a pawn by whites who weren't interested in him, only in his talent. Asked if he hated whites, he said he did. There were still the memories of Mississippi, and now these new, bitter experiences. Even Ross? "No, not Ross," Spencer said. "He helped me. He put himself on the line for me."

But, as Spencer became a star in the NBA, the outstanding star on the Seattle team and a hero in the city of Seattle, he became a different man than he had been. He had been hardened by his experiences. He was exposed to more mature black stars. He himself was maturing into the man he would be. He was being educated by life, becoming sophisticated. He became a militant black. He broke with Ross. Spencer went his own way, which was with his black brothers.

"This is a black man's league," he observed. "Most of the best players are black. Without the black players, it would not be much of a league. But there are not many black coaches. And no black owners. Well, it is no favor to us to free us from slavery. That was supposed to happen a long time ago. That is not a favor; it is our right. And we are going to fight for our rights. I will not beg from whites. I will work with my black brothers. I will be the best basketball player I can be. But I will do it for me, not for the owners."

He is an individual now, strong and tough. He may be wrong. But he may be right. Each man decides for himself what is right or wrong.

He says, "I have no bitterness against the ABA. It gave me my chance. It gives a lot of black men a lot of playing jobs. It gives all of us in both leagues a choice. The ABA was good for basketball. It did not treat me right. I had to fight to get free of it. But you have to fight for your rights in the NBA, too. You have to fight the establishment. The ABA is now part of the establishment."

Following the success of his Haywood transfer, Ross broke the contracts of Jim McDaniels, John Brisker, and Charlie Scott with the ABA and sold McDaniels and Brisker to Schulman in Seattle and Scott to Dick Bloch of Phoenix. He made money and they made money. But if Haywood did not disappoint Schulman in Seattle, McDaniels and Brisker did. New coach Bill Russell benched them, and Schulman sought to sell them in 1974. He could not, and remained stuck with fat, long-term contracts with them. Scott satisfied Bloch in Phoenix, but the prices being paid unproven players had begun to seem a gamble beyond reason.

Ross said, "No matter how much you do for some of these fellows, they always seem to want more. Sometimes I think nothing will satisfy them." He was beginning to sound like the Ringsbys.

AL ROSS

He sits, polishing himself like a jewel, in a setting of splendor, high atop the city. He would own it if he could. As it is, he'll take what he can get, piece by piece. He is Al Ross, who manages athletes, one of the men who has revolutionized sports. He has been called "immoral, a hollywood hustler, a quick-buck artist," and worse. He was bothered when an adversary called him "a Beverly Hills bastard Jew lawyer." This was getting personal. He broke the man's back, in a polite business way, of course. He ducks the bad names as though they were bullets and carries on as though he were a medic on a mission of mercy at the front.

97

What really bothers him is when he is called an agent. "Don't call me an agent," he says, as though it were a dirty word. "I am an attorney and a business manager, and I head up a large organization with a full-time staff of experts and access to the best brains in the country. First United Management offers by far the most complete service in the field to our clients. We get them business, negotiate their contracts, bank their money, budget it for them, invest it for them, provide tax shelters for them, pay their taxes. . . ." In a pinch he will deliver their babies for them and bail them out of jail when necessary, which it has been at times.

He says, "We do a helluva a job for the guys. Sure I make a buck off them. It's business. But they know where every buck goes. They know I care about them. That's the difference between me and some of the other guys in this business. I care. I worry. Some nights I don't sleep." He is white and some of his clients are white, but because most of the top athletes are black, most of his clients are black. He says he feels for them as only another member of a persecuted minority could feel. He says, "The black guys have been put down more than the white guys in basketball. It's as if they have no other way of earning a living and should be grateful for whatever they're offered by the owners.

"The owners resisted negotiating with managers until they saw it was inevitable. It was unfair for them with their staffs to draw up a contract and expect a young guy, maybe one without a lot of education, to just sign it without knowing what it said. They won't admit it, but the managers have got a lot more for the players than they ever got for themselves. But we couldn't have got it if the other's hadn't been willing to pay it. I didn't have a gun to hold at their heads. I only had the talents of my guys.

"New leagues are the greatest things that could happen to sports. When a Gary Davidson or a Dennis Murphy comes along with a new league he provides new opportunity for the players. And the players are the leagues. The leagues wouldn't exist without the players. The ABA was a godsend. The players were in slavery until the ABA came along. They had no choice of where they could play. They had to take what pay they were offered or not play. In a competitive situation, the salary offers rise to their highest point. The player commands the most his talent rates.

"The ABA people thought I was an NBA guy because I took guys out of the ABA and signed them with the NBA. The fact is I signed guys with the ABA, too. I signed guys where I could get the best deal for them. The best deal wasn't always the most money. It was the most money guaranteed at the best terms. And I win my cases. Rick Barry lost his. I didn't represent Rick.

"The ABA money wasn't guaranteed. The Dolgoff Plan was a joke. Take Spencer's case. The most the ABA had to pay Spencer in real salary was $400,000 over six years. The only other thing they had to put out was $10,000 a year for ten years—another $100,000. This was supposed to generate $1.5 million from mutual investments by the time Spencer was sixty. For an expense to them of half a million, they advertised a contract worth $1.9 million. And there was no way they could guarantee it. Who knows what's going to happen in the stock market? It's ridiculous. Also, they filled their contract with loopholes. Any time Spencer left them, he lost the money he had coming to him. He had no vested interest in any part of the future sums promised him.

"The owners blame me if a guy doesn't come through for them. I don't oversell my guys. I don't wrap them in a surprise package and try to sell them without the owners knowing who and what they're getting. The owners have general managers and coaches and scouts to tell them what a guy is worth. I try to get the most money I can for my clients. The top price an owner will pay, that's what I take. Sometimes a coach gets down on a guy. Bill Russell wasn't playing McDaniels and Brisker. How could they play good for him? They had some super stats some games they did play for him. They couldn't get good stats sitting on the bench. The NBA doesn't know how good these guys could be. Ask anyone in the ABA. They know.

"I'll admit sometimes money spoils these guys. They never had much money in their lives, and when they get some they get greedy. And sometimes they don't give a man his money's worth. Well, you can't control human nature. The more some people get, the more they want. The players compare notes, and every one wants to make more than the next one. Well, they can't all make the top salary. Conditions differ from owner to owner, from city to city, from player to player.

"I manage the money for my guys so they're set for life. But sometimes no matter how much you do for someone it's not enough. Some of these guys forget fast. The job has its headaches. I did a lot for Spencer and I lost him. Some fellows aren't grateful. Well, what can you do? All you can do is your best. The best guys appreciate you and make it all worthwhile. But I can assure you I'm no fast-buck artist. I put in a lot of hours and a lot of sweat and a lot of thought into my work, and the money comes in slow sometimes. It pays off, but I pay a price for it."

SAM SCHULMAN

A Brooklyn boy, educated at New York University and the Harvard School of Business, Sam Schulman made it big in business. He was the chairman of the executive committee of the National General Corporation conglomerate at the time he signed Spencer Haywood and other stars for his Seattle franchise in the NBA. In his sixties, hard and shrewd, he says, "The fans in Seattle have supported me and my team beyond any rewards we have given them, and I have made it a mission in life to bring them any rewards I could. I decided in my own mind that the youngster had the right to rebel against his ABA contract and we had the right to sign the youngster against existing NBA rules. I will fight for my rights when I feel I am in the right. Well, we were right on every count and we won every decision in the end.

"It was one of the most frustrating periods of my life because I found myself losing respect for men I had respected. No sooner had they lost their own fight to acquire Haywood than they turned on the winner. There were times I toyed with vengeful pursuits. I never considered signing Spencer for any city other than Seattle, but I did seriously contemplate the establishment of a new professional basketball franchise in the Sports Arena in Los Angeles with such UCLA stars as Sidney Wicks and Curtis Rowe, whom I felt I could sign as our stars. The Lakers do not operate in Los Angeles, you know. Their home Forum is in Inglewood. I did not pursue the project because I recognized my motives as spiteful and did not consider that a proper basis for beginning a business venture.

"I predicted four years ago that if the American Basketball Association remained in business it would pose a threat to us by the early 1970s, and my forecast proved correct. In any such venture, owners inevitably suffer heavy losses at first. If they have the resources to persevere, their chances of succeeding in the end grow increasingly greater as time passes. My fellow owners ignored both the lesson the NFL learned in the success of the AFL and my warning, and they did not begin to act appropriately until the ABA had begun to hurt the NBA heavily in the acquisition of new talent and the cost of this talent. Now I think a merger is in the best interests of both leagues and can be achieved without denial of legal rights to the individual players, and I have worked and am working to this end.

"Strangely, I have harder feelings for some of my fellow NBA partners than for some of my real opponents in this his fellow owners operated understandably and ethically in seeking to keep a valuable property within their province. I think Al Ross is an intelligent and imaginative person who can represent athletes responsibly and to their mutual benefit without working any hardship on management.

"In wars there are casualties. A war such as the ABA brought the NBA inevitably produces casualties. The weak will fall by the wayside, while the strong go on. There is nothing wrong with competition coming to the NBA or any other business operation. So long as it is fairly fought. But it is bound to be costly. And when the costs get out of hand and threaten the future of franchises and thus of leagues, peace must be sought so some economies can be practiced. The players and their representatives must realize that if they let greed get the best of them, that if they do not put some reasonable limits on their financial aspirations, they will kill the goose that is laying the golden eggs. The men who have operated the ABA have proven their right to exist alongside the NBA. The two sides should seriously pursue coexistence rather than prolonging a war which could kill off one or both of them."

CHAPTER 6

As Others See It, II

BILL SHARMAN

"I had coached in Abe Saperstein's old American Basketball League and was well known in southern California, so it was not surprising when Dennis Murphy and his associates approached me for an opinion when they were considering the start of a new professional basketball league. I told them I thought a new league could work if it was run right and the old league hadn't worked simply because it hadn't been run right. Saperstein had been so successful with his Harlem Globetrotters he just couldn't conceive of not succeeding with another basketball enterprise. But the ABL wasn't the Globetrotters. You couldn't just put the team out on the court and expect the fans to fill the seats. You had to spend money for players and promotion and build up a following. I warned Dennis it would not be easy, but it could be done. He had to get good owners. He had to get owners who had money and were willing to spend it the first few years to make money in later years. The problem in the ABL was that Abe was the owner of most of the teams. If he wasn't the man up front, he was the man behind the men up front. He didn't have enough money to make all the franchises go, and he wasn't willing to spend what he had.

"Although I am now an NBA man, I really consider myself a basketball man. My real loyalty is to basketball. I left the NBA to go into the ABL because I felt there was room for another basketball league, or at least more basketball teams on the professional level. There are more young players playing basketball in this country than any other sport. Hundreds of fine players graduate from the college ranks every year, and there was limited opportunity for them to play professionally. When I was with the Boston Celtics and Bob Cousy and I were playing the guard positions with Sam Jones, K. C. Jones, and Frank Ramsey behind us, a young guard had no opportunity to break onto our team for many years. Some might have been better than us, but they never got the chance to show it. Although basketball is my profession and I am in it to make money, to make a living for myself and my family, I really do feel a loyalty to the sport which has given me everything I have in life. That loyalty to the sport is greater than any loyalty to the NBA. I really felt an opportunity to do something for my sport by going into the ABL and helping it go and creating job opportunities for players and coaches, and major-league franchises for cities that didn't have them.

"The ABL didn't go, but when the American Basketball Association came along I felt again the opportunity to do something for basketball and for young players. I felt there were large cities in this country which could support two major-league professional basketball teams and many others which did not have one which could support one. I did not go into it with Dennis and Gary Davidson, because I had an opportunity to go to San Francisco to coach in the NBA while it was still not clear the ABA would begin in business. But after two years in San Francisco I did go into the ABA to coach the Los Angeles team, and I stayed with the team when it went to Salt Lake City, where we won the championship. I am proud that I am the only man who ever will have coached championship teams in the ABL, ABA, and NBA. No one else will get that opportunity. I got my chance to win a championship in the NBA, which I had narrowly missed in San Francisco, when I returned to the NBA in Los Angeles. I returned because it was an opportunity to return to California, which I consider my home, and my wife's home, where my children are. And the ABA was standing on its own and no longer needed me. It was a better professional opportunity for me.

"However, I wish the ABA well, even though I may be in the NBA now and may be considered in competition with it. As much as I came in contact with Dennis Murphy and Gary Davidson, I came to respect them enormously. I think they did a tremendous job of getting the league going. I wish they'd heeded my warnings more to take in only the top prospects as owners, but I guess as a practical matter that is easier said than done. I think they made some mistakes. I don't think they should have left Los Angeles, frankly, although my boss with the Lakers, Jack Kent Cooke, no doubt does not mind that they did. I think the team we were putting together in Los Angeles would have become a big team at the Sports Arena. But Jim Kirst just did not have the financing to keep it going, and a buyer here could not be found. It may have been a mistake. Bill Daniels bought the team which became a champion in Salt Lake City the very next year.

"The fact that the league still kept going is proof it had its place. It has had its problem spots. So does our league. We have more strong teams in more of the big cities. But it has some strong teams, some players that are as good as most of those in our league, and some cities that are as good as most of those in our league. After Gary Davidson and George Mikan left, the ABA ran through a number of presidents and commissioners. The league needed strong leadership. It needed a better break from the news media. Once there no longer was a team here in Los Angeles, we hardly heard of the ABA and its good teams and good players here. It needed a good television package which would give it national exposure.

"It posed some problems. I'm happy for the players that they are highly paid. I was a player myself not so long ago in an era when we were not highly paid. I do think they may be so highly paid they may be spoiled now. I think they must see that there are limits in the economics involved. The owners cannot continue to pay for a package that does not pay off. The leagues badly need a merger and some system worked out between them so salaries level off at a reasonable point. The system is faulty where untried players are paid more than proven stars. Most of the money must go to veterans, not newcomers. As a player proves himself and contributes to a club over a period of time, his salary should rise. The collective salaries should represent a fair return of the money being made by the teams.

"I look forward to a time when professional basketball is on a sound basis in many cities across the country, coast to coast, and the opportunities to players and coaches is in proper proportion to the popularity of our sport, which I think is the fastest growing of all sports."

GEORGE MIKAN

"We worked hard to get the ABA going. I think we laid a solid foundation. New leagues like this are good for sports.

They give more opportunities for more young men. I was one of the first men in the early days of organized pro basketball leagues in this country, and at that time only six or eight players out of college ranks had a chance to turn pro every season. As the pro game grew, more and more players got their chances. It is just now approaching the point where the supply equals the demand. It is not at the saturation point yet. There still is room for growth. People forget there have been mergers of basketball leagues from the beginning. The NBA grew out of mergers of the old National Basketball League and the Basketball Association of America. The NBA and ABA should not stay at war. The NBA should welcome the ABA as a partner. It has proven its right to exist. A merger is inevitable. If I am wrong, I think they will kill themselves off.

"I was the best-paid player of my time. I have no complaints. But I did not earn anything near what ordinary players earn today. As an old player, I am sympathetic to players' problems. I think they should get as much money for themselves as the traffic will bear. Most of them will have short careers. But a merger is necessary to stabilize salaries. You can't have unproven players being paid more than proven players. You can't stick owners with salaries for players who can't play. And the players have to recognize their responsibilities to their salaries. They have to settle their salaries between seasons and think only of basketball during the seasons.

"I don't like to see players tempted to turn pro before they complete their college careers. Life is cruel enough for a well-equipped person without throwing kids out in the world without the background of an education to help them when their short basketball careers are over. There isn't room for that many coaches. And coaching is an unsatisfactory profession. I tried that, and I know. A lot is done for players, but not much for coaches. Players have to be protected from themselves. This jumping from league to league is ridiculous. They're wined and dined and sign new contracts when they already have contracts. Contracts mean nothing to these guys. And the judges go along with them. As a lawyer, I can't understand court rulings in these cases.

"The day I took over the ABA and saw what condition the league was in I almost had a heart attack. I can't understand how businessmen can go into a sports business and not apply sound business principles to it, but to them it isn't business, it's a toy. And the founding fathers of the ABA didn't demand anything of the men they accepted as owners. If a man could produce a $5,000 check he was in. When I became league commissioner, the league had no money. I put out $35,000 of my own money to operate my office. The league later repaid me, but it shows how poorly structured it was.

"I had to hustle to keep teams going. I remember Art Brown, who owned the New York team, saying to me he didn't know how I kept the league together. Teams would be about to fold and I'd go to town and prop them up. I'd tell owners how to operate. Unfortunately, they wouldn't always listen. They were worried about things like having a league office in New York. It was unnecessary. I wanted it in Minneapolis, which is my home, where I have my business interests. It was as good a place for an office as any other. I still had to fly to the towns in the league. When I operated the league I operated it for half a million dollars. Today they spend a million and a half and it's still rising.

"I did a lot for the fans. I tried to give the game back to the fans. The red, white, and blue basketball was my idea, and I had to fight Gary Davidson to get it in. It proved popular with the players and fans and gave the league an identity. Shooting clocks were set at thirty seconds to speed up play and cut out stalling. The three-point long shot brought the 'home run' into basketball and is a fans' favorite. The

NBA is foolish for not adopting it simply because the ABA has it. It helps the small player stay in the game. Although I am a big man, I recognize the appeal to the fans of the fast, scrappy small man. He has a place in the sport, too. They're just getting around to rules I wanted, rules which cut down on free throws and keep the players from fouling out. Fans don't pay six or seven bucks to see stars foul out and sit on the sidelines.

"It's expensive for fans to attend games. You have to give them their money's worth. You have to make it attractive for families to attend. You have to give them a good game, good food, half-time entertainment that is something more than some kids shooting baskets. You have to give them postgame entertainment, even if it's only a small band or a singer. At most arenas the concession stands close before the game ends. A guy is stuck with having to take his wife or girlfriend or his family out for a postgame snack. Why shouldn't he be able to sit in the arena and have a hot dog and a cup of coffee and listen to some music and not feel he has to rush out into a traffic jam? That's why the pros went up to twelve-minute quarters. You can't charge a guy top prices and turn him loose at nine thirty to find some way to finish off the evening. You have to give him a complete night's entertainment at the arena.

"I got along with Gary. We had our arguments. We had a lot of differences of opinion. We thought different things should be done. And divided authority rarely works. He's a fine young man. He's a fine attorney. I don't know how good a businessman he is. I know he doesn't know a thing about basketball. I thought a basketball man should run a basketball league. Is that unreasonable? He said he thinks the future of professional basketball is limited because of the domination of black players. That shows how much he knows about basketball. Who wouldn't pay to see an Elgin Baylor play? What difference does color make? The University of Minnesota basketball team didn't start a white man last year and were sold out for the season.

"I don't go for controversial players, black or white. I don't go for the guys who wave their fists in the air and sneer at their country. I don't go for the guys who say, 'I've got talent, screw you.' I do go for the young man, regardless of color, who displays ability and conducts himself in the true spirit of sports without bringing in racial or religious issues.

"I think when you bring a group of young men into a town to represent a town you have to introduce them to the community so the community can embrace them and feel they are part of them. I think most teams enter a town and say, 'Hey, we're pro basketball, here we are, support us.' That's a bunch of baloney.

"The ABA remained alive all these years despite all the mistakes it made because there was a need for it, but if the players in the ABA and NBA go around biting the hands that are feeding them, and the owners don't give the fans their money's worth, they won't last forever. I left because they didn't want a boss. Everyone wanted to run the show for himself. They better get together. They can still fall apart."

MIKE STOREN

"The product is there. It is our job to sell it. Our teams are totally competitive with the NBA. But from the public's standpoint, the ABA is in trouble. I mean I have guys tell me, 'Hey, that mess down in Memphis is awful. You aren't going to make it.' But I never heard the guy on the street say, "Geez, that mess in Houston is awful. The NBA isn't going to make it.' Our attendance figures, with the exception of

New York and Los Angeles, are comparable. We might move some franchises, but only on a very sound financial basis with a lot of research.

"Owners have a habit of saying in public they want a man who will run their league, then the first time he does something, they say, 'What the hell do you think you're doing?' I think the owners in this league understand the problems; they understand where we are going and what we have to do to get there. There's no magic formula. But I don't view this as the commissioner versus the owner. They are not running me, and I'm not running them. Maybe I'm the first commissioner to convince the owners we have to stand together to get things done.

"The agreement we reached with the NBA is finished. It just frustrates me completely that the NBA is unable to look at its balance sheets and say, 'We have a problem.' I don't care about indemnities. I don't care about television. I don't care about jumping. If I'm the NBA, I've got problems. They say they'll do everything except give up the reserve clause. That is the single issue blocking the merger. Well, we have reinstituted our antitrust suit. If they want war, we'll give it to them. We have our rights, too. Right now I'm concerned only with our own problems. We'll solve them. And we'll have a merger with the NBA some day, too. It is an inevitable economic necessity for both leagues."

[Storen resigned as commissioner in 1974, to straighten out "the mess in Memphis."]

DON REGAN

"I met Gary Davidson in 1955 at UCLA. I was a senior and he was a freshman, but we were the same age. He'd bummed around at other colleges first. He's never been as stable as I am. I rushed him for my house, but he pledged another fraternity. He never has learned to accept my advice, although I'm usually right. I went into the service and for two years served as a small-boat officer in the Navy in Japan. When I came back I went to UCLA Law School and was in the same class with Gary. By then he'd caught up to me.

"We played intramural basketball and touch football together at UCLA, which hardened our friendship. In later life, he gave up football when he almost lost his life playing it. He was rather reckless. But I still play basketball and tennis with him. I should say he plays these sports with me. He can't carry my jock. I'm much better, but he's dirtier. He loves sports, but if he was as good in business as he is on the tennis court, we'd both be broke.

"He has more guts than good sense. One day Barbie, who became his wife, had a Christmas party at her parents' home. They had a swimming pool and the guys got to fooling around and he got pushed in. Well, he couldn't swim. So I had to jump in and save him. I don't know if he'd have drowned or not, but after giving it careful consideration I decided to save him just to play it safe. And it paid off, because now he owes his life to me and can't prove otherwise. I keep reminding him how he was floundering in that pool that day, our future about to go under.

"We both got married while we were still in law school, and our wives got as close as we were and our kids began to come along at the same time, so we were really tight with one another. We also were broke. Gary had this brilliant idea to invest in the commodities market. I thought he was crazy, but I went along with him. We bought soybeans. It was a bull market for soybeans. We made enough money to get us through our third year of law school. That was the first time I realized he might be good for something besides being a buddy. And someone I could beat at basketball or tennis. We even had money left over. But then we blew that on some other harebrained scheme, and I started to have doubts about his wisdom again. We blew our first few investments, and I figured he was just lucky that one time, but then he came through for me.

"He really is the creative side of our partnership. I'm the conservative side. He's more of a gambler, but I've come to trust his instinct. He has vision. I don't trust anything I can't touch, but I let Gary look ahead for us. I try to keep him within reasonable bounds. We don't agree on anything. But we are able to reach an agreement on which way to go with everything. We complement each other. I'm a much better lawyer because I'm much more interested in details. I graduated in the top 10 percent of my class. I don't know where Gary was. He was so far back I couldn't find him on the list. I guess he graduated. He said he did. And he showed up at the ceremonies and they didn't kick him out. Actually, he's a helluva lawyer, but no one knows it anymore, because he doesn't work at it anymore. He's a financier now. Sounds fancy.

"After graduation, I joined the largest law firm in L. A. County—Rutan and Tucker. I don't know how they got so large. They were terrible judges of young talent. I'd been working there a year or two when I told them I was worth more money than they were paying me. They told me they'd already decided I wasn't worth what they were paying me. It seemed a smart time to take my leave. I'd learned a lot from them, anyway, and I felt ready to go out on my own.

"I asked Gary to go in with me. But he'd just joined another firm and felt he should stay with them awhile. When he left them, he asked me to go in with him, but I'd just joined another firm and felt I should stay awhile. We never got too far apart. In those days, we lived near one another, each family had only one car, and we took turns driving each other to work and leaving the other car behind for the girls. Eventually we decided we really should go into our own firm to cut down on the driving time. It was as good a reason as any. We talked Pat Nagel into going in with us by letting him list his name first. Our firm name is Nagel, Regan and Davidson. You'll notice who's last. That tells a lot.

"However, he likes the limelight, so I let him have it. I hate him for it, but I let him have it. We're partners right down the line. At the end of every year we throw everything into a pot, figuratively speaking, and split it evenly. We don't try to figure out who did more. We can get along like that, which is rare. It was his idea to go into sports, I agreed, and when we went he was out front. He's never let me get in front of him for a minute ever since. When the news guys come, he locks me in my office. He has a passion for politics. He'd like to be president. Or king. Or dictator. He has a bigger ego than I do. I know I'm the brains behind him, but he won't admit it. It's all right. It's worked.

"I try to keep guys happy. Dennis Murphy, who's been in with us on a lot of things, does, too. We sweet-talk them until we've got them cornered. Then Gary comes in for the kill. He says, 'You bastard, you break your word to us, we'll break your back.' He says, 'Screw you, you can't have it your way, you have to have it our way.' Not our way. I'm sure he says 'my way.' Well, it works. Anyone who's been in with him finds he's right 90 percent of the time, which is a helluva batting average in any league.

"He'd fall on his face if I didn't build a solid base beneath his schemes, but he erects a helluva structure on top of the base. We've made a lot of money together. I can't knock a good thing. We're closer today than we've ever been.

"Roland Speth brought Dennis Murphy and John McShane together with Gary and me to discuss their idea for a new pro basketball league. Gary thought it was a good idea and sold me on it. But once we got into it we could see the way it was being developed it wasn't such a good bet. Gary almost bolted the first big meeting we had, but they pacified him by making him president. I became general counsel for the league, but about eight other guys thought they were the general counsel. That ship had about twenty-two captains. It would have sunk on launching if Gary hadn't kept it afloat himself. In business, he can swim. He's got guts, and he gets answers to questions.

"As soon as Mikan signed a contract as commissioner he shoved me aside and moved in his own attorney as legal counsel for the league. I didn't write the player contracts. Mikan's attorney wrote them. And approved those the franchises signed with players. Which is what got the league in a lot of trouble, because the contracts weren't any good.

"Mikan argued every decision that had to be made with Gary. I guarantee you Gary was right more than he was wrong. Without him, I don't think the league ever would have got going. It's been going ever since, but it's floundered ever since, also. I guarantee you if Gary had remained as president with the power to make the final decisions the league would have been healthier today and would have forced a merger or at least taken its place in the sun with the NBA long ago. Once Gary left, Mikan didn't last long.

"Our part decreased so rapidly we decided to get out while the getting was good. We'd learned a lot. We didn't know what we were going to do, but we knew we were going to be the boss of any venture we went into from then on. We weren't going to get involved in an investment that meant big money without a say in how it was spent."

HOCKEY

CHAPTER 7

As Others See It, I

Clarence Campbell, NHL PRESIDENT, *June* 1971: "The 1974–1975 season is the closest realistic date for future expansion of the National Hockey League."

Clarence Campbell, July 1971: "The World Hockey Association? What is it? I don't know anything about a new league."

Clarence Campbell, August 1971: "I would think it would be hard sledding for the World Hockey Association or any other new league in our game."

Clarence Campbell, September 1971: "As far as the NHL is concerned, the WHA is welcome. We don't presume to rule."

Clarence Campbell, October 1971: "I say God bless them, if they can be successful."

Clarence Campbell, November 1971: "We will take a normal competitive position and we will not take an obstructive position in any way toward the WHA."

Gary Davidson, WHA PRESIDENT, *December* 1971: "We have ten cities in our league. We hope to get at least two others. Atlanta and Long Island have been two we've wanted all along."

Clarence Campbell, January 1972: "The National Hockey League definitely is interested in Atlanta and Long Island as two of its cities for the future."

Clarence Campbell, January 1972: "I cannot conceive of any important players making a move from our league to the new league. A few fringe players may seek to transfer, but we will insist our contracts be upheld."

Bernie Parent, January 1972: "I'm satisfied with my salary and my place in the NHL, so why should I go somewhere where I don't know what's going to happen?"

Bobby Clarke, YOUNG NHL STAR: "You have to consider it when a new league offers you a lot of money, but you have to consider a lot of other things, too. Things like family, teammates, security. People say players have no loyalty anymore. I think we're loyal to our team, but I think loyalty to your family comes first. Before jumping leagues you'd have to consider your teammates and friends—what you'd be doing to them. But you also have to consider that teams in sports do not hesitate to trade players away. I don't think hockey players are underpaid. I think basketball players are overpaid. But every player has to decide this for himself. This is what I think. Others may make the move. As for myself, I'm making a lot of money now. My family eats good. I've got a new car. I'm happy where I am."

Phil Esposito, VETERAN NHL STAR: "I think the WHA is great. There will be competitive bidding for players' services. Salaries will rise. The player will be out front where he belongs. Up to now the player had no choices. If the WHA works, the player will have choices. He will have a say in his pay, in the place he plays, in his future. Any working man is entitled to that. Any working man is entitled to bargain for the best he can get for himself. I think every player wants the WHA to work. The players are taking the WHA seriously, even if most of the NHL isn't. I doubt that I'll go, but I think you'll find some good players will go. There's a lot of players who aren't happy with their lot in life and just want to better themselves."

Gary Davidson, February 1972: "It gives me great pleasure to announce the signing of Bernie Parent of Toronto of the NHL to a contract with Miami of the WHA."

Howard Casper, PARENT'S ATTORNEY: "Bernie has been given one of the best contracts ever offered an athlete. I have seen that it is guaranteed. It assures his future. He had to make the move."

Harold Ballard, TORONTO PRESIDENT: "How could we deny a kid like Parent a chance to pick up the kind of money we can't pay him? If Miami can pay it, I want him to have it."

Bernie Parent: "I had to take the deal the WHA offered me for the sake of myself and my family and our future security."

Clarence Campbell, March 1972: "We will do everything in our power to protect ourselves. We will insist that our players live up to their contracts. I do not think many major players will take a chance on the new league."

Bobby Hull, April 1972: "I don't plan to make a move, but if the WHA offered me, say, a million dollars up front and a million dollars in salary for the next few years I'd sure have to think about it."

Clarence Campbell, April 1972: "I can't conceive of Bobby Hull making a move into such an uncertain situation as the WHA. I think Bernie Parent may admit now he made a mistake. His Miami team is no more."

Gary Davidson, May 1972: "Bernie Parent will remain in our league. The franchise which was to have been in Miami will be in our league. Bobby Hull may be in our league. We are prepared to offer him a million dollars up front and a million dollars in salary for the next few seasons."

Gary Davidson, June 1972: "We welcome Philadelphia into our league. Bernie Parent will play for our new Philadelphia franchise."

Bernie Parent, June 1972: "I am happy to be back in Philadelphia, if not in the NHL. When I was in the NHL, Philadelphia traded me to Toronto. Now that I am in the WHA, the team that signed me, Miami, did not make it, but I will sign with Philadelphia, which will make it. We will make it together, the WHA and I."

Gary Davidson, June 1972: "I am happy to announce that Bobby Hull has signed a contract for more than two million dollars with our Winnipeg team in the WHA. He will receive a million dollars as a bonus and more than a million dollars in salary the next ten seasons. We will be in business for ten seasons and many seasons after that. We will be in business to stay."

Clarence Campbell, June 1972: "We will fight to keep Bobby Hull in our league. Players must see that they must honor their contracts."

Clarence Campbell, June 1972: "It is my pleasure to announce the addition of new National Hockey League franchises for Long Island and Atlanta for the 1972–1973 season."

Alan Eagleson, NHL ATTORNEY, PLAYERS' ASSOCIATION: "I suggest that the owners of professional sports enterprises always have considered themselves to be business entrepreneurs. They have taken political steps to ensure their preferred status, and until recently they have been successful in running their business in a crude, cunning, and deficient manner.

"Don't make the mistake of assuming that the World Hockey Association is a joke. It isn't. Even if the WHA goes no further, which I'm sure it will, it already has made a substantial contribution to the careers of NHL players. The NHL Board of Governors recently decided to remove a clause from the standard players' contract which allowed any club to give a player two weeks' notice and outright release.

"At the present time, the NHL contract provides that a club owns a player for life. The club can deal with a player at its whim, but the player has only two choices—play when and where the league advises or retire from playing.

"Owners say that the hockey player is so highly paid that he must accept the reserve clause as a condition of his payment. This reasoning is going by the boards. With competition for his services, the player is becoming what he should be—the most priceless commodity in the sport."

Bill Hunter, EDMONTON OWNER, AT A PRESS CONFERENCE:
Question: "Do you expect to make money this season?"
Answer: "I expect to lose a few dollars."
Question: "How much is a few?"
Answer: "None of your (expletive deleted) business."
Question: "How will you get players?"
Answer: "Steal them!"
Question: "Will you hurt the NHL?"
Answer: "Here's a red-haired (expletive deleted) who doesn't give a (expletive deleted) about the (expletive deleted) NHL."

Ben Hatskin, WINNIPEG OWNER: "We have Bobby Hull. We got him by offering him more money than they did. I don't consider it stealing. It was a straight business arrangement between two businessmen. If Chicago and the NHL had paid him more, they'd still have him. He went to work for the new firm, that's all. It took a lot to get him. He'll make money this year. I won't. None of us owners will. But we will in the future. Signing Hull assures our future. How can the NHL say it has the monopoly on the best hockey now that we have the best hockey player? We expect a lot from him."

BOBBY HULL

The time that comes to mind was when his jaw was wired shut and he had to feed himself through a straw and it was painful for him to speak, but when the fans went to him in the corridor just off the ice, he stopped on his way to the dressing room and talked to them and signed autographs for them and tried to smile. Most other players push on through. Even when it was unreasonable for him to do so, he paused for the fans. And, after games, after fifteen years of games in the National Hockey League with the Chicago Black Hawks, after hearing and answering every question over and over again, the same questions over and over again, he still sat in the dressing room in his sweat-soaked underwear and listened to the questions and answered them again, refusing to take his shower until he had satisfied the newsmen who were there, then taking his shower and finding new guys there and listening to the same questions an danswering them again while he dressed, and staying with the guys and making his teammates on

124

the team bus wait until he was sure the guys had got what they needed.

Bobby Hull is special. He always has been. He has been the most explosive and colorful performer of his time in his sport. After Maurice "The Rocket" Richard and Bernie "Boom Boom" Geoffrion, Hull became the third NHL player ever to score 50 goals in a single season. Then he set a new record with 54 goals. Then another with 58. Five times he scored 50 or more goals in a season.

The fastest skater and hardest shooter hockey has known, he slammed slapshots like bullets at goaltenders and fought not to duck them (he had nightmares over them, feared death from them), or he faked them and drove in on them with defenders draped on him and wristed short, swift, sharp shots into the nets.

He was hurt many times. He often played in pain. When Bobby had his broken jaw, John Ferguson, the meanest man in the sport, picked a fight with him, and Bobby stood up to him and returned punches as John jarred Bobby's broken jaw with blows. Hull preferred to play, not fight. He won the Lady Byng Trophy as the most gentlemanly player of excellence in his sport, as well as the Hart Trophy as the Most Valuable Player. But, after fifteen years, he sighed and said, "I've left a lot of blood, sweat, and tears on NHL ice."

The Hawks held his contract. They paid him well, but not what he felt he was worth. He held out one season, and they demeaned him as disloyal, and when he gave in and came back the fans booed him for having stayed away from his team. He never forgave his bosses for having put him in that position. And when the WHA asked him what he wanted and he told them and they got it up for him, he signed with them. He smiled and said, "I asked for so much I was sure I was safe, but when they came up with it I had to take it. It is a lot of money. I have my family and our future to think about. It is a lot of money and a lot of security." It was a lot of money and a lot of security—a $1 million bonus up front and $1.75 million in salary over ten years, the first four at $250,000 a year as player-coach, the last six at $100,000 a year to be determined. Plus side benefits such as a house and farm adding up to an estimated extra $175,000.

He was thirty-three. The long, curly, yellow hair, which caused him to be called "The Golden Jet," had long since begun to fall out and he had begun to go bald. His face was spider-webbed with scars from stitches from wounds suffered in the hockey wars. His nose had been bent in. But that magnificent mug of his, that ruggedly handsome athlete's face with the eyes shining through narrow slits and a smile that illuminated for a mile around, and that incredibly rugged body, like slabs of cement, were still intact on June 27, 1972, when he went through the formalities of signing his contracts with his new employers.

First, he accepted a certified check for $1 million from WHA Properties for promotional services to be rendered to the league. This was his bonus and was his unconditionally. There was a blow-up of it as big as he was to catch the eyes of the cameras. Flanked by his pretty wife and three sons from among his five children, who were smiling but seemed stunned, Hull said, "This is the happiest day of my life. This is the day my family's future life is safeguarded." He smiled and signed his contract with eleven different pens, symbolic of the eleven other league members who contributed to the pot to make the deal. Hull waved one of the pens at Ben Hatskin. He said, "Benny wants these pens back. He's gonna' sell 'em. He needs the money." Hatskin just smiled. Gary Davidson, the president, beamed. "This is a great day for all of us," he said. "This is the day our baby, the WHA, comes of age. No baby ever grew up faster."

Hull shook hands with everyone as he was hustled to a chartered plane for Winnipeg. Here, he was to sign his playing contract, presumably safe, by signing in Canada, from Chicago court action in the United States. Hatskin popped for steak and champagne. Hull thanked everyone on board for everything. At the Winnipeg airport a huge throng had turned out to greet him. People lined the streets along the motorcade route to the Fort Garry Hotel. Here, Hull signed his second contract. Then they all adjourned to the corner of Portage and Main, the town's busiest intersection, where thousands of fans stood and cheered as Hull held the giant reproduction of the check aloft. Again, he said, "This is the greatest day of my life. I'm going to try my darnedest to make the WHA go." Gary Davidson grinned and said, "The WHA is on its way." Hatskin stood with his hands in his pocket as if counting the change he had left.

Chicago fought to keep Hull but lost. The courts delayed the start of his season, but once he started, he went as before. Some had said he would be too good for the league. He was good, the best in the league, but he did not tear it apart. He wound up with 51 goals, but he'd scored more than that in the old league, and he was voted Most Valuable Player, but he'd been that in the old league, and while his team came close, he could not carry it to the title.

Late in the season, he came off the ice from a game his team had won and he paused to sign autographs for fans before going into the dressing room. Inside, he paused to talk to a writer.

He took off his soggy uniform and sat on a stool with the perspiration pouring down his flushed face and said,

"If I told you the millions had nothing to do with my signing with this league I'd be lying. The money was the most important thing. You take a lot to make the most of yourself in sports, and you have to come out with as much as you can because it doesn't last long—you don't last long and the money doesn't last long. It was something to be able to do something to help a league get going that would bring more jobs for players and other people in hockey and help everyone get a better deal and bring big-league hockey to more fans, and that counted for something. But I'm as selfish as the next fellow, and I wouldn't have made the move if it hadn't been so much money that it meant security for myself and my family for the future."

He was asked if he felt bitter toward his old team. "No," he said, "I'm not. They made me a very nice offer, but it was not nearly as nice as this one. I didn't want to bargain with anyone. I told the WHA what I wanted and they told me I could have it. I listened to the Hawk offer and I decided to take the Winnipeg offer because it was a lot better. It took the Hawks a long time to start paying me big money. It's taken the NHL a long time to start paying players big money in general. We all had to fight for what we felt we were worth, and we didn't have many weapons. Our talent is a weapon, and now we can use it. Most of the time the Hawks and the people in Chicago treated me very well. There were times when they didn't, but I don't want to talk about that. I'm happy to be here, and I'm not bitter about the past. I've had a good life in hockey, all things considered."

In Winnipeg he had a fourteen-room, $185,000 mansion in the suburbs and a large farm. Was he happy here? "Yes," he said. "It's a smaller city than Chicago, and while I love Chicago, I'm really a small-city boy. We live right on the edge of the city, and we can be in the country in a few minutes. I love the farm and wish I could spend more time there. I'm a farm boy at heart. I look forward to the time when I can retire and spend all my time working my farm. I really do. I love hockey, and I'll miss it when I leave it. I'm committed to it for a long time now. But I regret the time I can't spend with my family, with my growing children, out in the open air. I don't need a lot in life to be happy. I know that sounds funny coming from me. If the money's there for you, you take it. It means a lot to me. But it doesn't guarantee happiness."

He seemed tired. There were discolored bruises on his skin and a slash on a forearm that was oozing blood. He said, "It's harder for me than it used to be. I'm older and things don't come as easy as they used to. It's hard work now. And I feel the bumps more and don't recover from injuries as fast. Coaching is a lot tougher than I thought it would be, especially while I'm still playing. You have a lot more to worry about, and things don't always go the way you want them to. At first I had to do quite a bit of running around with the court cases and all, and it took its toll. I lost more than ten pounds. I don't carry any fat—that loss was all in muscle and meat. I felt weak and was worried for a while. I'm just getting my strength back."

Yet, he had not stopped doing all the extra things he had been doing for the league—making personal appearances and giving interviews and giving of himself to the fans. He smiled and said, "Well, they're paying me a lot of money and I owe that to them. I always figured I owed it to my sport, anyway. Without the fans, we wouldn't be anything. I don't mind the players getting the big money, but I do mind them not giving of themselves to the fans. A lot of them think all they owe anyone is what they give on the ice. I figure they owe their team and their league and their sport something off the ice, too, that off the ice is part of our sport, too. I think especially players in a new league owe it to the league to help it because the league has brought the players a lot.

"The league and the team have not asked as much of me as they might have. They've been sympathetic to my situation. I give everything I can. Changing leagues hasn't changed me. I'm still the same person I always was. It's not hard for me. Maybe it's just my personality. Maybe it's not in the personality of some other players. But the league needs it. I've been a bit disappointed by the attendance, but, then, attendance is down in the other league, too. I don't think it's expansion or the second league; I think it's all the squabbling in print and all the talk of money. I think the fans are only interested in the players and the playing, and I think both leagues had better start to stress that or they'll be in trouble."

Wearily he arose and stripped off his underwear and padded softly into the shower. The other players already were pulling on their fancy civies. When he returned, drying himself, they were almost all gone. He dressed slowly in slacks and sports shirt and sports jacket and brushed back his thining hair in front of a mirror. Did he have any regrets? "No," he said. "Not yet. I have no regrets. It was more than just a good business deal. It was a chance to be a part of something new, a pioneer. It will be hard for a while, harder maybe than I thought it would be, but it will work. The league may have needed me when I signed, but the time will come when it does not, when it can stand on its own feet, and that will be good for hockey."

He was very tired. He walked out, saying he was just going to collapse in his hotel bed. But the fans were there, outside, waiting for him, so he stopped for them and stood smiling at them, answering their questions, touching them, signing their autographs. It was very late, past midnight, but he was still Bobby Hull.

KEN DRYDEN

"I think the Rick Barry case in American basketball has set a precedent. Any NHL player who receives a decent offer will make a move. Some of us may not be in a position to make a move. Not right away. Some of us are committed by contracts for a while. The worst thing that can happen to a player is that he will be forced to sit out one year and then the WHA will guarantee him that one year's salary. Some players will jump back. But then others will jump. At least we will be able to make our own decisions about our own moves; we have alternatives to consider now; we have an opportunity to better ourselves."

OTHER PLAYERS

Derek Sanderson, who followed Bernie Parent into signing with Philadelphia, jumped back, as did Parent, but Gordie Howe and his two sons, Jacques Plante, Pat Stapleton, Marc Tardif, Rejean Houle, Mike Walton, and other top personalities from the NHL jumped to the WHA its second season. Ken Dryden, Paul Henderson, and Frank Mahovlich were among major NHL stars reported ready to go for the dough in the WHA the third season if a merger did not bar their jump. But Dryden decided to return to Montreal and the NHL. Salaries were still skyrocketing, which might force a merger.

CHAPTER 8

The Salaries

In most cases, the hockey salaries which evolved as a result of the war the World Hockey Association waged on the National Hockey Association, were, contrary to the cynicism of skeptics, as large as or larger than advertised. It is difficult to establish the worth of most of these contracts beyond the base salaries because most were complicated beyond belief by bonus clauses which resulted from extended negotiations between management and players. A survey of some of the contracts is revealing, however.

The contracts given Hull and Parent were simple by comparison with some of the others. Sanderson signed with Philadelphia for a base sum amounting to about $2,325,000 for ten years. He was to be paid $300,000 each of his first two seasons, $200,000 each of his next two, $300,000 for his fifth season, $200,000 for his sixth and seventh season, $225,000 for his eighth season, and $250,000 for each of his last two seasons. He was to be paid $100,000 in advance and then the remaining $200,000 in salary for his first season. He was to receive a loan of $100,000 by September 1, 1972, which was to be repaid by September 1, 1977. He had an option at the end of his last years to turn from playing to scouting, or representing the club in management or public relations at a reduction of his base pay of $100,000 a year. While he was playing he would receive bonuses of $2,000 if his team finished second in its division, $5,000 if it finished first, and $5,000 if it won the playoff championship.

From Cleveland, Gerry Cheevers got a contract calling for $1,400,000 for seven seasons at $200,000 per season, but this would be increased annually according to the increase in the national cost-of-living index. He was to receive a $10,000 interest-free loan to purchase a home and free rental on a new car each year. He also was to receive seasonal bonuses of $1,000 if his team finished third in its division, $3,000 if it finished second, $5,000 if it finished first, and $25,000 if it won the play off championship, $200 per point for each point his club was above fifth place in its division, $250 for each shutout he scored, and $2,500 for a goals-against average below 2.75. His goals-against the first season was 2.83, but he had five shutouts.

J. C. Tremblay's contract with Quebec was rather straightforward. It called for $125,000 up front and $600,000 in salary for five years, and he agreed to serve as coach or assistant coach if called on at no additional cost to the club. Tremblay, Cheevers, and Hull gave excellent service and were named the first all-stars at season's end. Parent gave excellent service and was a second-team all-star, but left at season's end. Sanderson didn't give much service and was gone before the season even ended.

Up front on the first all-star team with Hull were Andre

Lacroix and Danny Lawson of Philadelphia, neither of whom was established as a star when he signed.

Lacroix scored 50 goals and assisted on 74 and led the team and the league in scoring points with 124, which boosted his base income considerably. He signed for $312,000 for five years to be paid at $62,500 a season, with bonuses of $1,000 for 20 goals; $500 more as he reached each plateau of 25, 30, 35, 40, and 45; $1,000 extra at 50, 55, and 60; $1,250 for 45 points and $250 more for every five additional points; $1,000 for leading the team in goals; $1,000 for leading it in points, and some extra $100 bonuses for marks in between. You figure it out.

Lawson, who was first in goals with 61 and third in points with 106, signed for a base of $120,000 for three seasons to be paid $35,000 the first season, $40,000 the second, and $45,000 the third. He had an incredibly complicated bonus system which called for, among other things, $1,500 for his twentieth goal; $100 for each goal between 21 and 25; $150 for each goal between 26 and 30; $175 for each goal between 31 and 40; $200 for each goal between 41 and 49; $2,500 for his fiftieth; $750 for 40 points; another $750 for 50; $50 for each additional point; $2,500 each at midseason and season's end if he was first in team scoring; $1,250 if second through fifth; $750 if sixth through tenth; $4,000 if a first all-star; $2,000 if a second; $1,000 each at midseason and end if his team was first; $750 if second; $500 if third, and so on.

Clearly, these figures called for computers. If a player tried to figure out where he stood after a game, he'd have no time left to sleep. There isn't space to detail them all. Ron Ward, who went from two goals one season at Vancouver in the NHL to 51 the following season in the WHA and was second in scoring with 118 points and a second-team all-star had a fairly simple pact. It called primarily for $122,500 for three seasons to be paid with a $10,000 bonus, $40,000 salary each of the first two seasons, and $42,500 the third season. He was one who did so much more than expected that he wound up dissatisfied; he was getting less than others who had been expected to do more.

Tom Webster of New England, who scored 53 goals and was fourth in points with 103, helped his team to a divisional pennant and playoff title and was a second-team all-star, signed for $150,000 for three seasons at $50,000 a year and had a complicated array of bonuses which included $1,250 each for 20 goals or 40 points; $500 extra for 25 or 50; $750 for 30 or 60, $1,250 for 35 or 70, and $1,750 for 40 or 80, plus $2,500 if in the top five in scoring in the league, and $2,500 if his team won the title.

Larry Hornung of Winnipeg and Jim Dorey of New England wound up second-team all-star defensemen.

Dorey signed for a base salary of $230,000 for four years to be paid $40,000 the first year, $60,000 each the second and third years, and $70,000 the third year. He also got $50 for each game he dressed that the foe did not score more than two goals, and bonuses of $3,000 if the team had a 1.5 goals-against average; $2,000 if 2.0; $1,500 if 2.5; $1,000 if 3.0; $500 if 3.5. He also got $1,000 each at the halfway point and end if his team was first, $750 if second, and $250 if third.

Hornung got $130,500 for three seasons at $43,500 a year, plus $100 for each shutout; $1,000 if his team's goals-against was under 3.00; $1,000 if it finished first; $750 if it finished second; $500 if it finished third. He also had a complicated bonus system based on his plus-minus record, which hockey teams figure out on the basis of goals for and against while a player is on ice. He got $300 if he had a plus record, and an extra $100 for each five points plus.

Wayne Carleton of Ottawa and Norm Beaudin of Winnipeg were third-team all-star wingers. Carleton scored 42 goals and 91 points, Beaudin 38 goals and 103 points. Carleton had created a fair reputation. He signed for $155,000 for three seasons at $50,000 a year with a $5,000 bonus. He was to get $1,000 bonus each for 25 goals or 50 points; $2,000 more for 30 or 60; $2,000 more for 35 or 70. Beaudin signed for $70,000 for three seasons at $22,000 for the first season, $23,500 for the second, and $25,000 for the third. He was to get $500 for his twenty-fifth goal and $1,000 for his thirtieth. Presumably, they were not expected to score what they did.

Rosaire Paiement had scored 34 goals and 62 points two seasons before in the NHL, and he was expected to score more in the WHA when he signed with Chicago. He concluded with 33 goals and 69 points. He was paid $200,000 for three seasons, divided evenly, and had a complicated bonus system that called for $1,500 for his twenty-fifth goal; $150 for goals 26 to 34; $500 for 35; $200 for 35 to 44, and so forth, plus $75 for each assist above 50 points; $1,500 for 50 points; $1,000 to $5,000 for finishing fifth to first in scoring, and $500 to $1,000 for his team's finishing from third to first.

Gary Veneruzzo surprised everyone by scoring 43 goals for Los Angeles. He had signed for $40,000 for his first season and $45,000 for his second season, plus team performance bonuses which the team did not pull off. Signing early with L.A., goalie George Gardner got $50,000 for his first year in the WHA, $55,000 for his second, and $60,000 for his third, plus team performance bonuses. Bart Crashley signed with the Sharks for $45,000 a year for two years, a lot of it in advances.

Two former Los Angeles NHL players—Gordon Labossiere and Wayne Rutledge—signed with Houston of the WHA. Another former Los Angeles NHL player who signed with Edmonton was Eddie Joyal. All had fair years. Joyal was paid $141,000 for three years at $42,000, $47,000, and $52,000 plus a lot of bonuses ranging from $100 to $1,500 for goals, points, and placing in the scoring standards, which he could not collect with only 22 goals and 38 points. Labossiere signed for $105,000 for three seasons at $33,000, $35,000, and $37,000 plus an awesome array of bonuses for goals, points, assists, and standing in league scoring and his team's league standings, most of which he could not collect. Rutledge, a good goaltender, signed for $30,000 for his first season and $35,000 for his second, plus bonuses of $150 per shutout, of $1,000 for a goals-against under 3.00, another $1,000 for 2.75, another $1,000 for 2.50. He finished at 2.96 and squeezed in.

Bobby Sheehan, who led New York with 35 goals and 88 points, signed for $180,000 for three years at $25,000 up front, $50,000 for each of his first two seasons, and $55,000 his third season. He had bonuses calling for $1,000 each for 20 goals or 40 points, another $1,000 for 30 to 60, another $1,000 for 40 or 80, $100 per goal at the way points to 40, and $125 for each goal above 41. There were disappointments. Gary Kurt, who was hammered for 4.78 goals per game in the New York Nets, had a contract calling for $32,500 his first season, $35,000 his second, and $40,000 his third. He missed out on bonuses of $1,000 for playing more than half the minutes, $300 for each shutout, and $500 to $1,500 for averages of 3.50 to 2.50.

Gene Peacosh of New York surprised with 37 goals and 71 points. He was contracted for only $14,000 for his first season and $16,000 for his second season, $1,000 for 20 goals and $500 more for 30, and $1,000 for 50 points. Tim

Sheehy of New England was signed for $100,000 for two seasons and came through with 33 goals plus another nine in the playoffs. He got a $30,000 bonus and $35,000 a year salary and collected around $4,000 in bonuses for individual and team performance.

Brian Perry of New York disappointed with only 13 goals and 33 points. He was contracted for $30,000 for his first season and $35,000 for his second. Brian Conacher scored only eight goals and 27 points for Ottawa. He had signed for $35,000 for the single season, with $15,000 in advance, plus performance bonuses he did not collect. Ron Anderson of Chicago scored only three goals in 74 games. He had signed for $20,000 his first season and $25,000 his second, with $5,000 in advance each season, plus bonuses he did not get. Richard Brodeur, Quebec goaltender, was riddled for a 4.75 goals-against average. He was contracted for $2,000 bonus plus $20,000 for the first season and $25,000 for the second.

The big payoffs continued the second season. For example, the Howes signed with Houston for a $500,000 bonus with Gordie to get $125,000 a year for four years, son Mark $140,000, and son Marty $110,000. Mike Walton signed with Minnesota for $100,000 a year for three years. Marc Tardif signed with Los Angeles for $100,000 in bonus money and $350,000 over three years' service to be paid at $70,000 a year for five years. Rejean Houle signed with Quebec for $110,000 a year for three years. Jacques Plante signed as general manager and coach in Quebec at $100,000 a year for ten years. Pat Stapleton signed with Chicago for $125,000 in bonus, $50,000 a year for five years, plus bonuses for team performances, bonuses to match league bonuses, almost $100,000 invested in life insurance for him over a period of years, ten tickets to every game, and so forth and so on. Many of the contracts contained such complicated clauses. They are incredible contracts.

Henri Richard, VETERAN NHL STAR: "There's so much money in hockey now that you just keep raising your demands until your wife says you're crazy. Then you know you're asking for something you'll get."

Aurel Joliat, SEVENTY-TWO-YEAR-OLD FORMER NHL STAR: "I'm insulted I haven't had an offer from the World Hockey Association."

Neil Shayne, ORIGINAL OWNER OF THE WHA'S NEW YORK FRANCHISE: "Even in war, there has to be some sanity. You can't pay players more than you possibly can take in and hope to stay in business."

Bill Hunter, OWNER OF THE WHA EDMONTON FRANCHISE: "What this league needs is less lawyers and more businessmen. Player salaries can't keep going up. You can't go broke and make money. What's the point?"

Phil Esposito, NHL STAR: "The new league has been great for the players. As long as it lasts. I don't know if it will last without a merger. It hasn't been so great for the owners. I don't know if they can keep paying us more and more. Can the customers keep paying more and more for tickets?"

Tommy Ivan, MANAGER OF CHICAGO'S NHL FRANCHISE: "There has to be a limit to what you can pay a player, or a manager or a coach, for that matter. The WHA may drive the NHL to the wall, and I don't know if that would be good for hockey."

Clarence Campbell, NHL PRESIDENT: "We have the financial clout to put the WHA out of business by 1975. We will not sit back and wait for them to drive us out of business, I can tell you."

Emile Francis, MANAGER OF NEW YORK'S NHL TEAM: "Does Gary Davidson know what he's doing? I don't know. You'll have to ask him."

Gary Davidson

Don Regan

Dennis Murphy

In happier days, Spencer Haywood and Denver Rockets owner, J. W. (Bill) Ringsb announce the signing of Haywood's third and last contract with the ABA team, for $1 million, in April 1970.

Oakland Oaks co-owner and singer Pat Boone serenades Rick Barry at the piano after signing him up for his ABA team in June, 1967. Boone and his partner, Ken Davidson, later sold the franchise.

ABA *star Julius Erving (Dr. "J"), shown here playing for the Virginia Squires, was later picked up by the New York Nets.*

George Mikan, former basketball great and first Commissioner of the ABA.

Opening night for the World Hockey Association, October 11, 1972: League Presiden
Gary Davidson drops the first puck for Quebec captain, J. C. Tremblay, and Clevelan
captain, Paul Shmyr, while Quebec owner Paul Racine looks on.

Bobby Hull, his wife, three of his children, and Gary Davidson pose behind the blow-u
of the $1 million bonus check the WHA paid Hull to join the league in 1972.

Gordie Howe and his sons, Marty and Mark, in Houston Aeros uniforms after signing wi
the WHA team in Houston, June 1973.

Bobby Hull signs autographs before WHA game in Winnipeg, October 1972.

Derek Sanderson—with his lawyer, Bob Woolf, and Philadelphia Blazers owner, Jim Cooper—inks his $2.6 million contract with the Blazers in 1972.

Oakland Raiders all-pro quarterback Daryle Lamonica and former Los Angeles Ra[m]
linebacker Marlin McKeever get an embrace from Southern California Sun general ma[n]
ager, Curly Morrison, after joining the new WFL team, April 1974.

Tom Origer, owner of the
Chicago Fire football team, and
Gary Davidson, president of the
new World Football League,
announce the team's entry into
the new league, October 23,
1973.

Mayor of Detroit Coleman Young holds aloft the franchise for the Detroit Wheels, awarded by the founding fathers of the WFL, December 1973.

Miami Dolphin stars Paul Warfield, Jim Kiick, and Larry Csonka announce in March 1974 that they have signed to play for the Toronto Northmen of the WFL. Behind them are Northmen president, John Bassett, the players' agent, Ed Keating, Mrs. Alice Kiick, Mrs. Pam Csonka, and Northmen general manager, Leo Cahill.

Calvin Hill of the Dallas Cowboys and Ted Kwalick of the San Francisco 49ers are entertained Hawaiian style after signing to play with Honolulu of the WFL.

Gary Davidson exhibits some of the football designs he considered for the new WFL.

The Davidson family—Gary and wife, Barbara, with daughters, Jana and Katie, and sons, Eric and Peter.

CHAPTER 9

As Gary Davidson Sees It, I

Like the American Basketball Association, the World Hockey Association was made up in the mind of Dennis Murphy. He called me in January of 1971 to ask me what I thought of starting a new major league in hockey. He was general manager of the Florida franchise in the American Basketball Association, but was leaving Miami at season's end to return to southern California. He had got little out of his first-born sports infant, carried no clout in the league, and was tired of living away from his home. But he felt he had learned some lessons which would prove profitable if we went into another such venture, and he had decided hockey was a perfect project. It sounded interesting to me. I hadn't got much out of the ABA, either. I had learned lessons, too, which I felt I could profit from. I said I'd look into it and think about it and we'd get together again in the spring to talk about it.

Since I had left the ABA, I'd been busy. I'd come to

see clearly how much it meant to have money when you were dealing with money men and how important it was to have businesses going for you when you went into business ventures. I'd started several businesses, including a string of retirement homes, a manpower service, and an outdoor recreational project, and all were succeeding. I'd gained a lot of know-how in financing projects and putting together corporations. I'd made some money, which I'd invested in stocks and securities, which were making me more money. I probably was worth a quarter of a million dollars, which was more than many men make in their lifetimes, and which was a solid base on which to build a personal fortune. I enjoyed what I was doing, but I wasn't captured by it. I'm a restless sort of guy, always looking for something exciting. My experiences in the ABA had been frustrating, but exciting, and had whetted my appetite for another such venture.

I have to admit I had never been to a hockey game. Strange as it may sound, that made me even more interested in going into hockey. Here was a tremendously popular major-league sport which had not had sufficient exposure. It was supported by a smaller group of fans than those who support other sports, but a more loyal group who were more likely to buy season tickets than those who follow other sports. The average baseball fan may go to one or two games a season. The average hockey fan probably goes to twenty or thirty games. And there were, I felt certain, a lot of sports fans like myself who never had gone to a game who easily might get hooked on the sport if exposed to it.

When I saw how well supported the National Hockey League was, I was amazed. For many years it had been an exceptionally profitable operation even though it was being conducted in only two cities in Canada and four in the United States. In cities like Montreal and Toronto it had been impossible to get tickets to games for many years, and those who owned season tickets willed them to their survivors to keep the precious property in the family. Boston, Chicago, New York, and Detroit had developed very similar situations. Even after the league expanded by doubling in size to twelve cities in 1967, then later added two more to reach fourteen franchises, the league was still playing to almost 90 percent capacity. Unlike basketball, some new franchises made money from the start. St. Louis, Philadelphia, and Minneapolis started to sell out right away and went for hockey as they never had for basketball. Vancouver and Buffalo boomed right off. Only in Oakland, Los Angeles, and Pittsburgh were the franchises struggling. But these all had bad teams. And the sport was new to Oakland and Los Angeles, really. And Oakland had a bad ownership situation. The potential seemed high even in these places.

The National Hockey League was grossing $50 million a year. It had not faced any competition and was spoiled. It had only scratched the surface of potential television returns. It had only begun to invade new markets and put franchises in major population areas that were available. Many more remained available. And many of its cities had more fans who could not get into the games in town than could get in. NHL players were the lowest paid in sports, averaging only about $25,000 a season. Some superstars were making less than $50,000. The players were getting only about a fifth of the operating monies. Obviously, they were ripe for the picking. All my research soon told me that a new major hockey league had unlimited potential.

Hockey had many advantages over basketball. It was a more exciting game to watch, for one thing. Obviously some fans preferred basketball, but in most cities where they

143

had a choice the fans preferred hockey. In every city except New York and Los Angeles, the hockey team was outdrawing the basketball team. When Boston had a championship basketball team every year and a bad hockey team, hockey brought in more business. In Chicago and Minneapolis, where many basketball teams folded, hockey teams prospered. In some cities, such as San Diego, minor-league hockey teams outdrew major-league basketball teams. Hockey was more addictive than basketball.

Hockey had some disadvantages. While it had an appeal for a mass audience, it was not yet a prestige sport in the United States, which could expect big support from the business community. Since there were few black players, it got little support from the black community. Almost all of the players came from Canada, a smaller country, and many felt there was only a limited amount of top talent available.

However, these things often become a matter of supply and demand. Expansion could promote its popularity. The more opportunities there are at the top, the more young men who will go into it. I felt hockey had only scratched the surface of the talent pool that was available or could be developed in the United States and in college ranks, as well as in foreign countries, in many of which this is a big sport. Also, there were enough players around to stock a great many minor-league teams. You can say these were minor leaguers if you want, but pin a major-league label on a player and he becomes a major leaguer. The bottom 25 percent of players in the NHL were interchangeable with the top 25 percent in the minor American, Western, or Central leagues, for example. They went up and down between the majors and minors regularly.

At one time there were only half as many major leaguers in hockey as in any other sport. When the NHL was a six-team major league, it had superteams, but it was operating unrealistically. Compress football, baseball, or basketball leagues into six-team major leagues and these teams will be far superior to those playing now. But it would be a farce, as the NHL was for years. It would deprive good players of opportunity at the top, as the NHL did for years. Who is to say 150 is the correct number of major-league players? Why not 300? Or 450? The line is where you draw it. I do not know if our league raised the line too high, but I know it was too low before. There still are a lot fewer players in the major leagues in hockey than there are in football or baseball.

We got a copy of a standard NHL players' contract to see how sound it was and what our opportunities might be for raiding the league of established talent. We were surprised to find the contracts were weaker than we even might have hoped. Like the NBA contracts, the NHL contract bound the player to the team for an option year beyond the expiration of his contract. Unlike the NBA contract, it did not specify that he play that year for a specific salary. Theoretically, he could have been compelled to play for them for token sums or play for no one. Also, the essence of the contract was that he was tied to the team which held that contract for life.

We felt that such a contract was worthless. We felt that the courts would consider the option clause unfair and would rule the player free to sign with another team once the term of his original contract expired. We felt that the courts had considered the NBA contracts binding through the option year because the terms were reasonable, but that they would not consider the NHL contracts binding through the option years because they were unreasonable. You can't enforce slavery these days.

145

We took it to another law firm, experts at such matters, and they agreed with us.

Don Regan and I discussed this and everything else in detail, and he agreed with me that it was a good gamble and we should go into it. When Dennis came in with his basketball team in March, we met and agreed to go. We figured we had more experience at this sort of thing than anyone else by then and had a good chance. We had money to put into it now and a chance to come out of it with a lot more. I knew enough to protect myself by now. I would be president and Dennis vice-president. The election was unanimous. It was our league, and no one was going to take it away from us.

If it was such a good bet why didn't others go for it? I don't know. They just didn't. We did. That's all there is to it, I suppose. I'm sure a lot of people thought about it, but we were the ones who went ahead with it. We're doers. We put up our money and take our chance. We roll the dice.

In April, Dennis left Florida for good and returned to California and we went to work. We decided we'd each take a franchise. Dennis wanted Los Angeles. The Sports Arena was available there. The Anaheim Convention Center was not equipped for ice. The team wound up as the Sharks, but was originally to be the Aces. I took San Francisco as the next best bet in our part of the world. The Cow Palace was available. We were going to be the Sharks. We decided to seek eight to ten other franchises, and we decided to charge a reasonable amount of money for each franchise. We agreed to divide this money as our founders' fees. We weren't going into this strictly for the fun of it. If the league got off the ground, we would be the ones who got it going. If it worked, we would be the ones who made it work. This was a business venture, and we were entitled to a return on our investment in time, money, and energy, which we knew would be considerable.

We settled on $25,000 a franchise. It was better than nothing, which was what the ABA franchise had cost, essentially. I don't know why we didn't make it $50,000. I think we could have got that just as easily. And it would have helped. Not that we had to make more money. The additional amount could have been poured into the league treasury to support the troubled clubs which were bound to develop and to back up any contractual guarantees. This we did do with extra monies, anyway. This is the integrity of a league as we set it up. We took over a team when it got into trouble and didn't pay its bills. And everyone got every dime due him.

Most important, we knew that the more a man puts into a team and a league, the more he has to protect, the more he is committed, the more he is determined, and the more we're likely to get only men who can make it. However, the men we wanted were the ones we could get, and we were worried about scaring any prospects away.

We did get ten franchise holders to ante up $25,000 each to us as it turned out, which came to $250,000. Several paid more, and the excess went to the league. Dennis and I divided the base sums, $125,000 each. As we always do, Don Regan and I threw our return into the year's return, so we got about $62,500 each. Don did not take a team this time. One for us was fair enough. We took the San Francisco team this time and wound up selling it to Quebec City interests for $215,000. Mike O'Hara was our partner in this franchise. Divided, this brought our law firm about $107,500. I was paid $60,000 as league president for the year. And Don and our firm were paid legal fees. We got a fair return for what we put into it.

In the beginning, Dennis and I anted up $5,000 each

for travel and other expenses, and we began to talk to as many people as we could trust to see what sort of interest there was without tipping our hand too soon. Dennis did a lot of traveling, and I did a little and kept the telephone lines busy. With the ABA we had made a lot of contacts with monied sportsmen we could approach now, and these led us to others we could approach. Once you're known, you can get to such people. We were known. The ABA was still going, and now we were professional promoters.

We figured out a sound structure. In June, Don filed articles of incorporation in Delaware simply because legally that state had the best basis for forming a company. We set up a corporation to operate the league and a partnership for operating the league's intangible assets, such as team names, logos, and such, which might be marketed on a number of items. Handling the legal end, as usual, Don drew up the player contracts, bylaws, and so forth. We three—Dennis, Don and I—formed the first Board of Trustees which signed approval to the bylaws which gave us each one equal vote in the operation.

Now, we had to tie up franchise holders. Ideally, you pick up most promising territories and get a single, sufficiently wealthy, accomplished, and businesslike man to operate a team in each territory. Practically, you cannot pull this off. You take the best men you can get in the territories they want. You know that inevitably some will not work out and will have to be replaced. You also know that if you set the highest possible standards for your owners, you'd wind up with no one. You're not selling a proven property. You're selling a risk venture and your own ability to make it pay off.

You can use salesmanship, but no one will say I deceived them. I laid it out for them as I saw it, the potential for losses as well as profits, the potential and the risks. We warned them legal battles might be long and costly. We figured salaries at about $750,000, travel at about $150,000, equipment at about $50,000, and other expenses bringing the yearly budget to between $1.25 million and $1.5 million. We figured income at from $750,000 to $1,000,000 and probable losses at $500,000. Depending on how much a team invested in salaries and how well it operated, we were reasonably accurate.

We figured the losses could be cut in half the second year and some teams might break even by the third year and begin to show a profit by the fourth year. We encouraged action by stressing that those who come in on the ground floor could come in for the base price of $25,000. Anyone who waited until our league was a reality, until it was safe, would have to pay $200,000. You have to do this or everyone waits.

As always is the case, some of the first franchises that seemed set were the first to fall out. Some of the men who made the most noise about being part of our league went away without a word. You win some, you lose some. You keep hustling. We went after cities we didn't get. Some cities came after us that we didn't want. Where two or more groups in a city asked for franchises, we tried to figure out the best one. Where no one wanted a franchise in a city we wanted, we tried to find someone. When we couldn't find a single strong individual, we settled for a strong group. When we couldn't find a strong group, we settled for a weak one. If they were interested in us, we were interested in them. If they were warm and breathing, we were interested in them. If they died on us, we went back to work looking for a live one. If a man said he could support a team and looked as if he could, we didn't look any further because we didn't want to be disappointed.

Dennis had originally made contact with Herb Martin

149

in Miami, who wanted a franchise in Florida. Dennis left Florida feeling he had a club that could be the cornerstone of a league and a man who was a sort of partner in the project. Martin was supposed to be a millionaire. He was a builder who was going to build an arena in Miami, which did not have a decent one. He had a unique plan. He was going to build four office buildings on four corners of a plot of land he owned. The inner wall of each would serve as an outer wall of the arena. A roof for the arena would be draped between the buildings. We had been advised it was a workable and attractive concept. And he was already completing two of the buildings.

A guy Dennis had met in his ABA business, Paul Deneau, wanted to locate a team in Dayton, which he felt could be in hockey what Green Bay was in football. Two substantial Chicago businessmen, Harold Anderson and John Syke, wanted a franchise there. Lou Kaplan wanted a Minnesota franchise in St. Paul. A New York attorney, Neil Shayne, wanted a team there. With our Los Angeles and San Francisco franchises we were closing in on a nucleus.

It was a Canadian sport, and we realized we needed Canadian teams. We didn't want to take on the NHL in its Canadian strongholds of Montreal, Toronto, and Vancouver, but there were other cities in Canada we felt could support teams. We also wanted teams elsewhere in the world where hockey was popular—the Scandinavian countries, for example. A European division might be developed. Mexico City might support a major-league hockey team. As we investigated it, we saw it was possible, but perhaps not immediately. We couldn't set up operations in other countries as easily and swiftly as we could here. We did investigate Honolulu for a franchise. It is, of course, part of the United States, but it is virgin territory for major-league sports and has a sort of foreign glamour. However, it did not have an adequate arena for ice hockey, and the project was dropped. It may be picked up another time.

We did expect to get a lot of foreign players. Russia's success against Team Canada's NHL all-stars proved how powerful hockey is becoming in other countries. Czechoslovakia and the Scandinavian teams have won major international tests. And if their players are not really amateurs, they are not paid the sort of money the NHL and WHA pays and presumably could be tempted to emigrate.

The NHL has been getting some foreign players lately, primarily from Sweden. We got a few. Our Chicago franchise signed Swedish Olympian Ulf Sterner. But we failed to get the numbers we expected when Al Casmarik failed to come through for us. A flesh peddler of European talent, he was our contact overseas and gave us more promises than production. Others also tried to provide us with players from overseas but did not produce. We were sent some signed contracts. But the signatures turned out to be forgeries. We didn't want to get into that sort of hassle. So we forgot about that avenue to talent for the time being.

However, an international league was an important part of our concept. We even called ours the International Hockey League at first. But there was an International League in hockey, a minor league, in fact an amateur or semipro league, which operated in the U.S. Midwest. Don Regan's wife came up with the name World Hockey Association, which we adopted. Today, the U.S. and Canada. Tomorrow, the world.

We needed to get Canadians into our league, hockey men. Walt Marlow, a Los Angeles sportswriter, suggested Bill Hunter to Dennis. Marlow made an important contribution to the formation of our league and later replaced Lee Meade as league publicist. Marlow was a Canadian originally, a hockey writer, devoted to hockey, and he knew many hockey men. He recommended Hunter as a respected hockey man, but not an establishment man, a maverick who would not be afraid to defy the NHL establishment.

Hunter operated the junior team in Edmonton, and he'd had many battles with the NHL. He was a man who was not afraid to do battle. He might be a man who would be hard to handle. He was an explosive personality, a controversial character in Canada, but he had money and contacts with men who had money. He had brains and guts. After we met with him, we knew he was a man we wanted with us, no matter how much trouble he might cause.

He wasn't so sure he wanted to be with us at first, but we brought him to Los Angeles, where we met with other prospective franchise holders. Here, he became convinced we were for real and agreed to go with us. He brought in Ben Hatskin, who operated the junior team in Winnipeg, and Scotty Munro, who operated the junior team in Calgary. The junior teams are very important in Canada and in the structure of hockey. The men who operate junior teams in the bigger cities are powerful people. Some make a large profit from these operations. Many are wealthy. More than Hunter, Hatskin was independently wealthy. Munro was not, but he was powerful and he had access to men with money. Getting these Canadians in with us gave us credibility with Canadians.

Over the objections of Don Regan, I started to put out stories about our league. It was no longer a secret within the hockey establishment, anyway. But headlines and stories are very important to any new league. Like announcement meetings and so forth, they contribute credibility to your efforts. They make the budding league seem real. They bring people who might be interested to you. You can't find everyone you need. You have to put yourself in a place where they can find you. They began to find us. Prospective owners began to pop out of the woodwork. I do not mean to make it sound easy. Most of the men who approached us had very few real thoughts of going with us. It was just a possibility. Most of the men who had serious thoughts about it would not go with us. You have to wade through them all.

Late in September we had our first formal meeting of the new World Hockey Association in Los Angeles. Fourteen prospective franchise holders showed up. We asked for money for the first time. We asked them to put up $5,000 of their $25,000 entrance fee as deposits on their deals. Eight put up their money. Six held out or backed out. We weren't sure which way some of them were going to go. A group from Atlanta came in headed by Thomas Cousins, part of the group who owned the NBA Hawks. He expressed interest in joining us, but would not put up any money. We wanted Atlanta badly. The South had no major-league hockey.

I suspected from the start that Cousins was just using us as a wedge to get an NHL franchise. Obviously, there were advantages to going with the NHL if an owner could get a team in. The NHL was the only existing major league. It had the tradition, the great cities, the colorful franchises, the superstars. But it was going to cost an owner $6 million to get an NHL franchise, and for that money he would not get any superstars—he would get the leftovers from the established team's rosters, the players others in the league didn't want. He would get poor players and a poor chance to do well in the league for years to come. It would cost an owner $25,000 to get a franchise in our league, and if he wanted he could spend three or four million and acquire some of the greatest and most glamorous players in hockey. He would be starting out even with his rivals and have a chance to be the best. He would have two to three million left over to operate handsomely with. Or he could keep the money.

That was part of our sales pitch, and while it worked up to a point, it is too bad more men did not go along with it. No one really invested three or four million in talent. Everyone has to pay salaries. Used as front money and an investment toward paying future salaries, three or four million would have brought a man a team comparable to Montreal's or New York's. It could have bought two superstars, four top players, and a dozen other solid major leaguers. No matter what happened to the league, the owner would have had property worth more than he had invested in it. His franchise would have turned a profit from the first. His franchise would have been welcomed into the establishment at any time.

Instead, Cousins went into the NHL with Atlanta for $6 million. He didn't have a single outstanding player, and he won 25 of 78 games. Roy Boe went into the NHL with a Long Island franchise in the new Nassau Coliseum, which we wanted very much for our New York operation. It cost him not $6 million, but $12 million, since he had to pay an additional $6 million to the Rangers for use of their New York territory. He didn't have a single outstanding player, either, and won only 12 of 78 games.

When these moves took place, we filed a multimillion-dollar antitrust suit against the National Hockey League. It was not for spite, but for real. It was a weapon in our war with the NHL, but one we had every right to use. The one thing the NHL could not do was interfere with our right to start a rival league. They could fight our taking their players from them, but not our right to play in their buildings if they were public buildings. They could not roadblock our right to operate.

Clarence Campbell had said publicly that the NHL was years away from further expansion. By immediately expanding into territories and arenas we were seeking, his league betrayed its efforts to stop us. All right, I admire them for fighting dirty. This was war. The antitrust suit was one of the ways we had to fight back. And we weren't afraid to fight dirty, too. Unfortunately for them, they didn't fight hard enough and dirty enough. Their moves into Atlanta and Long Island were two of the few smart things they did. They should have done much more. They should have taken us seriously. They did not.

I never will understand how such an educated, experienced, and intelligent man as Clarence Campbell underestimated us so badly. Possibly he did not underestimate us as much as it seems. He is no dictator. The owners in his league do not give their president a great deal of power. He can voice his opinions, but he is limited in what he can actually do on his own.

The powerful men in the NHL are the owners. Bruce Norris, the owner in Detroit, whose family once owned half the NHL, is supposed to be the most powerful man in the league. He is chairman of the board. Bill Jennings in New York, Bill Wirtz in Chicago, Wes Adams in Boston, and Jack Kent Cooke in Los Angeles are among other powerful men in the league. Most of them underestimated us.

If they had gone at us full bore, they could have broken our backs. They could have killed us off fast. They did not. We counted on that. We counted on the overconfidence of men who have had a monopoly for a long time, who have operated so arrogantly they could not conceive of anyone's being able to challenge them.

It was not easy for us at first. I held the league together with spit and string. That was where I was important. I'm

155

tough. Dennis will try to sweet-talk people, so between the two of us we were able to keep everyone in line.

Paul Deneau came to our meeting with Lefty McFadden, who had been running the International League team in Dayton. McFadden started to take potshots at us. He wanted to know why we should be the ones to be forming the league. He wanted to know why they had to pay us any money. He wanted to know why he and some of the other guys didn't go off and form their own league. I told him why. I told him because they should have done it all these years and hadn't and could still do it, but wouldn't, because it wasn't that easy, it took more hard work and hustling and contacts and guts than they had.

I could see what he was trying to do. He was trying to undermine us with the other potential owners. He was an establishment guy from the NHL who was doing their dirty work for them and reporting back to them. Eventually, I had to tell him to take a flying leap. He walked. And wound up in the NHL with the new Washington team. Deneau hustled around and got the support of a powerful family, who operated the newspapers in Dayton. But it had become a hard haul for him in that town. McFadden was big in sports there and a powerful opponent.

We had plenty of problems within our own ranks. The Canadian block of Hunter, Hatskin, and Munro gave us all sorts of trouble. No sooner were they with us than they wanted to take over. They resented the fact that I knew nothing about hockey. They didn't see that we didn't have any hockey problems at that time—we had business problems. They started to make all sorts of demands. They wanted the league office in Canada. They wanted a Canadian commissioner. They wanted to say who came in and who didn't. They didn't want one vote each; they wanted all the votes.

156

Hatskin was reasonable. He became my friend and booster. Munro wasn't too bad. But Hunter was tough. He was the most outspoken, and he made himself the spokesman for the trio. He kept making demands on their behalf. He kept threatening to walk out and take the other two with him. Finally at a meeting at the Airporter Inn in Newport Beach, I said, "Bill, I'm sick and tired of the Canadians' trying to dictate terms to us and threatening us. If you want to walk, walk. But if you stay, I'm running the show. I'll listen to you. You have a vote along with all of us. But you're not going to be the boss, I am." And he got angry and asked, "What are you going to be, a Hitler?" And I said, "Yes, in a way that's just what I am going to be." Well, he sputtered, but he backed down and stayed.

The Canadians kept stalling about putting up their other $20,000, but finally they came through. Others stalled and came through. Others did not. Herb Martin was stalling not only on his $20,000 but the first $5,000. Dennis was in this with Herb. He'd cut Herb in for half his end. He thought Herb had a lot of money. He kept saying, "He'll come across, don't worry." But it was hard not to worry about him. Then he came across. At a meeting in Chicago late in October, the owners also had to ante up an additional $10,000 each to cover league expenses.

At this point, we had negotiated with a great many people in a great many cities, run up terrific travel expenses, and no longer recognized our families on sight. A lot of deals had fallen through, and others were shaky. Erwin Merar and Bill Chino had put up the $5,000 first money for a franchise in Milwaukee, but had been dissatisfied with the dates they had been offered at the arena in town and decided not to go for the additional $20,000. When they pulled out, we refunded them their original $5,000 because we felt they had come in early and gone all out in their attempt to make it.

We had come close to getting Dick Tinkham and his partners to put in a franchise in Indianapolis, Nick Mileti to put one in Cleveland, Abe Polin in Baltimore, and Carl Eller in Phoenix, but in each case they said they wanted to wait to see if they could get an NHL franchise first. Sam Schulman talked to us about putting a franchise in Seattle, but decided against it. He'd invested heavily in his basketball team and wanted to turn the corner on that first. We talked to individuals and groups about franchises in Philadelphia, Baltimore, Cincinnati, Columbus, Louisville, Charlotte, Albuquerque, Dallas, Oklahoma City, Kansas City, Denver, Houston, San Diego, Salt Lake City, Portland, and other cities, but for one reason or another these fell through.

I was having trouble finding backers for a franchise in San Francisco. Mike O'Hara, who'd done a good job for me in finding buyers for my ABA franchise in Dallas, was having a lot of trouble tying up money men. The Oakland franchise and its failures across the bay scared away people. Dennis was having trouble finding backers for his franchise in Los Angeles. The Kings weren't doing that well in their suburban Forum, and there was tremendous competition for the sports dollar in southern California. Neil Shayne was having troubles financing his New York franchise. Still, we felt these would go. We felt we had ten teams lined up.

It was time to make a move to give our league the appearance of a reality. The last two days in October, we met at the Americana Hotel in New York to tie up as many loose ends as we could and line up our franchises for a formal announcement. The first day of November we called a press conference and made the formal announcement: The World Hockey Association was in business with ten franchises in New York, Miami, Chicago, St. Paul, Dayton, Los Angeles, San Francisco, Edmonton, Winnipeg, and Calgary. Then we went back to work to make them real.

Doug Michel, an electrical contractor, came to us with a plan to put a team in Ontario. He said he had a backer who was worth $30 million. Howard Baldwin, a young man who had money from a clothing business, came to us with a plan to put a team in New England, either in Providence or in Boston. We wanted $210,000 each from them. They wanted to know why they had to pay so much more than the others. We told them because they had not come in with the others. They pointed out they were coming in before the league began. We wanted them. We agreed to take them in for the $25,000 up front and the $10,000 for league expenses plus the $100,000 performance bonds all the rest of us had produced, and let them pay us the additional $175,000 when they found backers. They went back to raise this.

Baldwin found a superpartner in Bob Schmertz, who had built a real estate firm specializing in retirement communities into a nationwide operation and had bought the Boston Celtics of the NBA. By throwing in with us, he was going against some of his NBA partners, who were in the NHL, but that didn't stop him.

We didn't know it until later, but Michel couldn't get the backers he thought he could get. Michel mortgaged his house in Ottawa to raise the $25,000 front money. Considering what it would cost to operate and support a team, the $25,000 was only a drop in the bucket. It is incredible that a man would mortgage his house for just the first payment of a project that would cost forty to fifty times that much the first year alone. But such is the desire of some men to own a sports team. He went into hock for everything he had to get into hockey. He scrambled around, borrowing money and raising letters of credit. He got the ante up. And he got an ulcer. He lost his health, and he almost lost his home, his family, and his senses. And he was far from finished. Martin Fishman was found to put up $250,000 for him. Later, he decided he didn't like the dates they'd got in the Ottawa building and he backed out, refusing to accept the responsibility he'd assumed for any further operation of the team. He lost his quarter-million. It wasn't until Nick Trobovich came in that Michel got a partner who would pay the bills. Trobovich took over, but he was not a well man as it turned out, and he later died. Eventually Michel had to sell out and bow out.

Late in November, we accepted Ontario and New England. Ontario later located in Ottawa, New England in Boston. That gave us twelve cities that were set. Or at least we thought they were. The New York ownership was settled when Shayne sold his interests to New Jersey law partners Dick Wood and Sy Siegel in January. I disposed of my franchise when I gave up on San Francisco and sold it to a group in Quebec City headed by Paul Racine and Jean Lesage in February. Control of the Chicago franchise changed hands in March and eventually landed in the laps of brothers Jordon and Walter Kaiser, wealthy realtors, who stabilized it. In March, Paul Deneau gave up on Dayton and transferred the franchise to Houston, where his partner became young Jim Smith.

Most of these franchise owners had several partners, but I am just naming the main ones or the men up front, as the tangled web of some of these structures is impossible for anyone to sort out.

Deneau had tried his damnedest in Dayton, but had failed. The Cox family withdrew support from him. An arena proposal fell by the wayside. There was a lot of political intrigue involved. And strong suggestions of anti-Semitism. I am not Jewish. Neither is Don. Neither, obviously, is Dennis. Deneau is Jewish. So are some of the other owners in our league. There was a lot of loose talk revealing feelings that were not kosher. McFadden's original International League team still operates there in a 5,600-seat arena. But the city might have been a major-league city today.

Problems keep arising which have to be solved, one way or another. Herb Martin had made a lot of noise by signing Bernie Parent of the Toronto Maple Leafs to a lavish contract in February. Parent was not the first player to sign with us, but he was the first "name player." But Martin still was not set. I was hearing stories that he was in trouble. I flew to Miami to see him. I flew most of the night and arrived Sunday morning. I called him up. He knew I was coming, but he said he'd see me Monday. So I wasted Sunday in a hotel. He was able to spare me an hour and a half on Monday. He showed me his arena site and the two buildings he'd erected on it. He showed me the projections of his plan. He avoided my more penetrating questions. Then he put me in a taxi and I went back to the airport and flew home, knowing we were in trouble here and had better start digging up alternatives.

In April, we held a league meeting at the Continental Plaza Hotel in Chicago at which franchise owners were to post $100,000 performance bonds. Some of the guys didn't have the clout to get a bank to give them a bond in that amount, so we accepted personal bonds from them in order to keep them in. Deneau put up a personal bond. So did Dennis, for that matter. He didn't have bank backing. But, more than anything else, these bonds were a symbol, a sort of sign that the members were serious and committed. Ten of the members put up bonds of one kind or another. Two didn't. Calgary and Miami were notified that they had two weeks to get back in good standing. They did not. Two weeks later, we decided to default their franchises. It was a hard decision to make, but it had to be made.

Calgary was a bummer. Bob Brown, Scotty Munro's money man, had died of cancer. Apparently, he had not known he had it when he went into the hockey deal with Scotty. Discovered too late, the disease finished him fast. Scared off, Scotty walked away without a word to anyone. Either he did not any longer feel we were going to make it the way he wanted or he could not find another sponsor. We could have found one for him. He could have got his money back or even turned a profit. But he went away without a word. He didn't say anything to anyone, and he never contacted us. He is still running his junior team in Calgary. But this might have been a major-league town, too.

In Miami, Martin had got himself in over his head. He was in a bind. He didn't have enough money. He'd neglected to buy adjacent land for parking for his offices-arena complex. He'd neglected to get city approval of the arena project. Without adequate parking, the city would not approve an arena. The two buildings he had put up had sent the cost of the land he might have purchased for parking skyrocketing beyond his reach. He never built his last two buildings or the arena between them. This booming city remains without a modern indoor arena. Because of this, the University of Miami gave up basketball. The Floridians of the ABA folded not long after Murphy left them. And the Screaming Eagles, as Martin called his hockey team, never got off the ground. Other men want to erect an arena there, and professional basketball and hockey teams may yet settle there, but for now the town is dead.

We found buyers for Miami and Calgary franchises. New

Jersey businessmen Jim Cooper, a banker, and Bernie Brown, a trucker, put up $210,000 for the Miami franchise and moved it to Philadelphia. Cooper gave me a check for the full sum. We gave them the rights to the players Miami had or had sought. Fortunately, for what it was worth for a while, Parent agreed to remain with the WHA. He signed a new contract with Philadelphia for about what he would have got in Miami. It would have looked bad for us to have lost a player of his prominence at that time because one of our owners had defaulted on his deal. Cooper soon signed another glamorous figure, Derek Sanderson, which helped.

Rejected by the NHL, for reasons that defy analysis, Nick Mileti was now ready to throw in with us. I flew into Cleveland, and he met me at the airport, spent the entire day with me, made the deal with me, drove me back to the airport, and personally put me on a plane home. I could not help contrasting the treatment I received from Mileti to that time in Miami when Cooper consented to give me ninety minutes of dodging my questions after making me wait alone in a strange city more than a day. Maybe it is a small thing, but maybe the stature of a man can be measured by the manner in which he deals with people.

Mileti is very heavy. We needed him, and he knew it. We were deep in the deal to get Bobby Hull, which we felt could make or break our chances of success, and we didn't have the dough to swing it. I leveled with Nick, which he appreciated, especially since word already had reached him of this. He agreed to pick up the twelfth spot Calgary had vacated for $210,000 and to loan us $40,000 in addition. We gave him rights to any players any members in the league had been unable to sign, and he soon signed another superstar, Gerry Cheevers, from the Stanley Cup champion Boston Bruins. Swiftly, he put together a tremendous team.

I will discuss the Hull deal in detail shortly, but just now

I want to point out that Mileti's franchise fee and the money he loaned us and some money Jim Cooper loaned us enabled us to sign Hull. The owners had agreed to share in the payment of the $1 million front money Bobby wanted and got, but not all had come across with the cash.

The league was in financial trouble from the first. That was my fault for not charging more for franchises or not assessing more for operating costs, but who knows if I could have got it? The way it worked out, we swung it somehow. At one point, Don and I personally posted a $250,000 bond that was demanded as insurance against damages in one of the court suits. At another point, Don and I personally loaned the league $100,000 for operating expenses. We got our money back. Mileti and Cooper were repaid for their loans. Everyone got everything he had coming to him. The sums for franchises above the original $25,000 went into the league fund, took care of these costs, and provided sufficient cash to carry us through a costly crisis which developed in New York during the first season.

Finally, we were set with twelve franchises for our first season. They were not all the ones we had thought we would have. Strangely, some of those who had made the most noise were not the ones we wound up with. We got more press at the start out of Miami, Dayton, and Calgary than almost anywhere else. There are doers and there are talkers, I suppose.

In New York, Neil Shayne was a big talker, but he could not get the job done when it came down to it. However, he created a lot of curiosity in our league by talking about it so much. He got us a lot of press. He got a lot of people interested. And there was someone else to take over for him, so we did have a franchise there when it was most important. I'm not sure you need a New York base, but if you do, you need it most at the start. So much publicity stems from New York that an operation there helps to establish the reality of a project. Once everyone can see it is real, once a project is established, the importance of New York is lessened. It is such a vast market that it always is valuable, of course.

We never got a Miami base, but what we got from Herb Martin was tremendously valuable to us. He got us a lot of publicity, especially with the signing of Bernie Parent. Parent was an important player in hockey, and the fact that he was willing to jump to our league encouraged other players to do so. And Martin quit at a time when Nick Mileti was available to replace his Miami franchise with a Cleveland franchise. It is not so much that Cleveland was a better territory, but that Mileti was a better owner.

We knew we had some territories that probably would have to be replaced. We knew we had some weak owners who probably would have to be replaced. You get guys who will get you going somewhere, anywhere. Natural attrition helps you weed out the weak, which can be replaced with the strong. If you can last through the first year or two, you will get stronger in the second and third years. The values of franchises as a going business are much greater than in a beginning venture. A lot of promoters came in at first, speculators looking to make a fast buck. As their property appreciates, sound businessmen buy into it.

The last owner to join us our first year, Mileti, was one of our strongest men. He is independent and wealthy. If he brings in partners, you can be sure they are strong. He sees the long-range picture and understands that selfish self-interest can do damage to all. He will use his money to support not only his own team but his league. Schmertz and Baldwin in Boston and the Kaiser brothers in Chicago were independent, wealthy men who were behind not only teams but the league. Though more rebellious, the Canadians Hunter and Hatskin also were strong owners. They were independent and did not have to buck a hundred partners for permission to do this or that.

If not all healthy, all of our teams were ready to go into operation. Nicknames had been selected and arena leases signed. The New York Raiders and New England Whalers were going to do business in competition with NHL clubs at the 17,250-seat Madison Square Garden and 15,000-seat Boston Garden, respectively. The Philadelphia Blazers, Chicago Cougars, Minnesota Fighting Saints, Houston Aeros, Ottawa Nationals, Winnipeg Jets, and Quebec Nordiques all had buildings seating 9,000 to 10,000 persons, which were adequate for the start if not for the long run.

The Alberta Oilers became known as the Edmonton Oilers when they decided against Calgary as an alternate location. They had only a 5,200-seat building, the only stadium, which was insufficient, even to begin with. However, Edmonton had a new arena on the drawing board. Chicago and Houston also had arenas on the drawing board. Minnesota had a 16,000-seat arena which would be ready at midseason, and Cleveland had one about to go into construction.

Unlike the teams in New York and Boston, the ones in Philadelphia, Chicago, and St. Paul were bucking established NHL clubs in their area in separate buildings. The other seven were pioneering more or less new major-league territories.

Locating men to back franchises and fight the legal and practical battles that lay ahead was only the first step. The battles already had begun, and the war had to be won. The league had to be staffed properly, as did the teams.

CHAPTER 10

As Gary Davidson Sees It, II

The World Hockey Association, "comin' on strong!" That was our original motto. At the start, I was president and Dennis vice-president. Dennis said he didn't want to be an executive of the league—he wanted to run his own team. He'd had trouble lining up a solid sponsor for his team, though he had got some financial support. He wanted to devote himself to the team. So he left the vice-presidency of the WHA to become general manager of the Los Angeles Sharks in May. Jim Browitt, a very bright guy who had been helping us as a consultant, was appointed league administrator and executive vice-president. He handled a lot of detail work in the front office. Don Regan was the general counsel.

Ed Fitkin, a veteran hockey man from Toronto, who had been an assistant to Jack Kent Cooke in Los Angeles, became my assistant, the president's assistant in charge of hockey matters. He was going to be general manager of my San Francisco franchise until that fell through. But his appointment as director of hockey affairs pacified Hunter, who'd wanted a Canadian hockey man high in the front office. Lee Meade, who'd been publicist of the ABA, became our publicity director. All the time we'd been hustling around rounding up franchise holders, we'd been forming our front-office staff to administer the league's affairs. You will note that the staff I formed did not include a commissioner. You have a president or you have a commissioner. One man has to be on top to make the final decisions. In our league, I was the one man.

Bill Hunter had stressed the point that it was important to acquire experienced officials with established reputations. I didn't think it was that important. I was wrong and Bill was right. This was a matter of hockey, and I bowed to his judgment. And I'm glad I did, because hockey is a fast, rough game, and while fights are accepted, you can have chaos without competent men in control. And respected referees provide respect for the integrity of your games. The fans may boo the refs, but they respect the well-known ones. The players may curse them, but they respect them, too.

At Hunter's urging, we went after the best and we got one of the best, Vern Buffey, a veteran of more than twenty years in the NHL, to be our referee in chief, for $75,000 a year. That's a lot of money, but he was worth it. Buffey brought Bill Friday in for another $50,000. Friday was paid $5,000 when he first started in the NHL. He once said no referee was worth $50,000 because referees don't sell tickets. In that, he was wrong. He was worth it because the integrity men like him brought our operation sold a lot of tickets. It gave us a big-league image. And brought in players, believe it or not. And other officials.

Veteran NHL officials Bob Sloan, Ron Ego, and Brent Casselman were among others who formed our first staff. The ABA boosted itself enormously when it went high to get Norm Drucker to jump from the NBA to supervise its refereeing staff. He brought in others, and it increased the major-league image of that league. Just as Buffey and Friday worked wonders for us.

Max Muhleman, an outstanding publicist who'd been active in the commercial car-racing field, came in with us as executive director of our separate arm, the WHA Properties Company. Jack Long joined up as his assistant. Max brought in a lot of business with commercial ventures that incorporated the WHA name or team logos on various products which not only made money for the league but promoted our image. He also laid the groundwork for future television returns.

Let's face it: no one from the television world was beating down the doors to carry our games nationally and internationally. Long set up deals that I closed with the CBC network and Global Sports in Canada and with CBS in the United States, which got some games on the air—our all-star game and some playoff games in particular—and brought us maybe $1 million in profits and set the stage for increased coverage as the league grows. These brought in sponsors such as the AVCO Financial Corporation, Sears, and Chevrolet, who backed us and boosted us in many ways.

Sports are business operations, and they are costly. We conduct our business in commercial countries. Any commercial support you can get from major members of the business company boosts you in many ways and brings in bucks which cut the costs you have. AVCO took over sponsorship of our World Cup Trophy, our counterpart to the Stanley Cup. And many of our teams had many television and radio contracts within their communities, which brought in sponsorship support and gave them exposure as well as profits, a fact which often is overlooked when the television situation is studied.

The charter owners became trustees—Ben Hatskin, Bill Hunter, Paul Deneau, Paul Racine, Doug Michel, Jordon

Kaiser, Jim Cooper, Nick Mileti, Howard Baldwin, Lou Kaplan, Dick Wood, and, of course, Dennis Murphy. Each with his partners had to form a front-office staff, hire general managers and coaches, acquire players, promote his product, set ticket prices, and sell tickets.

The leagues, the league president, even a dictator, cannot dictate to the owners how they will operate. Once owners are accepted into the fraternity, they are on their own. Some operate wisely and well; some do not. Some work hard and spend freely to get the best people on their teams; some do not. How much potential there is to the property and how much should be spent to build it up is something each owner has to decide for himself.

Coming in, all the owners talked big about buying the best. Some did; some didn't. If it had been up to me, each team would have invested heavily in getting the best general manager and coach possible and in getting at least one outstanding name player as a colorful attraction and as many quality players as possible. Some did; some didn't.

We did not have anywhere near the trouble the ABA had getting quality players. Whereas the ABA had only a single fringe NBA performer its first year, Wayne Hightower, we had sixty or seventy comparable NHL players in the WHA and we had some superstars superior to or comparable to a Rick Barry in basketball. The hockey players were not as bound by their contracts, they were paid less, and they were more conditioned to making a move for money. We had more owners who could afford to pay top dollar than the ABA had originally, and the agents flocked to us to talk business, either to force better contracts from their players' NHL owners or to make a move to the WHA for better contracts.

Steve Arnold, who had represented both professional basketball and hockey players, seized the opportunity to become a member of management, which later led to his becoming a franchise holder in our football league. He is a smooth, tough, but honest man, and we made him our director of player personnel. He served as the go-between among many of our owners and the agents and their players. We could not make deals for the owners, but we could set some up and help on others.

We paid some finders' fees to men who brought us prospective owners who took on franchises. The usual amount was $5,000, though sometimes different deals were worked out. We also paid finders' fees of comparable amounts to people who brought us important players who signed. It is all part of the expenses that must be paid out to get a league going. We did business with a lot of agents and attorneys.

Alan Eagleson, head of the NHL players' association, set the standard for most of these negotiations by insisting on letters of credit and monies being put in escrow and similar guarantees for each player's contract. We had to go along with this, but it made it difficult to operate. Instead of having to put up a year's payments each year, we sometimes had to put up four or five years in advance. The agents seldom care about helping a league go, even though it will benefit their clients enormously in the long run if it does go.

Eagleson used us strictly as a wedge to pry more from the NHL for his players. He signed only one player with us. He is a sharp operator, but it is difficult to trust his sincerity when you deal with him. He talks out of both sides of his mouth, and he has a forked tongue. He spoke to the press as if he were impartial—dealing with both leagues equally on behalf of his clients. I deliberately started to attack him in the press so that people would see that he was partial to the NHL and an adversary of the WHA. I felt it was important that his clients understand this.

Bob Woolf, who represents a lot of hockey players, too, is an impartial man, on the other hand. He was very honest and open in all of his dealings with us. He made it clear that he was negotiating with the NHL on behalf of his clients, too. He did not lie about amounts being offered his players. He did not try to pressure us or con us. He leaned over backwards to be fair to us. Most of his players signed with the NHL, but most of his players were top players who could command top dollar with the NHL and understandably preferred to stay in the established league. I think he's a good agent, a resourceful fellow who does his best for his clients. He was caught in a bind in the Derek Sanderson situation. He signed Sanderson with us and tried to get Sanderson to live up to his contract. But he couldn't control Sanderson. No one can.

I don't know how much Bernie Parent listened to Howard Casper, his agent. They say Parent's main adviser was his wife. Whoever it was, he got some bad advice. He signed with us, then deserted us, which ruined his reputation. Casper was almost impossible to do business with. As soon as he signed his player he started to seek more for him. Right away he started to look for an out until he found one and left through it. If he called me today, I wouldn't pick up the phone to answer him. I wouldn't care if he was bringing me O. J. Simpson. I wouldn't have any faith in any deal I made with Casper. I do not respect him. No doubt he does not respect me.

In any event, I respect most agents. They are important to the players. An owner who has the best legal and financial advisers at his beck and call is unfair if he expects a player to negotiate a contract for himself. These contracts are incredibly complicated.

Charles Abrahams, who represented a lot of players, but not many names, did so much business with us that he turned the NHL against him. They became convinced he was a WHA man. He was not. He was just a man trying to do his best for his clients, and the WHA was offering the best deals.

We offered more money than the NHL in many cases, we offered solid contracts, which were not as gimmicked up as the ABA's had been, and we backed them up. As a lure to players, and because we were convinced sports pacts will go this way inevitably, we offered contracts without reserve clauses, which bound players to our teams only for the terms they agreed to.

There are a number of ways men can put a winning team together. One way or another, the pieces must fit together properly. One man, such as a superstar center, can turn a basketball team around, but not a hockey team. Too many men play. Superstars alone will not guarantee the owner a winner. The Los Angeles Lakers in the NBA found this out when they put Wilt Chamberlain with Jerry West and Elgin Baylor. Philadelphia found this out in the WHA when they put Bernie Parent, Derek Sanderson, John McKenzie, Andre Lacroix, and Danny Lawson on the same team and flopped. New England went without any great names, but still won our first title. It fit good players together properly. It barely beat out Winnipeg with superstar Bobby Hull. Management is what matters, really—what you do with what you have.

We had to go mostly out of the mainstream to get men who were not closely affiliated with the NHL to manage and coach our WHA clubs. Some of our teams landed some outstanding men. Some settled for less. Some sought names instead of solid people. Howard Baldwin, who had been cut from the Boston University freshman hockey team as a collegian, hired the man who cut him, Jack Kelly, to be general manager and coach of his Boston WHA team. He was an outstanding college coach. So was Glen Sonmor from the University of Minnesota, who became general manager and coach of the Minnesota WHA team. Both were well known and well regarded in their communities. Hunter, who brought in backers to head up his franchise, wanted to be his own general manager in Edmonton. So did Jim Smith in Houston and Dennis Murphy in L.A. A promoter, Annis Stukus, became general manager in Winnipeg. A brilliant baseball executive, Marvin Milkes, became GM in Chicago.

Former NHL stars Bobby Hull, Billy Harris, John McKenzie, Marcel Pronovost, and Camille Henry became coaches in Winnipeg, Ottawa, Philadelphia, Chicago, and New York. The most glamorous NHL name of all time, Maurice "The Rocket" Richard, became coach in Quebec, but soon quit and was replaced by little-known Maurice Fillion. Former NHL coach Phil Watson became an executive in Philadelphia. Lesser-known former major-league and minor-league figures such as Ray Kinasewich, Bill Needham, Bill Dineen, and Terry Slater became coaches in Edmonton, Cleveland, Houston, and Los Angeles. Lesser-known former minor-leaguers Buck Houle and Maurice Fortier became GM's in Ottawa and Quebec.

In mid-February of 1972 we held our first player draft at the Royal Coach Inn in Anaheim. Some clubs were ready for it and some were not. Some teams drafted only players they had contacted or had been given reason to believe they might sign, and some simply picked names off stat sheets, roster books, and history books. We drafted everyone in sight—1,037 players. It got us a lot of publicity, but some of it was sarcastic. This was understandable. Among the players we drafted was Wendall Anderson, thirty-five-year-old governor of Minnesota. But he was a former Olympic hockey player. A spokesman for the St. Paul team pointed out that politics in an insecure profession and a former player might be available to resume play at any time. Well, it got us ink.

Beneath it all, however, we were serious, and far more capable of carrying out our objectives than most observers realized. We had a pretty good spy system and bought some pretty reliable information. Steve Arnold built us a book on which players' contracts were expiring and would be available to us and which had an interest in us. We knew who was unhappy with their teams, their contracts, their teammates, even their wives. We knew which ones were in trouble in their towns, which ones had so exhausted the patience of their clubs that the clubs would not fight too hard to keep them. We got some fine people and some disreputable characters, but in our position you take what you can get.

A lot of people laughed at some of the players we drafted, but we wound up with some players some people never thought we'd get. And we came closer to getting a lot more of the others than most people realize. Minnesota had the first selection, and they selected Henry Boucha of Detroit. We didn't get him. The last player picked was Gordie Howe, by Los Angeles. We got him. L.A. didn't get him, but Houston did. The second season, of course. But we got him. No one in his wildest dreams thought we could, but we did. And in-between we got a lot more no one thought we could get. No one thought we could get Bobby Hull, but we did.

What you have to realize is that this is a business for the players, too. Just as I want to make money, so do they. And while I can do what I do all my life, they cannot. They have limited playing careers in front of them, and they're worried about their futures. They're running scared. Also, they've been in slavery in a monopolistic situation for a long time. They haven't been able to bargain with their bosses as equals. If they didn't sign for what they were offered, they didn't play. If they didn't want to play in the town where they were owned, they didn't play. We arrived, offered them alternatives, and made them men. If a player preferred to play in a given place, we did our best to accommodate him. We made deals among ourselves so that anyone who could sign a player had rights to him. Each of our twelve teams had a list of four players it had rights to before it even started to draft players.

Thus, four dozen players were parceled out right off. And we landed a lot of them. We landed about one-third of the players we negotiated with who were available to us, which is an extremely high average under the circumstances.

Arnold and other agents who brought us players we signed received bonuses—$5,000 for every superstar, $3,000 for every established major leaguer, $1,500 for every established minor leaguer. It was difficult to draw some of these lines, but we managed to negotiate each case without complaint. The amount of the finder's fee wasn't excessive considering the amounts players were signed for. Most of our owners agreed to pay excessive amounts of money for players as an investment in the future. As John McKenzie said when Philadelphia signed him, if you steal enough players from the NHL, who knows, the next thing you know you might be the NHL. It's a matter of supply and demand. There is a short supply of good players. The demand for them became high when we arrived to make the bidding competitive. Owners had to go high to sign players. No one forced them to do so. They did so because it was worth it to them for one reason or another.

In March, Mike Curran, a goaltender for the United States' silver-medal Olympic hockey team in Japan in 1972, became the first player to sign a WHA contract, signing with the St. Paul team. A month later, Wayne Connelly and George Gardner signed with Minnesota and Los Angeles, respectively, becoming the first National Hockey League players to sign with the WHA. Eventually, we signed 340 players our first season, and 78 of them were NHL players. We lost two of them back to the NHL. Our second season we signed 20 more NHL players, bringing the total to 96.

The California Seals lost the most players, ten. Charlie Finley was Scrooge there. He was running a penny-pinching operation. Everyone wanted to desert the sinking ship. Garry Young was the general manager. He signed players for substantial amounts. When Finley found out, he fired Young and refused to honor the contracts. The players came to us. People forget that the Seals were a rising contender at the time. When the players left, the team floundered and sank into the cellar.

Buffalo and Detroit each lost nine players. In Buffalo, general manager Punch Imlach scoffed at our new league and refused to offer players the sort of money they wanted. In Detroit, the owner, Bruce Norris, indicated he would not be intimidated. Detroit was hurt badly. Chicago was hurt badly. Management there treated the players as slaves. The players were unhappy. Over a two-year period the Hawks lost Bobby Hull, Pat Stapleton, Ralph Backstrom, Bryan Campbell, and Andre Lacroix, among others. It remains a strong team, but in the long run it has to suffer from the loss of so much talent.

Over a two-year period, Montreal has lost players such as Marc Tardif and Rejean Houle. It remains a power, but in the long run has to suffer. Boston's Stanley Cup champion Bruins lost Gerry Cheevers, Ted Green, John McKenzie, Mike Walton, and Derek Sanderson the first season, and it cost them the Cup. Toronto lost Bernie Parent, Rick Levy, Brad Selwood, and Jim Harrison, and it cost them a playoff position. These clubs could have kept their players by paying them the going rate, but they refused and they were hurt. When Philadelphia got Parent back, it won the Stanley Cup and he was the star.

Minnesota met the challenge. Wren Blair is no one's fool. He got out of a sickbed to get his stars tied up. He didn't underestimate us. He went to his players and he said he knew they were going to get some tempting offers to jump his team, but he wanted to keep them on his team so he was willing to pay them the sort of money they were going to be offered. He signed them to long-term contracts. He lost the fewest players of any NHL team, only one. Atlanta and the New York

Rangers lost only two each. The Rangers had to go high to keep their many stars. They have had disappointing seasons, so some say it did not pay off for them. But they still had their stars, with whom they could make moves and remain a contender.

The biggest stars we got the first season were Bobby Hull of Winnipeg, Bernie Parent, Derek Sanderson, and John McKenzie of Philadelphia, J. C. Tremblay of Quebec, and Ted Green, Rick Ley and Jim Dorey of New England. But we also got some developing stars or overlooked players of high potential who became stars in our circuit such as Danny Lawson and Andre Lacroix of Philadelphia, Paul Schmyr, Ron Buchanan, and Gary Jarrett of Cleveland, Larry Hornung, Norm Beaudin, and Chris Bordeleau of Winnipeg, Terry Caffrey, Tom Webster, Tim Sheehy, and Larry Pleau of New England, Ron Ward of New York, and Gary Veneruzzo of Los Angeles.

Our second season the biggest stars we landed were Gordie Howe of Houston, Harry Howell of New York, Carl Brewer of Toronto, Marc Tardif of Los Angeles, Mike Walton of Minnesota, Pat Stapleton and Ralph Backstrom of Chicago, and Rejean Houle of Quebec. Jacques Plante also came over as manager of Quebec. But this was significant. The addition of players like Plante and Howe and Hull, who are immortals, who are or will be Hall of Famers, who had, as Ed Fitkin said, "NHL" tattooed across their stomachs, brought us enormous prestige. It is true that Howe and Howell are in their forties, but the NHL has had many players in their forties in recent seasons. It is their identification with us that is so significant. We also began to get youngsters out of junior ranks, such as the Howe sons, Reg Thomas, and others who will be the stars of tomorrow.

The third year, the WHA added Frank Mahavolich, Paul Henderson, and other prominent NHL heroes.

Those who think the figures have been exaggerated are wrong. We paid a great deal to get these players. Some players were paid more than they were worth, certainly. But as it turned out, others were paid less. For the most part, each team made its own deals and we could not control the amounts paid the players. Hull was signed for $2.5 million for five years. Sanderson was signed for $2.35 million for ten years. Cheevers was signed for $1.4 milion for seven seasons. Plante was signed for $1 million for ten years. Stapleton was signed for $1 million for five years. Parent was signed for $750,000 for five years. He was the first to sign for a large sum. Our troubles with him started when he learned others were later signed for much larger sums.

These figures include front monies, but they do not include performance bonuses and side items, such as cars and loans. The players were promised real money, not the potential from investments, but some received loans of up to $100,000 so they could make their own investments. Much of the money had to be guaranteed in the form of bank deposits or notes. The agents insisted on gimmicking up most of the contracts with extensive bonus clauses for individual and team performances. Most of the contracts were set up so that the payments would be spread over ten, fifteen, or twenty years to ensure security for the players.

Most players received a lot less, of course, but a lot more than they had been making. Stapleton had been making $55,000 a season from Chicago's Black Hawks. He was offered $270,000 to sign a new contract for three seasons. His agent, Jeff Rosen, said he would have signed with the Hawks for half as much as we offered him, but when the club did not come close, he went to our league. Then the Hawks said he wasn't worth anything to them anymore. But he had been played forty minutes a game and helped carry the Chicago club to the Stanley Cup playoff finals the year before. Every time one of these teams maligned a jumper, it made it that much easier for one of our teams to sign another jumper. Players deserve to be treated with respect. Signing with another team which offers a player more money and more security for his family and the future is a respectable thing to do.

We signed a few stars who jumped right back—Bill Flett of Philadelphia was one. We failed to get many players who were not offered as much money by their teams as we offered but were offered enough to cause them to stay. Some figured we'd fail. Some couldn't bring themselves to break ties of loyalty to their teams and their towns. Some may have made mistakes; some may not have. We did not fail. And their teams will trade them out of town without any worry about loyalty when they can profit by a trade.

It is my understanding that the Rangers signed Brad Park for $250,000 a year, Rod Gilbert, Jean Ratelle, and Vic Hadfield for $175,000, Walt Tkaczuk for $150,000, Rod Seiling for $130,000, and Ed Giacomin for $125,000, each for three to five years. We came very close to landing some of these. At one time I thought we had Park and Tkaczuk sewed up. The Black Hawks' Stan Mikita wanted $500,000 up front and $2,500,000 over ten years, and we decided he wasn't worth it. He was offered $1,500,000 for five years. Backstrom was offered $500,000 for five years by the Hawks. He signed with us for an additional $250,000.

Mickey Redmond was offered $1,500,000 for five years. He signed with the Red Wings for $1,000,000 for five years. Henri Richard was offered $1,000,000 for five years. He signed with the Canadiens for the same sum. We came close to getting Bill White, Bill Goldsworthy, Hilles Meloche, and many other major stars. Dave Keon was offered a $1,000,000 five-year contract by Ottawa. He accepted $50,000 up front. When he refused to sign, he refused to return the front money. He contends it was a bonus given him simply to consider the contract offer. Poor Doug Michel. Everything he touched turned to stone. Keon signed a new contract with Toronto's Maple Leafs for $750,000 for five years.

Ken Dryden was being paid only $78,000 a season by Montreal. Because they won the Stanley Cup in 1973 and he'd had an outstanding season, he may have made $100,000 with bonuses. That was the first year of a two-year contract. He was offered $100,000 a season for two seasons to sign a new contract. He asked for $150,000 and was refused. He refused to play the second season of his old contract and sat out the 1973–74 season, supposedly earning $7,500 a year as a law clerk. I am sure he got what he wanted from Montreal to rejoin the club. Using a threat to join us for a full year as a wedge, he made a lot of money.

Hull was the biggest star to come into our league, of course. He made us. A lot has been written suggesting that his signing was cloak-and-dagger stuff. This is not true. It was as simple a business deal between businessmen as a multimillion-dollar deal can be. At a trustees' meeting early in 1972, Bill Hunter made a pitch to have us support him in a bid to get Hull for his Winnipeg franchise and for the World Hockey Association. Hull had had trouble getting what he was worth from the Chicago Black Hawks. He'd had one prolonged salary dispute and holdout with them, had been demeaned for it, and had never forgiven them for it. He was unhappy in Chicago. Hatskin figured he could make him happy in Winnipeg.

It was Hunter's contention that one or two players dominate every league in sports. Hull was a dominant figure in the NHL. Bobby Orr was another, but he was not as outgoing or as appealing publicly as Hull. We kicked it around and saw that Hull could help us not only as a superplayer but as a personality. We saw that getting Hull would hurt the NHL enormously and help us enormously. We saw the sense of what Hatskin proposed. We thought it was a long shot at best, but agreed to pursue it.

Hatskin had talked to Hull. I went to Chicago and met with Hull's agent, Harvey Wineberg. To my surprise, he said Hull would make the move for two million dollars. He wanted one million up front and one million in salaries. We wanted to tie Hull to us for a long time, as much for his image as for his ability. It was worked out that we would pay him the million up front, plus another million for four years as player and coach, plus $100,000 a year for six years as coach or executive. He wanted to play in Canada and was agreeable to Winnipeg. It was agreed Hatskin would help him get a home and farm there. Hull is a farmer at heart. We wanted him to represent the league as much as possible in publicity and promotions, so we proposed to sign him to a league contract covering the front money for ten years and to a Winnipeg contract covering the remaining $1,600,000 for ten years as player, coach and executive, and Hull was agreeable to this. It was worked out that we would share any endorsement deals he did. If he brought the deal to us, he would get 75 percent of it and we would get 25 percent. If we brought the deal to him, we would get 75 percent and he would get 25 percent.

That was it. As far as I know, he was making $150,000 a year with the Hawks, but he did not talk to them about making more while he was talking to us. I think a million dollars was a magic figure in his eyes. The million up front and the million behind it would make him happy. I could only hope it would make our league happy. I do not know if I could have got him for less. I do not know if he could have got more out of us. There was no haggling. The terms were set swiftly, and once they were set there never was any change in them. The only string attached was that we had to produce the front money and the contract by

June, before it was time for him to sign a new contract with Chicago. I still had to go back to the owners to get their approval of the deal.

We met and voted on a proposal for the league to pay the front money and Hatskin the remainder. The deal received almost unanimous approval. The only vote against it came from Bob Schmertz of New England. He thought it was just too much money. But he agreed to go along with the rest of us. And he since has agreed that we were right in going for this. It was agreed that the league would pay one-fourth the front money, the teams the remaining three-fourths. It was agreed that all such monies would be considered loans, repayable from future earnings, such as from franchise fees future entries into the league would pay.

However agreeable it all was, we still had to come up with the money. And as the deadline drew near, we did not have it. The league had to come up with $250,000. The teams had to come up with $750,000 at a rate of $62,500 per club. The Winnipeg club had to pay this, too.

I got the league's $250,000 from Nick Mileti's franchise fee when the NHL rejected him and he agreed to come into the WHA with a Cleveland team. Most of the teams antied up their $62,500 shares. New York, Los Angeles, and Houston did not. The day before we were to meet with Hull to close the deal, I was $195,000 short. In desperation, I telephoned Jim Cooper in Philadelphia, and he agreed to loan the league the money and wired it to us. Hatskin might have loaned us the money. He had posted a bank letter of credit for his million six. We were in. Later, Los Angeles and Houston came up with their shares. Only New York never paid. The rest received promissory notes which should be paid off from franchise fees paid by three new teams entering the WHA in 1974 and 1975.

I do not know how Hatskin feels about it now. He still

has to cough up a quarter-million dollars a year for these years. And he is not making money in Winnipeg. He will not lose money. He may have to move the franchise or sell it. He has had an offer of $4.3 million from Milwaukee for the franchise with Hull and earlier had a $5.2 million offer from Detroit. But he may lose Hull. Hull is unhappy.

It is not that Hull is an unhappy person by nature. He has as happy a nature as any man I ever have known. There is not an athlete in the country who is in greater demand from the press and the public, and no one I've ever known handles it as agreeably as Bobby. He has a marvelous athlete's face and a super smile and a quick wit. He is the greatest public relations athlete any sport ever had. He does more than you ask him to do.

He does so much that we didn't use him as much as we planned. He was wearing himself out. As a player, he is picked on by every desperate defender and he is punished unreasonably. And coaching has punished him mentally. It is tougher to coach than Bobby realized, and it is murderous to try to coach and play at the same time. It was all right when Winnipeg was going well. But when the team went bad at the start of the second season, Hull took it to heart.

I believe Ben would get more for his money if he would relieve Bobby of coaching and just let him play. I believe Bobby would be happier. As it is, he made a major move to Winnipeg. If he made another move, it might be back to Chicago. If the Winnipeg franchise shifted, Bobby might not want to go along with it. He feels he signed to play in Winnipeg and is not committed to play for the franchise elsewhere. The appointment of a "coach" to handle the bench during games, Rudy Pilous, should satisfy Bobby, even if he and Rudy had their disagreements in Chicago years ago.

184

I hope Hull stays with the WHA. I know how I feel about him. He repaid our investment in him the first season. From the first, he represented us marvelously well. From the moment the courts freed him to play with us, he played as hard as he could, he played well, and he was worth two to three thousand persons at the box office every game he played. Just his presence in the league probably was worth a thousand persons at the box office every game other teams played. He gave our league stature. He could not be everywhere at once, but in a sense he was.

Actually, he was under such pressure that we did not call on him for as many activities as we might have. He'd never have refused one. But his health and sanity were important to us. And he gave us our money's worth. So did most of the other stars we signed. Fellows like Cheevers and Howe were not only wonderful performers, but superb salesmen for a new business. As superstars, they were out front, and they conducted themselves with considerable class.

Sanderson and Parent were something else.

When Jim Cooper took a Philadelphia franchise in place of the forfeited Miami franchise, he took over the rights to Bernie Parent. He had to renegotiate a new contract with him, however, since Parent's original contract was with Herb Martin and a Miami franchise. These no longer were in our league. Parent not only had got $750,000 for five years, but a new house, a new boat, and a new car. In fact, he was to receive a new car every year of his contract.

He agreed to go for comparable considerations with Philadelphia, partly because he loved Philadelphia and considered it his home. He had his home in suburban Cherry Hills, New Jersey, which he kept when he was traded by the Philadelphia Flyers of the NHL to Toronto in 1971. Although a Canadian, he was broken-hearted when the

185

Flyers traded him. He wept at the press conference. He is an emotional fellow. He was not happy in Toronto, a situation which helped the WHA when he was invited to jump from the NHL. And the opportunity to return to Philadelphia helped when we wanted to keep him in the WHA.

Cooper, however, went overboard. He went high for many players. He invested beyond reason. He had one superstar; he wanted two. When he went after Derek Sanderson, Jim asked my advice. I advised against it. He went against my advice. Sanderson was not worth the sort of money it took to get him. He was a big name, but not a superstar. He was a good player, but not a great one. When he was inspired, he was a tough competitor, but when he was not, he was nothing. Even inspired, he could not score 40 goals in a season.

He got his big name from being a sort of imitation Joe Namath. He was one of the first players to let his hair grow long, cultivate a mustache, and don mod clothes. He was outspoken and rebellious. He hit his peak when he was photographed in living color in *Life* magazine with his girlfriend in bed. It's been downhill for him ever since.

He was already spoiled by fame and bound to be spoiled by a fortune. He invested a chunk of his dough in a twenty-eight-room mansion in plush Chestnut Hill. He said right off, publicly, that he wasn't going to knock himself out for any new league. He started to complain about a back injury. He wound up playing eight games for his team.

He complained that crowds were small and he couldn't play unless inspired. But it was his inspired play that was supposed to draw big crowds. Actually, color doesn't draw a dime at a box office unless it's backed up by ability and effort. Cooper should have erected a box office at the front door of Sanderson's mansion. More people would have paid to see Sanderson in bed with a broad than they would to see him in hockey at the arena. As he himself tells it, his real ability lies in bed.

Bernie Brown was so infuriated by Sanderson that he took control of the club away from Jim Cooper. Brown was determined to dump Sanderson. He didn't want team morale destroyed by a goof-off. And Philadelphia was floundering financially with low attendance. He offered him around the league, but no one wanted any part of him. Brown went to a trustees' meeting and asked if the other owners would ease his financial burdens by chipping in on Sanderson's payments as they had done in the Hull case. But buying Hull had been agreed on by the owners, not purchasing Sanderson. Hull was worth a lot to the league; Sanderson was worthless. Brown was flatly rejected. He was furious. The owners were outraged. Brown's lawyer and Quebec City's Paul Racine stood up shouting at each other and almost came to blows.

Brown wanted to release Sanderson and refuse to pay him on the grounds that he had not fulfilled his contract. But Sanderson threatened to sue for breach of contract on the grounds that his back condition did not permit him to play. Back problems are difficult for doctors to diagnose. Brown knew he could lose such a suit even if he knew he was in the right. Reluctantly, he bought Sanderson off. It took a million—$500,000 up front and another $500,000 to be paid out over an extended period.

It was ridiculous to pay him a million for the services he'd rendered. It may be the most outrageous payment in the history of sports. He couldn't care less. In his usual graceless way, he went away saying we were a bush league and Philadelphia was a city of losers and he was lucky to be out of it.

He went back to Boston and talked his way back into his $100,000-a-year contract with the Bruins. And promptly started to complain about his back again. His Boston bosses were quoted as being skeptical about his having a bad back. They sent him to the minors for a while to try to shock him back to his senses. They brought him back, then suspended him. Now they've unloaded him on New York. Losing Sanderson was embarrassing, but it didn't hurt our league. Everyone in hockey knows Sanderson and what he's worth. If anything, losing him helped us. It showed we were serious, not conducting a circus for clowns.

Losing Parent was something else. Whatever else he was, he was an outstanding player. He, too, was out at the start of the season. He was injured, and that hurt Philadelphia's chances of getting off to a good start, on the ice and at the box office. Once he got into action, he played well. He missed 15 out of 78 regular-season games but played the last 57 games in a row, which is an iron-man mark in today's game. He brought the Blazers from the bottom of the league to the top. But as soon as he realized others were being paid more than he was contracted for, he wanted more. He wanted to negotiate a new contract.

His attorney, Howard Casper, kept coming around, making demands, making life miserable for everyone around him. He'd call up to tell the coach how to play Parent. Parent kept saying he wanted to play, Casper kept saying Parent needed to rest. Finally, Casper said that if the contract was not renegotiated upward, Parent would not play.

This business of renegotiating contracts is a tricky one. Players who have good years always want contracts renegotiated upward. When they have bad years they do not agree to renegotiate contracts downward. Players and clubs negotiate long-term contracts to provide themselves with security, and both should stick to them. There are exceptions. A minor player signs for a small sum. If he becomes a major star, his salary should be made major. But renegotiating with one player opens the way for all the rest to want to renegotiate. It is a tricky situation. Parent was being well paid, and Brown refused to renegotiate.

Casper found a loophole to walk through. Parent's contract was guaranteed by a letter of credit at Cooper's Atlantic National Bank. Cooper was an owner of the bank. But it was not a big bank, and it did not have a large limit of credit permitted by federal law. When the Blazers' contractual obligations exceeded the limit, some letters of credit had to be withdrawn by the bank's officers, and Parent's was one of them. Once this was done, Parent was contractually free to flee.

It has been supposed that the Philadelphia franchise failed to meet a payment to Parent, but this is not true. Every payment due Parent was made him. And I believe every one due him would have been made him. The league was behind the Blazers as it was all the member clubs' contracts. Every payment due has been made every player. And Brown and Cooper had and have the money to buy a dozen Bernie Parents. Combined, they were among our wealthiest owners. But Parent had his out and took it.

It was when he took it that hurt most. After playing the first game of the playoffs, he walked out. A player owes something to his teammates. Contract negotiations should be conducted during the off-season. Parent could have waited a few weeks and pressed his demands after the playoffs. Walking out when he did, Parent cost his teammates and the club considerable cash. They did not win a game after he left and were run right out of the playoffs. It finished off the franchise in Philadelphia. How can Philadelphia's fans cheer him now that he is back with the Flyers there? I guess they can because he is such an outstanding goal-tender and was the backbone of the team's pennant and playoff championship effort.

His coach and teammate in Philadelphia, John McKenzie, an honorable man, said he'd strangle Parent if he ever got his hands on him. It is said that not only Casper but Parent's wife persuaded him to walk out on his obligations. Whoever was responsible, Parent was the one who walked. He went across town to the Flyers and said he'd return to the NHL if they could arrange his return from Toronto. Naturally, the league worked it out. We are not the only ones willing to accommodate a desirable player. Doug Favell, a popular performer in Philadelphia, was traded to Toronto in return for Parent.

We tried to keep Parent. We knew he wanted to stay in the East, in the United States. We arranged for the New York franchise to take over the contract, backed by the league. We renegotiated the contract, and Casper and Parent agreed to the terms. Parent was in the team's offices reaching out for an advance payment when a telephone call was received with word that Parent already had signed a new NLH contract. The check was torn up, and he was sent on his way.

Well, whatever else he was, he was a good player, and losing him was a loss to the league. He helped us when he signed, for his coming to us caused others to consider coming to us. He hurt us when he left, for he hurt our reputation and may have caused others to reconsider making a move. He proved himself as a player by leading the Flyers to the Stanley Cup.

If we lost two, we kept the rest. We will lose others, because once a player makes such a move, he feels freer to make another move another time. But we will get others because the players now know the league met its debts. The World Hockey Association established itself its first season. It fought some furious legal battles to win the rights to play the players it signed, got into the inevitable tangle of weeding out weak owners and weak franchises to be replaced by stronger ones, and enjoyed a season few thought ever would materialize, and a better first season than any rebel league ever enjoyed. Into and through its second season the WHA became a booming business.

CHAPTER 11

As Gary Davidson Sees It,   III

The first year for any new league is rough sailing. You have to find your way home in a storm through mine fields. I had to be a nice guy to everyone when we were organizing, but once we began operations, I became a bastard. You have to take a bastard position as president. You have to figure you know more than the others do or you wouldn't be president. If you don't, you won't be president long. You have as many problems on the inside as you do on the outside. The infighting is murderous. After a while you wonder if you have more enemies among your friends or among your foes.

It's a game to these guys until the first game is played. Once the shooting starts one owner is as liable to shoot a fellow owner in the back as he is a rival owner in the heart. They're all jockeying for advantage, ready to screw each other to get ahead of each other. If I ruled in favor of one guy in a dispute it meant I was ruling against another. Every time I made a friend I made an enemy. Not too many guys are big enough to see beyond their own selfish interests. Well, this is the way I make my money.

Most of the owners make money in business, but they don't use good business practices in sports. They're in the spotlight in sports and concerned with their image. If they ran a chain of stores they'd want them all to succeed, but they don't look on themselves as owners of a league; they look on themselves as owners of a team. They want to win, and the hell with the other teams and the rest of the league. In our league a lot of the owners didn't want to offend the NHL any more than necessary. They'd been beholden to the NHL a long time and felt they might be again some day. They wouldn't take all the strong positions I wanted them to take. I was on the attack against the NHL. I could not have cared less about the NHL. I wouldn't have to flip back to them for survival some day. I didn't owe them a thing.

I needed support and I got some, but I didn't get as much as I should have got. Few of the owners were willing to take me on head-on, but there was a lot of bitching behind my back. They complained that I wasn't a Canadian or a hockey man and had the league office in Orange County. And then I had other interests. Well, money was getting tight, and most of my net worth was in other companies. I couldn't cut them off. But I didn't neglect my league duties. I did neglect the owners. I didn't spend all my time traveling around to our cities, breaking bread with the owners, holding hands with them. I guess you've got to do that, but it isn't worth anything real. It's the public relations side of being a league president, and it's all false front with nothing behind it. They called me a Hitler. I told them if they didn't like the way I ran a league they could leave. I didn't threaten to execute them.

Bill Hunter battled me, of course. Ben Hatskin came over to my side. Paul Deneau was another Canadian allied with Hunter, but he got into financial trouble, started to scramble to keep his head above water, and I helped keep him afloat. It got to be to his advantage to keep me as president, so we developed a sort of unholy alliance to protect each other. You learn to play these games. I had brought a lot of these guys in and stepped into their troubles, and after a while I knew where all the bodies were buried. This was a weapon I could use in a pinch. I think some guys were after my scalp at every league meeting, but I wriggled out alive every time.

Our teams took to the ice to play games for the first time on September 23, 1972. The New England Whalers beat the Philadelphia Blazers in Roanoke, Virginia, and the Minnesota Fighting Saints beat the Chicago Cougars in Hibbing, Minnesota. Most of our experienced players were not available. Many major leaguers still were not available when we opened our regular season October 11 with Alberta at Ottawa and Quebec at Cleveland. Our first order of business was to get all of our players eligible to play.

I felt the National Hockey League player contract was illegal, immoral, and unenforceable. Its reserve clause in essence bound the player for life to the team in that league which held his contract. He could not play hockey elsewhere for anyone else without obtaining his release. He was essentially in slavery. It was not a matter of his choice in having signed such a contract in the first place, for if he did not sign such a contract he did not play in the professional ranks. We did not know how the lower courts would rule because these often are influenced by local prejudice. We felt once we got the matter into higher courts we would win.

The NHL at first fought to retain its rights in its contracts. Clarence Campbell, the president of the NHL, said the NHL could not live without the reserve clause but could live without a few players even if they lost a few cases. His reasoning was the traditional reasoning—that without a reserve clause, the wealthiest teams would wind up with all the best talent and imbalance would wreck the league operation. The answer to this is that you must have balance among your owners if you are to hope to have balance among your teams. The owners must be competitive if the teams are to be competitive. No reserve clause, no legislation you can enact, will guarantee equality of competition. The smarter operators will win as often as the wealthier ones. Montreal's Canadians dominate the NHL, not the wealthier Rangers.

We offered contracts without reserve clauses because we believed such clauses inevitably will be declared illegal and because we felt it would be an attractive lure to players. The only way reserve clauses can continue to be legal in hockey is for the NHL to get a ruling from Congress exempting it from the antitrust laws as major-league baseball did. However, that ruling on behalf of baseball is considered by the legal profession the most incredible, illogical, and illegal case of preferential treatment that could have been rendered, one which could not hold up under pressure and one which is not likely to be repeated.

One way to live without a reserve clause is to sign players to contracts of two years or more and renegotiate the contract in its final year each time. You do invest time and money in players and need some sort of reasonable restrictions on losing them. If a player does not wish to sign a new contract and sign again with the team that holds his contract, he should be free to sign with another team.

If it can be worked out, it is reasonable that the team which loses a player should get reasonable compensation from the team which acquires him. This is the Rozelle

195

rule because the NFL's Pete Rozelle worked it out. It is a good rule and can be made to work. As Rozelle does it, when the teams cannot agree on the compensation, he sets it. This has worked because he has been granted dictatorial powers. But the NFL players are rebelling because they feel he is an owners' man. It has not worked as well as it should have because the club owners, the partners in the corporation, have seldom been willing to bid for another team's player, so the unhappy player lacked much opportunity to move. The rule needs an impartial arbitrator to administer it.

We set up an arbitration board to render majority rulings on contract disputes and compensations. Because we are so young, it has not yet been tested. Hopefully, we would not discourage the movement of discontented players from one team to another within our league and so keep players within our league. Hopefully, we could keep a lot of players content with their original teams. If too many players made moves, chaos would corrupt our operation.

Pat Nagel, the labor relations expert from my law firm, worked out a two-year contract with Curt Leichner, who was named general counsel of the WHA Players' Association, guaranteeing them the sort of working conditions the players wanted. This included such details as the amount of travel allowances, meal money, and such. Most importantly, it gave the players a pension plan comparable to the NHL plan and guaranteed them credit for any years in the NHL they might not get from the NHL plan. A pension plan is critical. The players consider it their security.

We set up an owners' council and a players' council to negotiate any disputes. We encouraged the players to unionize. It was inevitable anyway. The NHL players were unionized. Jim Browitt headed up the owners' council, along with Pat Nagel and a group of the owners.

Our owners had agreed to share the cost of the inevitable legal battles. In the first year, each WHA franchise loaned the league $200,000 toward these costs. Through the first season I'd estimate the cost to both sides to be between $2.5 million and $3 million. The cost to the WHA has been about $1 million, the cost to the NHL close to twice that much.

Our ace in the hole was that we were attorneys and my firm worked for my league less expensively than the average firm would have. Also we were able to retain other attorneys and law firms to do work for us for less than they would have charged men who were not members of the fraternity, and they didn't demand their money up front. Obviously, my firm profits by the work we do, so I profit from it. But, we had the incentive of wanting to protect our vested interests. It monopolized our time and resulted in far less profits than we would have realized from other work.

As I figure it, we were fighting this war on fourteen fronts. The NHL started to sue us all over the map all at once. Chicago sued to keep Bobby Hull. Boston sued to keep Gerry Cheevers and Derek Sanderson. Los Angeles sued to keep Doug Barrie, Jim Johnson, and Bob Woytowich. And so forth. We had correctly anticipated that instead of filing one major suit against us, the NHL would file a whole series of smaller suits. The theory was that they would kill us by causing us to hire so many lawyers to fight so many battles on so many fronts at such expense that we would be spread so thin that we'd come apart. It was sound strategy because they had a lot more money to spend than we did and could last a lot longer in such a costly combat. Also, instead of taking the chance of losing one major suit, they were covering their bets; if they lost some, they might also win some. Every player they prevented us from using would weaken our position.

Our retaliatory strategy was to file a cross-complaint, a single major antitrust action for $64 million asking an injunction that would prevent them from suing us in these series of small cases. Meanwhile, we had to handle the small suits that already had been filed. We sought first to get these suits transferred to cities where they would not be prejudiced by local interests. And, second, we sought to get the cases transferred to federal courts. In any case, where we lost on a local level, we were ready to appeal to a higher court where we felt we would win.

Frankly, we sought to avoid certain cities where we felt the courts were less impartial. We were fooled some on this. Los Angeles may have as admirable a court system as there is in the country, but the Kings won an injunction to prevent us from playing Barrie, Johnson, and Woytowich. We appealed immediately. But we did not stop playing the players. We just did not play them when their teams played in Los Angeles. We ran the risk of being declared in contempt of court, but we felt the decision was so patently wrong that we were sure to gain a reversal.

In Boston, U.S. District Court Judge Andrew Caffrey refused to order an injunction in a suit filed by the Bruins to prevent Sanderson and Cheevers from playing in our league. Some of his comments favored us. He said, "Because of its peculiar international character, involving several teams in Canada as well as the United States, professional hockey would seem to be the leading candidate for a ruling that is subject to federal antitrust rules. . . . I find the balance of hardship favors the defendants, who would suffer a much more serious hardship if the injunction was granted than the Bruins would suffer."

We didn't want to fight the Hull case in Chicago, but

couldn't get it transferred. And the Hawks were granted an injunction which prevented our playing Hull at the start of the season. The Hull case was so important to us that we didn't dare risk losing it by playing him, risking contempt citations. However, most interestingly, the judge who granted the injunction there, Cook County Circuit Court Judge Francis T. Delaney, turned around and said that if the federal court in Philadelphia upheld our injunction, they would not enforce their injunction.

The Philadelphia case was the key one. And we won the victory we needed to get going when Judge Leon Higginbotham of the U.S. District Court in the Eastern District of Pennsylvania issued a preliminary ruling on November 8, 1973, that enjoined the NHL from enforcing its reserve clause while the case was being tried. He said, "Despite the glory of the sport of hockey and the grandeur of its superstars, the basic factors here are not the sheer exhilaration of the speeding puck, but rather the desire to maximize the buck. . . . The NHL is no shaky institution which will collapse if it loses a few superstars or even many average players during the preliminary injunction. The NHL is merely sustaining the fate which monopolists must face when they can no longer continue their prior total dominance of the market . . . there is clear and substantial likelihood that at trial, the interlocking agreement among the NHL teams, the reserve clause in the standard player contract, and the agreement between the NHL and minor and amateur hockey organizations will be found to have given the NHL the power of a monopoly."

This was only a preliminary ruling, but it was binding until a contrary ruling might be issued. We had not won the war, but we had won a big battle, and there were strong indications we might win the whole shooting match. The NHL was staggered. We were free to play the players we had signed for the time being and might well be permitted to keep them. The NHL had thrown a lot of strength against us. It had sixteen attorneys on its side, headed up by Washington lawyer E. Bennett Williams, a close friend of Jack Kent Cooke, a co-owner of the Washington Redskins' NFL team and a member of the Board of Directors of the Los Angeles Kings' NHL team. And these lawyers were falling all over themselves. They simply were not as united as we were in this case. Most of the owners wanted simply to ignore us, to pretend we did not exist and hope we would go away. They thought that if worse came to worst they could sue us out of existence. Cooke was not one of these. Nor was Bill Jennings of New York or Wes Adams of Boston. But they'd lost a big round. We'd played a long shot and won.

The case was still in court, and the NHL continued to fight us in a lot of little ways. For instance, we had set up an international series with the Czechoslovakia National Team in Quebec, Winnipeg, and St. Paul in January which could be considered comparable to the "Team Canada" series with the Soviet Union Team in the preseason. "Team Canada" really was the NHL All-Stars. Canadian fans were deprived of a representative team when Bobby Hull and Gerry Cheevers were not permitted to play. This was petty on the part of the NHL. It almost cost them the series, which was closer than they arrogantly expected it to be. Anyway, the Czechs, not the Russians, were reigning world amateur champions at the time. But the Czechs could not obtain sanction for our series from the Canadian Amateur Hockey Association and the Amateur Hockey Association of the United States. We negotiated in good faith and offered a considerable donation to the programs of the CAHA and AHAUS, but these bodies were allied unfairly with the NHL and blocked our exhibition series. We had to cancel it.

Nevertheless, we went ahead with our season, and it was a success. Not that we did not have our failures. Our first game in Philadelphia had to be postponed when the ice-cleaning machine broke through the ice and ruined it. The least a hockey team can be expected to provide is a satisfactory surface of ice for games. Some clubs operated in chaos. There were the usual firings and hirings of coaches in midseason, but I guess this silliness is not restricted to our league or our sport. We had the Sanderson illness, of course, in which a player was paid $1 million not to play.

Some coaches and players were treated poorly. In Chicago, coach Marvel Pronovost said his player Jimmy McLeod was the greatest goalkeeper in the league. Pronovost later was fired and McLeod traded to New York. In New York, Ron Ward became a surprise star and a hero to the home folks. After the season, he was traded to Vancouver. He was hailed as a savior in Vancouver. He then was traded to Los Angeles. Los Angeles traded him to Cleveland. In Los Angeles, Dennis Murphy found a backer in a Kansas City physician, Dr. Arthur Rhoades. Late in the first season, he walked out. He just went away without a word to anyone. He just stopped paying the bills. In New York, when the owners could not pay their bills, the league had to take over.

We felt our new teams were comparable to NHL expansion teams. There can be no question our best could not be compared to their best, but our best may have been better than their worst. I doubt that the New York Islanders, who won twelve games all season, or the California Golden Seals, who won sixteen, could have handled our New England Whalers or Winnipeg Jets. That is not idle speculation. I'm sure the value of the players assembled for the New England and Winnipeg franchises was higher than what the Islanders and Seals had.

We had much better balance among our teams. We had more clubs who were competitive. We had fairly good pennant races in both our divisions—the Eastern, won by New England; the Western, by Winnipeg. Our three top teams, including also Cleveland, each won between 43 and 46 games. Eight others won 33 or more games. Only Chicago was far from the others with just 26 victories. Most of our teams were in contention for the four playoff positions in each division the last week or two of the season. Both battles went down to the last games. Eight points separated the four teams in the third through sixth places in the Eastern Division. Three points separated the four teams in the second through fifth places in the Western Division. Two teams tied for the fourth and final playoff spot.

New England defeated Cleveland in the Eastern Division playoff finals and Western Division playoff winner Winnipeg in the league finals for the AVCO World Cup trophy. The New England organization put together a strong team which was managed and coached superbly by Jack Kelley, who was voted the Howard Baldwin trophy as Coach of the Year. Bobby Hull did a fine job coaching and inspiring the Winnipeg club, and his outstanding individual play won him the Gary Davidson trophy (harumph) as Most Valuable Player in the league. Nick Mileti did a marvelous job putting together a contender in Cleveland in a short time, and his Gary Cheevers won the Ben Hatskin trophy as best goaltender in the league. Immodestly, we named the trophies after ourselves. In such a way, the founding fathers leave a mark on the league, though I wonder how long my trophy will continue to carry my name now that I am gone.

Ample proof that ours was a stronger league than observers expected came in the fact that Hull could not tear up our league. It was said he would score 75 goals. He did not. In fact, the only player ever to score that many goals, Phil Esposito, has done it in the National League. Hull did not lead our league in goals or in scoring points. He scored 51 goals and 103 points, but he had scored more in the NHL. Five players scored 50 or more goals in our league, but that is the trend today, even in the NHL. There can be no question that either major league is as strong as the old NHL was when it had only six teams, but then it was too small to really be a representative major league.

Danny Lawson of our Philadelphia team scored 61 goals, and Hull, Ward, Andre Lacroix of Philadelphia, and Tom Webster of New England each scored 50 or more goals. Lacroix had 50 goals and 74 assists and totaled 124 points to win the Bill Hunter trophy as scoring champion. It is true that some of these players were not superstars in the NHL. Lacroix had never scored more than 24 goals in an NHL season. Ward had scored two goals in the NHL the season before. But it is also true Rick MacLeish scored 50 goals in the NHL when he had scored one goal and been sent to the minors the season before. And Bill Flett scored 43 goals in the NHL when he had scored 18 the season before and never more than 26 in a previous season.

In some cases, the puck simply bounces right for a player in a given season. In other cases, a player suddenly arrives at his peak. These surprising performances take place in all leagues. A Danny Lawson and a Tom Webster were developing. They were regarded as future superstars when they were in the NHL, and they found their futures in the WHA. Such fine youngsters as Webster, Tim Sheehy, and Larry Pleau led New England's championship playoff push, although Winnipeg's Norm Beaudin led in goals with 13 and points with 28 in the postseason play.

It was said by NHL supporters that the WHA played loose, defenseless hockey, just as the NFL used to say it about the AFL. It simply wasn't so. The NHL averaged 6.5 goals per game, the WHA 7.1. That is less than a goal a game difference and simply isn't significant. In the playoff finals, the NHL averaged 9.3 goals per game, the WHA 9.6. That was less than half a goal a game difference. And our players were just beginning to get used to one another in team situations. They were bound to get better and tighten up. The NHL ridicule ran out when its playoff finalists Montreal and Chicago played 8–3, 8–7, 7–4, and 6–4 games. It had eighteen goals in one game and ten in one period. They didn't play tight hockey. They played like they were tight.

We had good defensemen. The former Montreal star J. C. Tremblay of our Quebec club was voted the Dennis Murphy Award as best defenseman in the league. He and Cleveland's Paul Schmyr formed the first-team defense in front of goaltender Cheevers on our all-star selection. Hull, Lacroix, and Lawson formed the forward line on the select team.

I think we played a colorful style of hockey. Some of our rules represented an improvement over the NHL game. Most significantly, we played 10-minute sudden-death overtime periods when games ended in ties after the regulation three 20-minute periods. We had overtime throughout the regular season, not just in playoffs as the NHL does. The NHL used to have them throughout the regular season, but stopped them during World War I when teams could not afford to miss scheduled travel times. They should have returned to them long ago.

It is not just that a tie is an unsatisfactory finish for the

fans, but the fans are cheated when teams coast conserva-
tively through the final minutes of play to protect a tie.
Knowing they will have to try to play off a tie, teams in
our league would go all out to win. We put the most
exciting moments back in the game where they belonged.
And overtimes are enormously exciting. If sometimes they
are won by a lucky shot, so, too, are all games. A lucky
shot is just as likely to occur in the last minute of regulation time as the first minute of overtime.

For a while, we experimented in the preseason with a
Wild West shoot-out to settle games still tied after overtimes. Players alternated skating in and shooting on the
goalie until one scored. But this proved unsatisfactory. It
violated the spirit of a team game and created a circus
atmosphere. So we abandoned the idea. As it was, our overtimes produced decisions in 45 out of 64 situations. We
had only 19 ties. The NHL had 82. Clearly, we came out
on top in this department.

We hoped to draw 2 million fans our first year. We drew
almost 25 percent more than we expected. Combining regular season and postseason, we drew 2,694,771 fans to 499
games for an average of 5,400 per game. I realize this is
far from the 9,200,000 who attended 662 games, an average of 13,897 per game, in the NHL. But the NHL has
been in business for more than fifty years. It had better
players, bigger names, and established teams. You can't buy
the tradition it brings with it. We drew far more fans than
anyone expected.

It is significant that we did not destroy the NHL. Their
claims that we would kill the market were disproved. The
NHL drew more fans than it had the year before. As we
insisted from the first, there was room for both leagues. In
a way, we helped the NHL, because we spread hockey
around our two countries, increased interest in our sport,

and brought in new fans. The potential for television soared. Competitive bidding brought the NHL a better contract from CBS in 1974 than it had from NBC the year before.

Of course, there can be no question that we hurt the NHL in many ways. We took them from a monopoly into a competitive situation. We brought the NHL teams into a dollar war of bidding for players which picked a lot of bucks from their pocketbooks. We hurt their prestige by taking a lot of players from them, including some superstars. We backed them up against a wall to the point where they had to start thinking of merging with us.

CHAPTER 12

As Gary Davidson Sees It, IV

We didn't want a merger. We really didn't. We wanted recognition and coexistence. We wanted to establish ourselves to the point where we could have a common draft which would arrest the upward spiral of player salaries at some level we could all live with, compensate for this restriction on the players by having a free exchange of players between teams and leagues, and boost both of us by scheduling some preseason or even regular-season interleague competition, culminating in a championship playoff between the league winners at season's end, a sort of Super Bowl of hockey. With inclusion of a European division, we could have true World Cup competition comparable to that so popular the world over in soccer.

We were at least five years ahead of any new league ever formed before. In a single season the value of our franchises shot up from $25,000 to $2 million or more. A new franchise now costs $2 million. Old franchises with players went for more. Yet, some owners panicked and wanted to get together with the NHL on any terms. Some owners in the NHL still stubbornly resisted taking in any WHA teams on any terms. And others insisted they'd merge only on stickup terms.

Late in our first season, early in April, some men from the WHA and NHL met at the Marriott Essex House in New York City to talk merger. They were not representatives of the leagues. They were there informally to feel out possibilities. I knew of the meeting, but NHL president Campbell did not. Our owners knew of it, but some of the NHL owners did not. Actually, NHL men approached us; we didn't approach them. Bill Jennings of New York telephoned Nick Mileti of Cleveland to set up a meeting to talk it over. Mileti, Bob Schmertz of Boston, and Ben Hatskin of Winnipeg of the WHA met with Jennings, Ed Snider of Philadelphia, Peter Block of Pittsburgh, and Jacques Courtois of Montreal of the NHL.

They worked out a tentative agreement that called for all of the owners of the WHA to enter teams in the NHL to form a twenty-eight-team circuit. However, our teams in New York, Boston, Chicago, St. Paul, and Los Angeles, which were in the territories of NHL teams, would have to move to other territories. Each of our franchise holders would pay $4 million to enter the NHL. The value of our franchises was set at $2 million. The cost of new NHL franchises was $6 million. The $4 million represented a compromise sum. Each of our teams would pay $750,000 down and the remaining $3.25 million over a period of time. We would drop our antitrust suit. They would drop their various suits, which were inactive because of the injunction we'd obtained, but which could have been reactivated later. We would adopt their contracts. We would keep the players we had taken from them, but would not take any more. We would participate in a common draft of new talent. To avoid antitrust charges, it would be called an "agreement" rather than a "merger." Knowing there would be objections from players, the NHL men insisted we had to sign the papers within two weeks.

It was not what I had wanted. To effect a merger within one year of opening operations would have been a feather in my cap, for sure, but I did not like the terms. I had been proceeding with the understanding that we were trying for a working agreement, not a merger. I felt we were at a point where we did not have to pay to join the NHL. I felt we could deal with them on even terms. I said this in an interview. I said we were pursuing our own growth plans and were not interested in becoming a member of the NHL family. Nick had not informed me that negotiations had taken a different turn. He was having lunch with Jennings when Jennings got a phone call informing him of my statements. Jennings was upset. He wondered if Mileti was empowered to work out any agreement with NHL owners. The fact was that Nick needed the approval of our owners, but so, too, did Jennings need the approval of his league's owners. He had no more power to effect a firm and final pact than Nick did. But Nick was furious. He felt I had let him down by not promoting the merger idea at this time. He since has come to understand the misunderstanding. At the time, the friendship he felt for me cooled. Later, we resumed our friendship. But the misunderstanding undermined negotiations.

Mileti had talked to our owners to sell them on the idea of pursuing an agreement. He felt it was the opportunity of a lifetime for our owners. But he didn't want to stuff the idea down their throats. He's not that kind of man. Mileti did not meet with us to report on the agreements that had been reached. He sent a representative, who was not nearly as persuasive a salesman as Nick was. Nick went off to be with his Cleveland Indians baseball team while we weighed the matter. We called in our counselor who had been representing us in the Philadelphia case, Harold Cohen, and he warned us the agreement we had reached was a dangerous one: the courts or Congress might consider it to be a conspiracy to restrict the rights of the players. He also said it was certain that the players would sue to protect their rights, to prevent us from removing their bargaining power from them. Our owners went against the agreement.

Their owners went against it, too. They didn't want Winnipeg, Edmonton, and Quebec in their league. One wonders what they did want. I'm sure they just wanted to get rid of us, our raids on their talent and our antitrust suit, which threatened their cash and their contracts. Some of them didn't want any part of us. Some were outraged when they found out the meeting had taken place without their knowledge. Clarence Campbell was outraged. Well, he was a retiring president on his way out, anyway, an administrator, not a dictator, and he had little tangible power in important matters. But he considered the meeting without his knowledge an insult, which it was.

Bill Wirtz of Chicago was against it. For one thing, he would be against anything which wouldn't bring Bobby Hull back to his side. And representatives of the players' groups screamed murder when word of the secret talks leaked out. We knew they'd be against it. Well, it would have been almost impossible to take care of all the paperwork in two weeks, anyway. You do not rush a project of such proportions. So it fell through, and it was just as well. I felt we were gaining strength every day and moving toward a not so distant time when we could deal from power and would not have to be begging anyone for anything. Which was true as it turned out.

Not that we did not have our problems. Some of our franchises were floundering and had to be righted and strengthened. This is what happens, though. You start with as much strength as you can muster. And then you must build up, strengthening yourself as you go.

Our first season, New England and Quebec averaged almost 7,000 fans a game during the regular season; Winnipeg, Los Angeles, New York, and Minnesota around 6,000; Cleveland more than 5,000; Houston, Chicago, and Philadelphia around 4,500; Edmonton around 3,800, and Ottawa around 3,200. This does not correlate exactly to the amount of success or failure a franchise had. Some operated more economically than others. Some had much higher player payrolls than others. Some had stiffer arena rental situations. Some had smaller arenas which could not accommodate the occasional exceptional crowd which helps teams so much. Some had no prospects for superior arenas in the future.

New York was our biggest problem.

Had the original owners in New York got their team into the new Nassau County Coliseum on Long Island, they might have made it. They were discouraged when the Islanders moved in with an NHL franchise and turned to Madison Square Garden in Manhattan. In Nassau they should have been offered a reasonable lease and would have had as a rival the worst team in the NHL. The arena refused, and we have an antitrust suit going there. In Manhattan they accepted the worst lease in sports, which compelled them to pay about $20,000 a game and denied them the rights to raid the Rangers of any local heroes. Then the owners refused to purchase name players or spend to promote their product.

Marvin Milkes was a solid general manager, but he couldn't compel the owners to operate reasonably. When they reached the point where they couldn't pay their bills, we had to take over. Jim Browitt went in to run the operation and find new backers. Lee Mattison and Ralf Brent arrived to save the ship the second season and promptly capsized in a sea of red ink.

Milkes, who had fled, was persuaded to return the second season to conduct a holding operation as the league took over again and started a new search for a new owner. To cut down on the overhead, the team temporarily was transferred to Cherry Hill, New Jersey.

I would say the league as a whole lost $15 million its first season. The least any team lost was probably $200,000 or so. New England and Quebec probably lost the least. The most any team lost probably was between $1.5 million and $2 million. Philadelphia lost the most. New York lost a lot because it had to pay around $20,000 a game to share Madison Square Garden with the Rangers, but it did not have a high player payroll. Los Angeles lost a lot, but it did not have a high player payroll. And it was sold for $2.5 million in 1974.

Most teams probably lost $500,000 to $750,000. But this is not pure loss. Vancouver interests paid $1.9 million to acquire the Philadelphia franchise. Toronto interests paid $1.8 million to acquire the Ottawa franchise. Most of the lost money was made up. Some investors may even have turned a profit. Others could. Winnipeg received offers of $4.3 million from Milwaukee interests and $4.5 million from Detroit interests. I don't think you could buy the New England franchise for less than $5 million.

If our clubs lost $15 million, their collective worth conservatively now could be set at $36 million, which represents a net gain in value of $21 million. And it will rise yearly.

Three new teams entering in 1974 are paying the league $6 million. From the start of the second season of the World Hockey Association I was laying plans for the first season of the World Football League. The WHA was working. It still had problems, but it will always have problems, as will any league. I felt it was time to move on to another venture.

I delayed because I wasn't sure I'd go ahead with the football project at first and because I wanted to be sure the hockey project was solid before I departed. I knew if the hockey league failed, even later I'd be blamed. And I knew if it was a solid success before I left, I'd get the credit. If you leave too soon, you are forgotten. Dennis Murphy isn't remembered much now as the man behind the ABA. Well, I wanted to be remembered as the man behind the WHA. I wanted desperately to establish it as a success, and I knew if I did I would deserve the credit and if I didn't I would deserve the blame.

Our first major move the second season was landing the Howes. This was a body blow from which the NHL has not recovered. Here was the top scorer and greatest all-around player in the history of the National Hockey League, Gordie Howe. He had two sons, Mark and Marty, who were considered among the greatest prospects to come along in years. Mark, especially, was rated a potential superstar. A forward, he had been the youngest player in the Olympics. He was eighteen. Marty, a defenseman, was nineteen. Neither was eligible to be drafted from the Canadian Hockey Amateur Hockey Association by the National Hockey League until he was twenty under an agreement between the two bodies. We had no such agreement.

It was Doug Harvey's idea that our Houston team draft them. A former Montreal all-star, an NHL immortal, Harvey was an assistant coach at Houston. He suggested to Jim Smith that he draft and seek to sign them. Smith telephoned Gordie. The retired star said, "Great." He laughed and said he might go with them.

At our draft meeting in Toronto, Smith came to me with the idea. I went for it. I felt we did not owe the CAHA anything. They had allied themselves with the NHL, notably in blocking our exhibition series with Czechoslovakia. The CAHA had no moral right to deprive a player of the right to play for pay because he was not twenty. If a young player had the ability, he should be able to move up.

Smith drafted Mark. The meeting went wild. The Canadians were protesting all over the place. Phil Watson was waving me away, as if to say go back to California, you Yankee. Ben Hatskin and Bill Hunter complained we couldn't do it. Hatskin said it would wreck our relations with the CAHA. I said we had no relations with them worth anything. Hunter said it would destroy the CAHA, which was a free farm system for us. I said I didn't know it would wreck the CAHA. Maybe we could work out a system of payments as compensation to them for players taken, similar to the one the NHL had with them. In any event, I did not believe in making anyone's difficult decisions for him. If we posed a problem for them, they would have to find their own solution for it.

When the situation was starting to get out of control I told everyone to sit down and shut up. I ruled that we were going to draft anyone anybody wanted to draft and that was that. Well, there we were, the Indians sneaking around behind bushes, picking the Redcoats off, one by one. Houston then drafted Mark. And, finally, Gordie. L.A. had the right to Gordie, originally, but let Houston have him.

Smith flew to talk business with the Howes. Harvey had let him know Howe was unhappy in Detroit, and Gordie confirmed this. After twenty years with the Wings, he'd been making $35,000. It was not until his twenty-fifth and last year that he made $100,000. Retired two years, he'd been given an executive position with the team for $50,000 a year. What he really was given was a desk with nothing to do. The league had found no use for him.

It had been his ambition all his life to play with his sons. He hadn't lasted long enough. Now he had a new chance. The arthritis in his wrist which had troubled him his last few years had improved with rest. He felt he could play another year. If his sons went, he'd like to go with them. He thought they should go. Why should they play for Toronto Marlboros for $60 a week the next year or two when they could play for the Houston Aeros for many thousands? For big money, they would go.

A deal was worked out. The money was big—$2 million for five years. Gordie would get $1 million, his sons half a million each. That works out to $200,000 a year for Gordie, $100,000 a year each for Mark and Marty. Gordie would be committed to play for only one season, but might play more if he wanted to. In any event, he would play the first game in the new arena in Houston. Other years he would represent the team in the front office.

Smith brought the deal to me, and I took it to the owners. By then they saw how shook the NHL was by it. The NHL had offered Howe another $125,000 to represent it. With his Detroit $125,000, Howe could make more staying in the NHL and not playing than he could playing for us. But he is a man of honor. If we got up the dough, he would go.

The owners agreed the league would loan Houston the $500,000 front money, to be repaid partly out of earnings he brought in through NHL properties. Smith went back to the Howes, and the contracts were signed. It was a master stroke. In two seasons we had signed the two greatest veteran stars in the NHL. They were an image any league could be proud of.

The signing produced tremendous publicity for us. Howe is much like Hull. He is a magnificent man, marvelous under pressure from the press and public. They are not all like this. These are two of the best. And anyone who thought he was washed up was wrong. A magnificent physical specimen, he was one of the leading scorers in our league and a powerful, complete all-around player. And Mark and Marty more than lived up to their billing as budding stars. They played impressively with older performers. The Howes hurt the NHL a great deal.

We followed up by signing other juniors, of age and under age. Our first season we had needed names to bring in business. We could not risk our investment on unproven prospects. Unlike the football and basketball players who come out of collegiate ranks with national reputations, hockey's graduating juniors are known only to insiders in the sport. But by our second season we had added new names such as Pat Stapleton, Ralph Backstrom, Mike Walton, Marc Tardif, Rejean Houle, and others and no longer were as much in need of more as we were building up our teams with the top talent who would be the stars of the future. We drafted a number of top junior stars and we signed a lot of them. Los Angeles signed Reg Thomas, coveted by Chicago's Black Hawks, for example. Cleveland signed Tom Edur, an eighteen-year-old defense star of the future. Cincinnati, coming into our league in 1975, signed Dennis Sobchuk, an eighteen-year-old forward regarded as the best bet for stardom among the amateurs. He will play on loan to Phoenix in 1974.

The CAHA came to us. Could we pay them for players taken from them? Yes, we agreed, we could if they could work out a deal with the NHL to pay the same prices. The NHL had been paying $10,000 for any of the top thirty-two selections it signed, $7,000 for each of the next thirty-two, and so on down the line. They were getting away cheap. We brought

216

the bill up to $25,000 for each of the first twenty players drafted and signed, $20,000 for the next twenty, and so on. The NHL went along with it. That was that. Dennis Murphy was president when the deal was finalized.

The aging Gordie Howe and the underage Mark Howe proved important players in the second season of the WHA. With Don McLeod, they led their team to the Western Division pennant and the AVCO Cup playoff championship.

Mike Walton, a marvelous acquisition for the Minnesota team, led the league in goals scored with 57 and points with 117. Winnipeg's Bobby Hull and Vancouver's Danny Lawson were second and third in goals with 53 and 50, respectively. New Jersey's Andrew Lacroix was first in assists with 80 and second in points with 111.

Gordie Howe scored 31 goals, assisted on 69 and was third in total points with 100. His son Mark scored 38 goals and was one of the two or three top left-wings in the league, selected for some all-star honors. McLeod beat out Cleveland's Cheevers statistically for goal-tending honors. Gordie was rated Most Valuable Player in the league, Mark the Rookie of the Year.

Some said Gordie would disgrace himself, but by the end even Nation Hockey League partisans admitted he was phenomenal. He helped coach Bill Dineen's team win 48 games, the most of any team in the league. Western runnerup Minnesota won 44 games.

Eastern Division winner New England won 43 games and the runnerup Toronto team 41 games. Cleveland and Chicago won out in a close race with Quebec for the final two playoff positions in the East. Losing out, Quebec's general manager and coach Jacques Plante resigned, and joined Edmonton to resume his career as a goaltender in the fall of 1974.

Again, we had close competition. Billy Harris was considered Coach of the Year for the job he did in Toronto, but Pat

Stapleton also did a super job, changing Chicago from the worst team in the league to one of the best. Not only did he make the playoffs with his club, but he took it all the way to the finals before it bowed to Houston.

Attendance increased in the second season of the World Hockey Association from 2.4 million paid fans to 2.7 million. Attendance increased in nine of the twelve cities in which the WHA operated in its second season.

Attendance increased from 168,600 in Philadelphia to 364,900 in Vancouver, a transfer that resulted in an improvement of 116 percent. Vancouver led the WHA second-season attendance with an average of 9,300 fans per game, followed by Quebec with 7,900 per game.

Houston averaged 6,800 fans, Minnesota 6,500, Winnipeg 6,400, Cleveland 6,200. New England averaged 5,900, Los Angeles 5,300, Chicago 4,900, Edmonton, 4,400, Toronto 4,200, but New Jersey only 2,500.

Some attendance was promising. Some was not. The team moved from New York to New Jersey fell off 56 percent from the first season. New England and Los Angeles dropped. All three had to be moved before the third season.

I would not have moved out of Madison Square Garden in New York, but rental terms were tough. Responsible ownership with satisfactory financing to support the team through a reasonable period of growth was never found.

Faced with a problem, Dennis Murphy made a difficult decision and transferred the franchise early in the season to New Jersey. However, he located in a small arena in Cherry Hills where the team could not draw well and now must settle financially with the original season ticket–holders in New York.

The franchise has been relocated in San Diego, where it should be a success. San Diego interests had been holding out for an NHL franchise, but it never materialized. This is the

NHL's mistake. There is a fine arena in San Diego, adequate population, and enormous enthusiasm for hockey. Minor league hockey has outdrawn some major league sporting ventures in San Diego.

Joseph Schwartz, a Baltimore businessman, bought the Jersey Knights, so many assumed the team would be moved to Baltimore. The WHA could yet wind up in Baltimore, where it could be competitive with the new NHL team in suburban Washington. Because of alleged connections with the Mafia, Schwartz was not approved as the owner by San Diego city representatives, and a new owner had to be found or the team moved.

There is talk of a new indoor arena in New Jersey in the populous Hackensack Meadowlands as part of the sporting complex which will contain a new stadium to house the NFL Giants. This has been hung up in political controversy, but it is possible the WHA may move back to the New York–New Jersey area.

I do not think the league needs a New York–area franchise to survive, but I do think one would be of great benefit to the league.

Similarly, I believe a quality operation would succeed in Los Angeles. Dennis Murphy did not have the finances to manage it himself. I was listed as vice-president of the Sharks until Dr. Rhoades took over the team, but I was just a figurehead. Dr. Rhoades did not buy the team. He took over its debts and obligations. I got nothing from the deal. Nor did Dennis.

Dennis had to assume responsibility for it again when Rhoades decided to take a walk at midseason. Dennis found San Diego dentist Lenny Bloom to take over the new debts and old obligations. Bloom denied that he owned the team, but it was his. His signature was on the checks and contracts. He did not bother to boost it. He ignored offers of television deals which would stimulate interest. He did not promote his product.

He wanted the team only to bolster his bid to have San Diego citizens build a new arena in suburban Chula Vista to house both his ABA Conquistadors and WHA Sharks. He bought Wilt Chamberlain for $600,000 a season to add to his ammunition. He felt that with Wilt he would not be refused, but he was fooled. Now he may move Chamberlain and the Q's to the Sports Arena in Los Angeles to do battle with the Lakers at the suburban Forum.

Dennis had bowed out of the Sharks to succeed me as president of the WHA, but he was kept busy selling the Sharks. He wanted to locate a money man in L.A. He almost landed Bob Hope. The comedian had his staff investigate the potential and got their approval of it as an investment, but he decided to pass. Perhaps he simply is not that much of a hockey fan. Larry Daniels was announced as a buyer for the team, but bowed out. Others were cornered, but escaped.

It was too bad. All the franchise required was solid backing, a name player or two and a contending club to prosper. Two major league hockey teams can live in the Los Angeles area. The Kings are just now getting entrenched. They have been vulnerable to a strong rival for many years and may still be. This is a major market which can be made to work for the WHA, but it hasn't been given a good chance.

I would have liked to have tried my hand at operating the franchise. I have a big ego, I guess. I've succeeded with leagues, I feel I could succeed with teams. Like a lot of other people, I sit on the sidelines and watch men make mistakes I feel I would not make. Maybe I'm right. Maybe I'm wrong. But I'm too busy to find out.

Basketball is Bloom's bag and he needed all his money to make it in the one sport. The Sharks were sold for $2.5 million to Detroit businessmen Charles Nolton and Pete Shagena. Dennis insisted it would remain in Los Angeles at least one more season, but a credibility gap arose when the new owners promptly fired the team publicist and dropped the radio broadcasts. They changed coaches for the second time during the season and team morale nosedived and what interest there was in the team locally disappeared.

Any fool could see the franchise was headed for Detroit, and as soon as the season ended it was announced it was going there as the Michigan Stags. It will not share the Olympic with the NHL Red Wings, but will move into a renovated Cobo Hall.

Detroit has been disappointed by the mismanagement of the NHL team there and may be receptive to the WHA entry. However, WHA public relations in Los Angeles may never recover and it would be difficult to return a team to this rich area now.

Dennis is enjoying the presidency of the WHA and would like to continue in that capacity. He can handle it, I now believe. He wanted to keep his office at home in southern California, which would have been impossible without a team here. Locating the New York-New Jersey franchise in San Diego may have filled the void created when the Los Angeles franchise landed in Detroit.

Attendance in Boston was disappointing and Bob Schmertz and Howard Baldwin got tied up with my new World Football League, so they sold part of the New England franchise to interests in Hartford, Connecticut, mainly the Aetna Insurance Company. A new 10,000-seat building is rising in Hartford and a franchise can work there.

Interestingly, the franchise located temporarily in Springfield, Massachusetts, for the playoffs and, while the building there holds only 5,500 fans, it was 100 per cent sold out for all four games the team played there.

It remains a struggle for some franchises, of course. None

have escaped headaches. But that is the business. Some are starting to prosper and their headaches are decreasing.

Chicago had a dreadful front-office situation until the Kaisers came in, asserted themselves, made some changes and straightened things out. Jim Tierney, former owner of the Cougars, was sentenced in U.S. District Court in Chicago to four years probation for using forged securities as collateral for loans he received to purchase the WHA franchise originally.

Jordon Kaiser took over as chairman of the board, his brother Walter as president. Ed Short was replaced as general manager. An outstanding individual, Pat Stapleton, was bargained away from the other team in town, the Black Hawks, as player-coach. Another fine player, Ralph Backstrom, was pried from the Hawks. The team started to rise as construction started on the $20 million, 18,000-seat O'Hare Arena in Rosemont suburbs, near the airport.

The Amphitheatre where the Cougars have been playing was built in 1934. Because a touring show had been booked into the building, it was not available to the team during the playoffs just when the Cougars were commanding considerable interest in Chicago. The Cougars had to play at Stapleton's suburban ice rink, which hurt horribly.

The popularity of the Hawks and hockey in Chicago is such that even though management permits superstars to escape, they sell out every game at top prices. But fans are fed up with the Chicago Stadium, an ancient arena in a depressed area. Chicago is a big city and can support two teams. I would not be surprised to see the Black Hawks begging their way into the new building one day. The NBA Bulls may move over. Or the Kaisers may put their own ABA team in there. The Cougars are a solid franchise.

I have decided that with some exceptions you are wiser to go into a big city where a major-league team is operating, interest is established, and fans have been shut out than to go into a smaller city where customers are not accustomed to paying big-league prices and you must create a demand. There are some cities such as Indianapolis where I would think we will go big from the beginning, but others where an owner would do well to go into competition with a thriving foe. I think this is the case in Toronto. Michel didn't have the money to make it in Ottawa. Trbovich blew $500,000 trying to cut it in a 9,300-seat building in what was really a small town. And the juniors had a hold on the town. I advised Buck Houle, the general manager there, to invest heavily in Denis Potvin, the hottest junior in Canada and a hero in Ottawa. He was ready to sign for a mere $50,000 a season. It would have broken the back of the junior operation, but they didn't go for it. It finished them. John Bassett, Jr., and John Craig Eaton bought the franchise for $1.8 million, so a profit was turned fast on what seemed a hopeless situation.

Bill Ballard wanted the WHA team to go into Maple Leaf Gardens as co-tenant with the NHL team. Bassett chose to mark time in 5,400-seat Varsity Arena while a $20 million, 20,000-seat stadium is constructed in suburban Mississauga. Now they may mark time in Maple Leaf Gardens after all. They played their playoff games in the Gardens and averaged 7,400 fans, 45 percent of capacity. It has been years since you could get a ticket to a Toronto game, but it may not be long before the new Toros are pulling packed houses from hockey enthusiasts who can't get into Leaf games. A similar situation could develop with a WHA franchise in a new indoor arena being built for the 1976 Olympics in Montreal, where the waiting list to Canadiens' games at the old Forum numbers in the tens of thousands.

The Flyers are fashionable in Philadelphia, and the Sanderson and Parent failures frustrated Jim Cooper and Bernie Brown with the Blazers there, but they bailed out by selling out for $1.9 million to a Vancouver syndicate headed by Jim Pattison. I don't know if Philadelphia was sufficiently enthusiastic to support big-league hockey teams, but I know Vancouver is. The new franchise moved in to share the 14,400-seat Pacific Coliseum with the Canucks of the NHL, swiftly sold 8,000 season tickets, and may make the mismanaged and controversial Canucks suffer. The WHA entry in Vancouver appears to be a solid franchise.

So, too, seems to be the Quebec City entry. This is in the heart of hockey country, but for years the citizens had to settle for second best—teams which sent their best players up to the majors, notably Montreal. Paul Racine, Jean Lesage, and Marius Fortier have operated effectively. They went high for a Canadian immortal, Jacques Plante, as general manager and coach the second season, but that didn't work out. The Nordiques' home arena, the Quebec Coliseum, could be larger. It seats only 10,000. However, enthusiasm seems to be running high.

The Edmonton entry, which was called Alberta most of the first season, is another with an excellent territory which typifies the growth in hockey interest. Less than ten years ago, it had 5,000 players registered. Today there are more than 30,000. The amateur ranks which provide the professionals of the future are broadening annually. A new 16,000-seat Coliseum is under construction. It has been a struggle so far with a 5,200-seat facility, but a better day is coming. Dr. Charles Allard and Zane Feldman are the money men atop the operation, but Bill Hunter, vice-president, trustee, and general manager, runs the show with a strong hand.

Nick Mileti didn't need the money, but is spread so thin he decided to bring in backers to share the burden in Cleveland. He really is a civic-minded soul who puts the interest of his community ahead of his own interests. He did not put a team in my new World Football League in Cleveland because

Cleveland has a solid and successful NFL team. He bought the baseball Indians because they were about to be moved from town. He brought in the basketball Cavaliers and hockey Crusaders because he wanted to bring all the big-league team sports to Cleveland. Clevelanders Robert Jackson and Ronald Gottfried bought 45 percent of the Crusaders stock for $1.67 million, bringing the net worth of the club to $3.7 million. Mileti's magnificent $18 million, 18,000-seat arena is rising in suburban Bowling Green in Richfield Township as a new home for indoor sports and entertainment in this area. It would seem to ensure the success of Nick's well-run hockey operation.

I would think the Minneapolis–St. Paul area in Minnesota could support two major league hockey teams. It is hot hockey country. And while the NHL North Stars play in suburban Met Center, the WHA Saints play in an even newer arena, one of the most beautiful I've ever seen, the 16,000-seat St. Paul Civic Center. It even has glass sideboards. John Finley, Fred Grothe, and Lou Kaplan are well-heeled and imaginative owners. But attendance was below expectations until 1974. They figure an average of 10,000 fans per game as their break-even mark, and their second season fell well short of that. The area is saturated with high school and college hockey, aside from the North Stars, and there was talk that the franchise might be shifted. During the playoffs, that talk died.

I felt all along it was possible that if the team stuck it out it might strike it rich. It was too good a territory to surrender too fast. This was proven during the playoffs when the team attracted two sellouts of around 17,000 fans and averaged close to 14,000 fans for three dates. Houston also had two sellouts during this playoff series, which may be the league's high point to date.

Houston has a substantial population, and the community is set on a new indoor arena, long overdue and badly needed. Irv Kaplan, who bought control of the NBA team in Houston, may be about to buy control of the WHA team from Paul Deneau and Jim Smith, and he is solid. But the franchise is not.

The Southwest is not established hockey territory. The Howes came high, and while interest increased after they arrived, attendance most of the season had not justified the investment. An average attendance of 9,100 fans per playoff game probably solidified the franchise in Houston and promises a bright future.

However, Bobby Hull may be wasted in Winnipeg. It is not a big or a rich city and while it is not near the bottom in attendance, fans have turned out as might have been expected from a contender led by a Bobby Hull. Ben Hatskin has about given up on hopes of getting a new building in town. He has hopes that a renovation plan will be approved which would increase capacity in his ancient arena from 11,000 to 15,000 persons, which would help. But he is not happy with his arena lease. The arena keeps all parking and concessions cash and shows a profit while Ben loses money. He paid a lot to bring Hull to town and may feel unappreciated. He could succumb to the offers he's had for his franchise. A Hull or a Howe would bring in big business in a big city. They could have turned the fortunes of our teams around in New York or Los Angeles.

It is a shame that you get some of your weakest operations in some of your strongest cities. I'd love to have had a Bob Schmertz operating his team in New York or Los Angeles.

In any event, through the first season and into the second season, the WHA made sufficient inroads to cause the NHL to begin to buckle. The first capitulation by the NHL came when it entered settlement negotiations with us.

Another came when it discarded the reserve clause in its contracts and replaced it with a one-year option clause comparable to the NFL system. Its players would have the right to play out their option year and move to another team with a panel of arbitrators to rule on compensation in cases in which the clubs could not agree. The players group, represented by Alan Eagleson, wasn't satisfied with it and was prepared to fight it, but it was a step in the right direction for their rights.

The crack in NHL opposition widened when Indianapolis, Phoenix, and Cincinnati joined us in the fall of 1973. Each paid $2 million for its franchise. Each would get to draft players from lists provided by our member teams.

It's funny, but Indianapolis could have come in with us for $25,000 less than two years earlier. The owners there waited and it cost them. At one time we were ready to take in all of the Western Hockey League teams for $200,000 each. This time it cost Phoenix $2 million.

In any event, the three new territories were all ones wanted by the NHL. Each has solid ownership.

John Weissert and Dick Tinkham head the Indianapolis operation, and they're the same fellows who've made the ABA franchise there such a success. It has the seventeenth largest market in the nation, larger than Baltimore, Buffalo, Miami, New Orleans, and other major-league cities. And it has an 18,000-seat arena rising downtown.

Brian Heekin and Bill Dewitt of baseball fame head the Cincinnati franchise, which is getting a 16,500-seat arena adjacent to the Reds' new Riverfront Stadium. Basketball has had a hard time in this town, but hockey will go here. And major-league basketball will return with the new building.

The Phoenix franchise is headed by Carl Eller, Bert Gaetz, and Jim Wells, the same men who operate the Western League Roadrunners. They have a head start on the others because they have players, some of whom may move up to the top. And they have a 12,500-seat arena already.

I have been asked if I'm concerned that taking Phoenix may kill the Western Hockey League. No more than the NHL did when it took L.A. and the San Francisco–Oakland area from the Western Hockey League. We both went into Vancouver, which was Western territory. Portland and Seattle are both ripe for major-league hockey. Portland might be a fringe franchise, but possibly could combine in an area operation with Seattle under the name of the Northwest Nomads. They could divide home dates, televise from their sister city, and maybe make out well. Denver is a ripe possibility.

The possibilities for future expansion are plentiful. If the NHL's Oakland franchise is shifted, San Francisco would rise anew as a big-league bet in hockey. Milwaukee remains in the running. Miami might rise again. It has the market. It needs only an arena. New Orleans is incorporating an indoor arena setup into its $150 million Superdome and will be in demand for major-league basketball and hockey, as well as basketball, in which it now has an NBA franchise.

The NHL could see that we would be competitive for such attractive territories. It could see it now might lose Bobby Orr or Phil Esposito or others stars. It came to us with a proposal for peace. I was bowing out, my mission accomplished, but Don Regan would work out the details. He worked them out.

We would drop our $50 million in antitrust suits against the league and agree not to challenge their new contract with the option clause. We still could sign players who played out their options, subject to arbitration on compensation. Players waived out of one league could be traded to or picked up by teams in the other league. I feel sure straight interleague trades will develop out of this in time. Interleague exhibition games would be played between the two teams, but not regular-season games or postseason games or postseason play-off championships. The latter two will come, too. They would not block us from any of their arenas, such as the one in Long Island. Nor would we block them from ours. Both leagues would drop all legal actions against the other, but the NHL would pick up the tab, by then $1.75 million for our legal costs to date.

Both the WHA and the NHL approved the agreement. In Philadelphia, U.S. District Court Judge Leon Higginbotham approved it and dismissed the case. In less than two years my league had effectively forced a working agreement from the NHL, and, frankly, I feel I can take some credit for it. I feel I have won an important victory.

You will note they were to pay us this time. We were not to pay them anything. Players' groups from both leagues say they will fight it. I can understand this. They feel their bargaining power is disappearing. They fear a common draft will come out of the agreement, and I think it will. But they will lose their fight against it. They have gained a lot of freedom. But competitive bidding for all players is too costly for the leagues to long endure it. At the moment it goes on. The agreement is not a merger and has not ended all skirmishes.

Players' salaries have about doubled. They are well paid. Many are spoiled. Edmonton's Jim Harrison went on strike in the middle of our second season because his team would not renegotiate his contract to $200,000 a year for ten years. Harrison is not Howe. He is a possible star, but when a player refuses to play unless he is paid $200,000 a year the warning signs to the owners are posted.

No doubt we are to blame for such irresponsibility. It is the price we paid for what we wanted. We are to blame for higher ticket prices. We are also to blame for three hundred major jobs for players that were not there before and many hundreds more good posts for managers, coaches, front-office personnel, scouts, arena helpers, and so forth. And we are also to blame for bringing a lot of sporting excitement to a lot of people in two countries.

We also were responsible for bringing into my office, Don's office, and Dennis's office people with wild ideas for new sports leagues. Suddenly we were considered the superspecialists in the unique field of organizing new major leagues. People brought us ideas for every kind of a league imaginable, including, believe it or not, tiddly-winks.

Someone went to Dennis with the idea for a team-tennis league. He went for it and it is a reality. And a table-tennis league. He likes that, too, and that, too, may become a reality.

I have my doubts about team tennis. I don't think there are enough top players willing to play in it to attract fans even in the biggest cities to 20 home matches, sometimes several a week.

Dennis points out his teams need only 3,000 to 4,000 fans a match to make money, but I doubt they'll draw that many. As his first season started, they weren't.

They could improve the format. They have more doubles matches than singles. Even good fans walk out on doubles. But even with the best possible players and best possible format it might be a struggle.

He asked me to get into it to help out, but I did only to the extent of placing a franchise for him. I bought the Phoenix franchise for $50,000 and sold it to Baltimore interests for $200,000. I can't complain, obviously.

I helped structure Mike O'Hara's International Track Association for him. I didn't have time to go into it full time, but that one will work, I believe. There was a need for it. There figured to be a place for pro track.

Average attendance the first year was 7,500, the second year 12,100, which produced a small profit. That's fast for a new big league to break into the black. They drew 15,000 fans to an indoor meet in New York and 57,000 fans to two outdoor meets in Tokyo. Track appeals to an international audience. Mike doesn't have to outbid another league for athletes. He's putting cash against gold medals. He got a lot of good athletes to begin with, and now that it's working he will get more.

When Sean Downey announced plans for a new baseball league, it was reported we were interested in one, too. We were not and are not. Walter Dilbeck came up with the idea of Global Baseball League in 1968. It was to have franchises in the U.S., Latin America, and the Orient. It started and stopped with a team of Japanese players stranded in Venezuela. Now Downey has come up with an idea for a 32-team league, also to operate in the U.S., Latin America, and the Orient. He was one of the original owners of the New Orleans franchise in the ABA and I wish him well, but I don't expect him to succeed.

It is possible it will work, although it will not work if he sticks to his announced intention to play during the winter in cold-weather cities, fighting football. I do not think baseball is as popular with the average fan as football is these days. And no one is going to sit in snow to see slow baseball.

However, the real reason we never have given a rebel baseball league a second thought is that the antitrust exemption organized baseball secured would make it extremely difficult for a new league to obtain talent. Also, baseball is played with a long schedule and the economics of mounting an operation in this sport are enormous. You can lose a lot of money fast trying to travel to play 150 to 160 games. Obviously, I have nothing against starting new leagues to compete with established operations, but baseball just doesn't strike me as a good bet.

Someone went to my partner Don Regan with an idea for a volleyball league. He's interested. That's his sport and it may have a chance as a major league team game. We're work-

ing together on a European soccer league. I had my own idea:
A new professional football league.

Once I got into the football, I saw I'd have to get out of the
hockey. I knew that once word of my football idea got out,
the hockey owners would want me out. They already thought
I was spread too thin. This would be too much. And I knew
they would be right. At midseason, I resigned. To my surprise,
they tried to talk me out of it. For the first time, they admitted I'd done a good job for them. They were a success.
They were afraid that without me they'd founder. Suddenly
they saw me as some sort of security blanket. But it was non-
sense. They were healthy and on their feet now. They no
longer needed their midwife. I'm far from irreplaceable. They
would suffer without me only if they picked a weak man to
replace me.

They moved Jim Browitt into the job on an interim basis.
But when they started to screen candidates to find a perma-
nent president, they saw they faced a difficult decision. They
asked Dennis Murphy to take over while they worked on it.
To my surprise, Dennis accepted the presidency. And maybe
to Murph's surprise, too. He'd never considered himself presi-
dential stuff. He said he wasn't an administrator. I felt he
wasn't either. I also felt he had too many other irons on the
fire. Which from me is like calling the kettle black. But Dennis decided he wanted to give it a try.

He decided his World Team Tennis League was organized
sufficiently and had enough satisfactory leadership for him to
step aside from it to concentrate on the World Hockey Association. He decided the WHA was his baby, and he wanted
to play papa for a while. He didn't want to lose his hold on
this one as he had the other one.

To this point he's doing a helluva job. He lets his enthusiasm run away with him sometimes. He announces this and
that, such as the sale of a franchise, before it's finalized. If

it isn't he has to eat his words. It hurts his prestige, and the league's. He's getting tougher. He'll glad-hand the guys, which they'll like. He'll hustle. He's got ideas. He's got an imagination that is twice as big as his belly. And the smile to sell them.

Meanwhile, a rolling stone who gathers moss, I was on my way.

CHAPTER 13

As Others See It, II

GORDIE HOWE

He had been the greatest player ever to play the game, but when Gordie Howe skated out on the ice to start his twenty-sixth major league season five minutes into the Houston Aeros opener in the Los Angeles Sports Arena at the start of the World Hockey Association's second season, a Sharks fan, one of those true sportsmen, shouted, "Go back to bed, you bum." And when Howe seemed slow and awkward for the first period, the gent hollered at him that he was washed up and should return to retirement and the WHA was a home for has-beens and should retire from competition. Howe never heard him. He'd heard it all, anyway. He just kept working, which is his way, and it began to get better for him, and Gordie was going good in the second and third periods. He could not know it then, but at the age of forty-five, after two years of retirement, it would get better for him through the season and he would contend for the league scoring championship.

Howe has been tremendously tough all his life. He was born in the small town of Floral, Saskatchewan, in March of 1928. He was nine days old when his family settled in Saskatoon. He was one of nine children reared during Depression days. No one around him had any money. When a lady who was desperate dumped a bagful of clothes at the family's door in return for a dollar, a pair of ice skates tumble out. Gordie grabbed them. He was five years old. He was playing on frozen ponds at six. He made the majors with the Detroit Red Wings in 1948 at eighteen.

He signed for a $500 bonus and $1,700 salary. This was a time when players played for the love of the game and for the opportunity to make more than a man could make digging a ditch. Howe spent his money to have plumbing put into his parents' home. Until he could afford a room in a boarding house, he slept in a storeroom in the stadium basement. He didn't have an alarm clock and was awakened for the first practice by the sounds of pucks pounding on the sideboards overhead. His first game, he got a goal. He also got two teeth knocked out.

At the end of his third season in the NHL, he crashed into the boards and suffered a severe skull concussion. He hovered between life and death for days, recovered, and became a star in his fourth season. He carried on through his career despite two knee operations, broken noses and cheekbones, and facial slashes requiring more than 300 stitches. He was tough, and he gave as well as he got, wielding his stick like a spear. He won his fights until foes were afraid to fight him and gave him room to maneuver, something Hull never got because he never dealt out the punishment Howe did.

Howe wasn't a fancy stylist, an explosive scorer, a colorful performer such as Richard or Hull, but he was a better all-around player. If Hull was built of concrete, Howe was slabs of steel. The 6-foot, 205-pound Howe always seemed to have

235

the puck and could not be moved off it. He controlled play, dominated games. He had a deadly shot and made marvelous passes. He played longer and set more records than any other hockey player ever. In 1,687 regular-season games he got 786 goals, and in 154 playoff games he got 67 more. He helped Detroit win nine pennants and four Stanley Cup playoff titles and was voted Most Valuable Player in the National Hockey League six times.

At forty-one he was still good enough to score 43 goals in a season. When he retired at forty-three at the end of his twenty-fifth season in the spring of 1971, he was still one of the best, but he had an arthritic wrist which made playing painful. And he had promised his mother he would quit. When she died, he retired. He and his wife Colleen had three sons—Marty, Mark, and Murray—and a daughter—Cathy. He had wanted to hang on until he could play in the majors with his older sons, but he felt he had just run out of time. "I first thought of it in the middle sixties as soon as they started to show signs of making it, but the rules prohibited amateurs turning pro until they were twenty, so I had to let it go. I had to tie my left hand to the bedpost at times to get any sleep and couldn't go on playing," he said.

Surgery and rest through two years in retirement made the wrist begin to feel better. By then, the World Hockey Association had arrived as a rival major league. In the last years of his career, Howe had become bitter after learning others far less valuable than he were making much more money. He did not make $100,000 for a season until his last season. He was paid $50,000 a season to serve as vice-president of the Red Wings, but he became bitter about this, too. He says, "I was given nothing to do. They kept me in the dark about decisions, and every once in a while someone would come in and throw garbage on me."

An old rival, Doug Harvey, had signed on as an aide with Houston in the new league, and he suggested the league go after the Howes. Mark had played on the U.S. Olympic team and was considered a superstar of the future. Marty was considered a good prospect. When Houston asked Gordie about getting his sons to turn pro before they finished their amateur careers, he said if the offer was right they could have him, too. They grabbed him.

Howe wanted to prove he could still play, and he did when he scored a goal 21 seconds into his new team's first exhibition game. He played with his sons in that game. Then he played wtih his sons in an exhibition game in Detroit, drawing a seven-minute standing ovation from a crowd of 17,000 fans, which was another thrill. Now it was the regular-season opener. He played on a line with Mark, a left-winger, and they were on the ice at the same time with Marty, a defenseman, a few times. Both Mark and Marty revealed lessons learned from the old man by slashing with their sticks a few times. The teacher was always around the puck, just like old times, and assisted on three goals, including the winner. He was selected first star of the game and got an ovation from the nearly 10,000 fans in attendance.

Afterward, he sat in the dressing room, gray-haired, flushed, and sweaty, and said, "I got tired, especially on one shift when I stayed on too long, but I think I'm in good enough shape to help a team. I can do some things and maybe help the other players do some things. The thing I don't want to do is embarrass the team or the league. I want to play a lot to repay them for their investment in me and their interest in my sons."

Like their father, long-haired Mark and Marty were unemotional. All eyes were on them, which at their age puts pressure on them. Marty was saying he wanted to play with his father, but mostly he just wanted to play and wishes he'd played

237

more. Mark was saying he couldn't see playing twenty-five years like his pop had, but he'd be proud to play anything close to as good as his pop, though his idol really was Bobby Hull. He spoke of what a thrill it would be to play against Hull. He said he didn't feel too young to have made the move to the majors and hoped it would help others move up faster if they could make it.

Gordie laughed and needled Marty about some penalties he'd drawn. He kept rubbing his leg, which was sore from having been hit by a puck. Close up, he showed his age, but his body was still hard. He laughed and said that a lot of guys in the NHL were playing into their forties, so it wasn't fair to knock the WHA for having given work to an old geezer like him.

He didn't undress from his soggy uniform and go for a beer until the last reporter had asked the last question. Then he stood outside and signed autographs for the fans until the last one had left. He is a lot like Hull in this respect. No other sport ever had two such superstars who were so kind to the press and the public.

BEN HATSKIN

"I was approached by Bill Hunter about the new hockey league. My feeling was I didn't think too much of it until I met in Los Angeles with Hunter and Gary Davidson and saw they had seventeen different groups at that time that wanted franchises. The numbers impressed me. I thought there were some Canadian cities that had a pretty good chance of supporting a second major league, but I figured the American cities were a gamble. I was operating the junior club in Winnipeg, and I wanted to be the guy to go with a major-league team there if one was going in there, so I threw in with the new league. I knew Hull's contract was up, and I knew he was the type of player needed to make a new league go. It was my idea, but I thought it was a long shot. I didn't know Hull. I approached him, and to my surprise he was interested. He gave me his manager's telephone number, Harvey Wineberg, and told me to talk to him. I did. He gave me the figures they wanted. I passed them on to Gary. He looked into it. We had to sell the league on helping me with it. I couldn't carry it alone. They took the front end; I took the rest.

"He has repaid the league. It wouldn't have worked without him. He has not yet repaid me. It takes years for a team to get back an investment such as I've made in Hull, and I might never get it in a town like Winnipeg. We have a small population. We have a small arena. It holds about 10,000. A major-league franchise needs an arena holding about 15,000. You have to be able to have a place to put the big crowds to balance out the small crowds. There is no chance of a new arena. There is a chance of rebuilding the old arena if the city shows enthusiasm for our team. Crowds haven't been bad, but not good enough and not building up fast enough. The arena people are enthusiastic, but we're not. They've got a good deal; we don't. We pay 13½ percent of our gate for the use of the arena. That's a lot. For them it's a lot more than they had before.

"We're a little discouraged. It's been tough for me. For me, it's a business I have to build up. I'll go with it as long as I think it's got a chance to go. We could go to another town. If we do, I believe Bobby will go with us. Or we could sell the team. We have had offers. If we sold it, I believe Bobby would go with new owners. But those are just possibilities. If I was looking to make a move, I would have done so already. I am looking to stay in Winnipeg and trying to build things up here. Our losses weren't as heavy as some teams'. We had a heavy salary with Bobby, but our management did a good job of operating efficiently otherwise. I think you need the Bobby Hulls. It is only with the superstars that the WHA can reach parity with the NHL, so within economic limits, we're still interested in adding other top players. It's an investment in the future so long as the promise of the future warrants it.

"I think the league is solid now, but all the teams aren't. There'll be some changes in some cities yet. I don't regret going with the WHA. Before I did, I phoned Clarence Campbell. He was very pleasant when I asked him what it would cost to get a franchise. He told me that by the time an opening for a Winnipeg bid could be considered I'd have to think in terms of more than $7 million, plus the cost of an arena that could seat at least 16,000, which is another $20 million. I thanked him and hung up. I'd invest all that money and get a team without Hull. Why not invest part of it in Hull? I don't feel I cheated everyone. I believe in free enterprise. That's why I say nuts to the reserve clause. The NHL may say it needs it, but I believe in free enterprise for the player as well as the owner.

"I make mistakes. I once fired Barbra Streisand when I ran a nightclub. She was plain-looking, and I didn't think she had much of a voice. But I believe in sports. I played pro football for the Winnipeg Blue Bombers in the Canadian League. I've paid to support hockey in the Western Canada Junior League. It's repaid me. I believe in the World Hockey Association as a business venture. But I don't throw my money away. That's why we don't have a yearbook this season. It would have cost $2,750, and the demand for them wouldn't make it worthwhile. But I'll invest a couple hundred times that in something that is worthwhile. I think we'll have a merger with the NHL. It's business. Don't forget, these are tough businessmen. That's what we have to be. They're not stupid, you know. They see what's happening in the courts. There is no love lost on either side. No one is doing anyone

240

any favors. From a sheer business point of view, we may be forced into a union of some sort in the future."

DON REGAN

"They approached us on the merger; we didn't approach them. If word hadn't leaked out, I think it would have happened already. They're sensitive about some things in it, but I think it will happen sooner or later. They want us to drop our antitrust suits. They can see they can lose in the courts. It could cost them a lot of money. They're willing to pick up our court costs. They're willing to take us in as partners at no cost, but they don't want to take all our teams in, and some of our owners aren't willing to drop out. And they don't want us in all their arenas, but we insist we should have that right. We don't want to be in most of their arenas, but there are some cities where it would be better for us, at least for a while. They're worried about being embarrassed by having a Bobby Hull show up in a WHA uniform in Chicago Stadium or a Gordie Howe in Detroit's Olympia. They want to keep their new contracts with the one-year option clause, but we're worried about antitrust there. The players are against any common draft, but salaries have to be brought to a reasonable level. I'm sure we'll work something out."

CLARENCE CAMPBELL

[No comment.]

FOOTBALL

CHAPTER 14

Tomorrow the World

Gary Davidson sits in new offices in a new building on Mac-Arthur Boulevard in Newport Beach in a booming business community near the Orange County Airport. The World Hockey Association's offices are here, along with the Nagel, Regan and Davidson offices—on the second floor of a two-story, wooden layout with an open-air walkway within. Soon, the World Football League offices will be here, too. The World Football League has not been born yet, but it is in its initial stages of conception. It is the fall of 1973, and Gary reckons the gestation period at less than one year, which is fast for a football league, if not for babies. Leagues are his babies now. He is on the phone talking to a prospective sponsor, and he is talking fast:

"The hockey league is really going good now. We're going into our second season, and we're established already. No one has made any money yet, but everyone will make money. To give you an example of what happens. Guys who didn't get in

on the ground floor of our hockey league for twenty-five thousand are buying in now less than two years later for more than
two million. Indianapolis could have got in for twenty-five
thousand, and now they're paying two million to get in. Milwaukee could have gotten in for twenty-five thousand, and
now they're the ones offering 4.3 million to Ben for his franchise, which has Bobby Hull of course. These franchises
appreciate fast, especially if you've invested in some name
players. . . .

"Anyway, I figured right now is the perfect opportunity to
form another pro football league. I kicked it around a little
bit with Ben Hatskin. Then with Bob Schmertz and John
Bassett and Nick Mileti. They're all enthusiastic about it. My
idea is to go into Anaheim, Seattle, New York, Phoenix,
Tampa, Milwaukee. . . . There are about twenty major
metropolitan areas that could support more major-league football. Anaheim has a stadium. Dates are available. A lot of
places have available stadiums. Seattle is putting up a stadium. Honolulu is putting up a stadium. The Giants are
leaving New York for New Jersey, which opens up Yankee
Stadium to us, which is perfect. . . .

"Who has a better opportunity to start a new football
league? I've started two leagues. Both are surviving and becoming successful. No one else has done that. The other thing
is I've got strong owners from hockey now, like Hatskin and
Nick Mileti, who has the NBA Cleveland Cavaliers, the
Cleveland Indians in baseball, and the Cleveland Crusaders
in our league, the World Hockey Association. Now it looks
like I've got Bob Schmertz, who has the Boston Celtics in
the NBA and the New England Whalers in the WHA. So
you've got some real heavies. That gives you a credibility
factor right off. . . .

"The football market is so large, the television market is so
large, it's a whole new animal from anything we've gone into

yet. Half of the United States doesn't know about hockey. But everyone knows about football. Ben said we should go into Toronto, Montreal, and Vancouver and go head up with the Canadian teams. The Canadian Football League teams have a formula that allows them to use only so many American players. We wouldn't have that. We'd go with American rules, except for improving them like maybe using the two-point extra point and changing the field-goal rules so the kicking wouldn't be so important and opening it up. There's no offense in the NFL. The fans are getting bored. They're ready for us. . . .

"Right now, I'm jazzed for it. How about you? I figure we'd go in 1974, right away. Our first year we'd probably use mostly rookies out of college and guys cut from the pros and maybe a few names who have played out their pro option. The NFL has a one-year option clause, and players are free to go to other teams after that, but if they go to other teams in the NFL those teams have to pay their original teams, where if they went with us that wouldn't have to be done.

"Yeah, yeah, we'd be back to a bidding war. But if you think about it, all the good players who come out of college with good reputations who don't make it for some reason or other, there's a lot of players available. Like Dennis Dummitt, a big name at UCLA, who was supposed to be too small, received no opportunity in the NFL, but might have made it if he'd been given a chance. And the little receiver, Randy Vataha, who was so big with Jim Plunkett at Stanford, was cut by the Rams because he was too small, but New England picked him up and put him back together with Plunkett, and he's been a sensation. And the leading receiver in the NFL now, Harold Jackson, was supposed to be too small and was cut off by George Allen when he was coaching the Rams. We'd offer a whole new market to these guys. . . .

247

"It's a wild concept, don't you think? Right now I'm putting together a founders' group, and I'm putting together a group for Anaheim. Anaheim's another market from L.A. We have 1.7 million to 1.9 million right here. And it's a pretty affluent county. In L.A. you've got the Bruins and Trojans and Rams playing football, but down here you don't have anyone. There's a great possibility this could be a very successful franchise. If you went after an NFL expansion franchise it'd cost you nine to twelve million. The Rams would cost about twenty million. I'm gathering all the stats now. It seems to me the figures are really favorable. A guy'd have a much smaller gamble going in with us than trying to get into the old league. You can't even get into that league.

"We'll be taking on the big boys, Lamar Hunt and friends. They'll probably have a contract out on me. But it's a phenomenal opportunity. If I went to a press conference in New York with this this weekend I'd get front-page coverage all over the world. So, anyway, think about it. I'll get some statistics to you. Maybe you'd want to go into Anaheim. I figure our teams will capitalize at about three million. The budget would be about 2.1. And then you'd want to buy some big boys.

"If we'd gone into business this year, we could've had Joe Kapp and Roman Gabriel. We'd have really been in business. And you won't have to pay top dollar for most players. The highest-paid sport right now is basketball. Second is hockey, and third is football. Almost anything you give a football player would be more than he's making now. Baseball is last. . . .

"Yeah, right, well you give it some thought. It's a helluva opportunity. But don't say anything about it because it's not time yet, and if it gets out now they'll have my ears." With a word of farewell and another of encouragement, he hangs up.

248

AS GARY SEES IT

Having prepped in basketball, and graduated from hockey, I was ready to go into the sports business in a big way in football. Compared to the others, professional football is the big time. Professional basketball is doing about $55 million in business a year, hockey is doing about $65 million, and baseball about $130 million. Professional football is doing about $140 million. The sports business itself is growing. In the decade beween 1962 and 1972, gross revenues in major-league sports grew by 201 percent, while the gross national product grew by only 88 percent. And football's growth has been the greatest in sports.

It is true that it had not been long since the American Football League rose to threaten the National Football League in 1960 and forced a merger in 1966. Was it too soon for a new war? Well, since the merger, the NFL has misused its monopoly. Like a fat cat, it has grown soft and content.

Its average salaries are the smallest in big-time sports. Pro basketball salaries average $65,000, hockey salaries $55,000, baseball salaries $35,000, and football salaries $28,000. There are fifty pro basketball players earning $100,000 or more, forty-five hockey players, thirty baseball players, only ten football players. Only 20 percent of pro football's income goes to players. Yet, without the players, you would have no fans. And pro football has plenty of fans.

Season-ticket sales are the basis of success in any professional sports operation, and pro football sells more than any other sport. Miami sells close to 80,000 season tickets, Kansas City 70,000, Philadelphia 65,000, Buffalo and New Orleans 60,000, Cleveland, Baltimore, Oakland, San Francisco, and Detroit 50,000, Los Angeles and St. Louis 40,000. Average

attendance to NFL games is close to 60,000, and total attendance tops 10 million.

I surveyed at least twenty major markets in the country
that could support new major-league professional teams. New
York was the only big city that had two teams, although the
sister cities of San Francisco and Oakland each had one. All
three major networks in the United States have to share television rights to the single major league. They paid $200 mil-
lion for the rights for four years, a rise of $20 million over the
previous period of four years. ABC's Monday night football
telecast received $80,000 a minute from commercial sponsors.

For all of its popularity, the National Football League was
asleep at the switch. Its hold on the public seemed to be
slipping. Defense had mastered offensive tactics. Every team
used the same offensive patterns. Defense dominated games.
Passing games were passing out of existence. Touchdowns
were becoming rarities. Many games, including some of the
most important and most watched games, were played without a touchdown being scored, or at most one or two. It was
not unusual to have three, four, five, or six field goals in a
game. Field goals decided games. And they are dull. Yet, the
NFL refused to restore balance to its games by revising its
rules. It stuck to some ridiculous rules.

As usual, the arrogance of an existing operation opened the
doors to a rival. The NFL had no strong rival. The Canadian
Football League existed, but it had small stadiums, a small
market, and small money and never had been able to move
successfully into the American market. It posed a threat only
for the odd player it pursued. And there were plenty of
players available. Not only were many NFL players discontented with their lot, but more than a hundred quality
prospects were cut each year without adequate tryouts. Many
CFL players were available. More than a thousand quality
prospects graduated from major college football powers each

season. Less than half were drafted, and fewer than one out of ten were given a chance to make an NFL roster.

The cost of acquiring an NFL franchise had risen 1,000 to 2,000 percent. The last franchise to be sold, the Los Angeles Rams, went for $20 million.

Most existing franchises figured to be worth that much. An expansion franchise figured to cost $14 million to $18 million. And it was almost impossible to land a new franchise. We could price franchises reasonably at from a quarter of a million dollars to a million dollars and turn a tremendous profit. We could make a new league go. Who had more experience or better credentials? A man could get a franchise from us for a fair price and have a fine chance of making a lot of money. And he'd be in the sports business, the most popular of all sports businesses, which so many men want.

I started to think about it during the first season of the World Hockey Association when I saw how well the hockey was working. I talked to Don Regan about it, and he agreed it was a project with enormous prospects. I spoke to Dennis Murphy about it, and he said he'd help but preferred to stick primarily to his tennis venture. When the season ended, I went into it in detail, trying to make a final decision on it. I had been playing with other people's money. I saw I would have to put some of my own money into this one—perhaps as much as $100,000. Well, I was moving up to the big time, and I needed some heavyweights into it with me. I needed big men as the base of a big operation, not promoters and fast-buck hustlers.

I went to CAHA meetings early in August of 1973 to work out our agreement with the amateur body and met with Ben Hatskin in the bar of the Georgiana Towers Hotel in Vancouver. He wanted in it. But he didn't want a Vancouver franchise. He wanted a Honolulu franchise. I guess the idea of Hawaiian winters appealed to him more than the Canadian version. We agreed to carry the proposal to other prime partners in our hockey league.

I spoke to Nick Mileti and Bob Schmertz about it. Mileti said Cleveland didn't need another pro football team, but another league could go and he'd help. Schmertz pointed out that the New York Giants were vacating Yankee Stadium to move into a new stadium proposed in New Jersey. Yankee Stadium was being refurbished, the baseball Yankees were going to play there, and a new pro football tenant would be a natural there and he wanted the franchise for it.

Schmertz also said he and John Bassett had talked about another football league. So I spoke to John at the next World Hockey Association meeting, and he said he wanted to be in our new league. He said his family owned the Canadian Football League franchise in Toronto, but U. S. interests in the NFL had already expressed interest in Toronto, Montreal and Vancouver, and in Canada in general, and if competition was going to come anyway, he wanted to provide his own competition. We weren't worried about wrecking the CFL. We didn't plan to invade all its territories. It either was strong enough to stand up against competition or it wasn't. We were operating in free countries, and the free trade system was in *effect.*

Steve Arnold was interested in a Tokyo franchise and came in as a founding father.

It is interesting that so many others had thought about another football league, but no one had done anything about it. Well, that was what I did. I did it. I named it the World Football League and started out with the concept of eventually expanding into South America, the Orient, and Europe with teams. I was sure professional football, American style, would go in Mexico City, in Tokyo, in London, somewhere in Germany.

I already had representatives overseas working out plans for a soccer league to operate in European countries. National teams played in international competition in soccer, but there was no existing league in which standing teams representing countries played one another on a formal league basis. It takes time to work out details for such an operation in foreign countries, but while we were doing so we could lay the groundwork for a division of American football teams for our World League. It was decided that the league would pay all travel expenses for all teams to encourage the entry of distant teams.

I had my base group of founding fathers—myself, Hatskin, Mileti, Schmertz, Bassett, and Steve Arnold. Don Regan was also going to be involved, but he wasn't going to take a franchise if the other founders put together their respective franchises. The six of us would each take a franchise and pay $100,000 for operating expenses. We would operate them or sell them.

Additional franchises would cost $250,000 to $750,000 the first season, with the first to come in paying the lowest fee and each following franchise higher fees. Each would have to pay an additional $100,000 in operating funds. We wanted ten to twelve franchises for our first season. We got twelve. The six founding fathers would split the fees equally. Hatskin had Honolulu; Schmertz, New York; Bassett, Toronto; and Arnold, Tokyo. Mileti took Chicago. I took a floating franchise which I planned to place in Philadelphia. I felt Orange County with an area population of between 1.5 million and 2 million persons would support a team splendidly, and it would be easy to find a franchise owner in my backyard.

I am president at $100,000 a year. My partner, Don Regan, a co-organizer, is the secretary and general counsel. Danny Rogers, a former USC basketball star, the first basketball coach at the University of California at Irvine in

253

Orange County, and a successful businessman in marketing as national sales manager of Nutrilite Company, is a young, good-looking, personable guy who has represented me in many of my hockey dealings, and was set as vice-president of my football league. Max Muhleman .was brought in as vice-president in charge of marketing and public relations. Later, Don Anderson from USC was appointed our public relations director and Bob Russo came in as publicist.

I told Rogers and Muhleman they could get franchises if they could get backing. Hatskin reported he was sick and had to drop out, so Rogers took over the Honolulu franchise and sold it to businessmen there. Since Hatskin dropped out of the operation, complaining of illness, we will have to figure out what his share in it is to be in the end.

I got together the necessary details. It was worked out that each team would be capitalized at $3 million. An owner had to have that much behind him. The first year's budget figured to be between $2.3 million and $2.7 million depending on the investment in players. The first year's losses figured to be between $500,000 and $1 million. We figured we could cut the losses in half the second year and again in half the third year and shoot for a profit by the fourth year. We planned to charge the going rate in each territory for pro football tickets. We were not going to be stamped as minor league in any way. At $7.50 an average ticket, a crowd of 30,000 would bring in a gross of $225,000, not counting parking and concessions. A ten-game home schedule would bring in a gross up top of $2.25 million. And 30,000 seemed a modest aim for the crowds we hoped to attract in a short time. Average crowds of 20,000 would bring in $1.5 million. Crowds of 40,000 would bring in $3 million. Then there would be such television monies as we could pull.

We anticipated problems with television. When the AFL was formed, CBS had TV rights to NFL games. ABC and NBC were available. NBC gambled on the AFL, and its money helped the AFL survive. After the merger, NBC picked up half the TV contracts. ABC was shut out until it was brought in with a Monday night prime-time telecast. As we formed, all three networks in this country were involved with the NFL. They couldn't legally refuse us simply because the NFL was doing business with them. The NFL legally couldn't threaten them against doing business with us. But we recognized that the networks were in a difficult position and might be reluctant to gamble on a new operation. Well, we can go to them later when we are established if we wish. Once we got going, we had good offers from independent networks which wanted to syndicate a "game of the week" in prime time with a $1.5 million offer. TVS Sports Network outbid the Hughes Sports Network for the rights. They would televise twenty-six games, mostly on prime time on Thursday nights, and promised us exposure to 90 percent of the market with bookings on at least 150 stations. Each team could negotiate its own radio and television contracts for its other games. In the future, when we are in action overseas, we will use telestar facilities for global exposure. To protect my future, I contracted for 10 percent of all television revenues for the next 10 years. I might point out NFL TV revenues have reached $52 million annually. We have the best first-year TV contract any new league ever had and we can grow.

Do ten-game home schedules seem a lot? Well, many NFL teams now play ten- or eleven-game home schedules, only three or four of the games are exhibition games they dress up by using the term "preseason games." In many cities, fans are required to buy the exhibition games to get season tickets. And the exhibition games do not count. The

NFL plays twenty-game seasons, but only fourteen of the games count, and the other six are meaningless. The regulars often do not play, yet the fans pay regular prices. Why not skip the exhibitions and play twenty games that count? Colleges skip the exhibitions and maintain their high level of play. So, I decided, would the World Football League. We would start play in July and end in November. Why not buck baseball, instead of football? Why face the NFL at its peak? We will get the football fan in the summer and reach the climax of our campaign before the NFL had peaked. Why duel football for fans and television money on weekends? Why not play in midweek, which worked wonderfully well in other sports and would be especially attractive during summer evenings! I decided to go on Wednesday nights and seek a Thursday night nationally televised game of the week, which we got.

We wanted an attractive game. We adopted a brightly colored blue and gold ball. I proposed rule changes which we adopted. Kickoffs from the 30 will improve field position for offenses. The goalposts will be moved to the back of the end zone as they are in college football. This will remove them as an obstacle to play and add 10 yards to the length of field-goal attempts. Missed field goals will be returned to the line of scrimmage if tried from beyond the 20-yard line. Why encourage cheap attempts at field goals? Why reward teams for misses? It is patently unfair for a team to try a field goal from the 50, miss by 30 yards, and gain 30 yards, having the ball placed on the 20. The NFL talked about this, but did nothing about it. We didn't just talk; we did it. After we did it, they did it.

In our most revolutionary change, we made touchdowns worth seven points and added a run or pass for an eighth "extra" point, eliminating the dull place-kick conversion entirely.

In another move to cut down on ties, we decided to add a 15-minute overtime period in an effort to provide decisions in most games. It would not be sudden death because the mechanics of football are not the same as basketball and hockey, when both teams have equal opportunities to score from the start. We didn't want the flip of a coin to give a team too great an advantage. And we wanted dramatic endings.

Other rules were set on the basis of finding a balance between offense and defense. We wanted to open up the game, but only to restore the balance the NFL had lost.

Shortly after we announced our new rules, the NFL created a sensation by announcing many new rules of its own, many of them identical to ours. They can claim coincidence from now to doomsday, but we know we pressured them into modernizing their game and they know it and every sports fan in the country knows it.

Now we had to find franchise holders and began to beat the bushes. We had kept our operation secret for a surprisingly long time, but word began to leak out in the fall. *Sports Illustrated* was the first to call. I stalled them because I was not committed to the project at that time. But as soon as I was, I spoke freely of it. This brought a rush of bidders to us.

As I expected, the first comments from the news media were sarcastic: *Who needs* it? *Another get-rich-quick scheme!* But sooner than I expected, the tide turned. As the writers and broadcasters considered the success of our other ventures we began to receive a favorable press.

I was as candid as I could be in all interviews. I am more candid than most men in my position. I do not try to conceal the truth. For the most part, honesty really is the best policy. There are exceptions. Not that I'll lie, but I will plead "no comment" on occasion. When a franchise spon-

257

sorship or a franchise sale is not closed, it is unfair to all concerned to report it as a reality. It destroys your image to have to reverse your field later. If a prospective owner does not want his name mentioned in connection with a project until he is committed to it, it is unfair to use his name. When you are considering a move of a franchise, it is destructive to attendance in the current city to announce it in advance. Usually, the transfer is not closed, anyway. Frequently, it does not take place. I report only on reality.

I am in these ventures to make money. I will not do anything that I am ashamed of, so I will admit to anything I do. I talked to thirty-five groups in twenty cities. I talked to groups from Chicago, Milwaukee, Detroit, Memphis, Birmingham, Orlando, Jacksonville, Tampa, Baltimore, Washington, Los Angeles, Seattle, Portland, Houston, San Antonio, Phoenix, Oklahoma City, Indianapolis, Norfolk, Charlotte, Columbus, Akron, Montreal, Vancouver, Madrid, Mexico City, London, Düsseldorf, Tokyo, and Rome, among others.

Arnold had wanted the Tokyo franchise, but found it would take more time than he had the first season to put it together, so he sought to locate his franchise in Memphis. City interests there, holding out for an NFL franchise, discouraged Arnold and he shifted to Houston, where he will be playing in the 50,000-seat Astrodome. He'll be bucking the NFL Oilers there, but they have been a disaster and have frustrated fans. If Arnold's Texans can be competitive in the new WFL, they should find a following.

Howard Baldwin bought a Boston franchise for $250,000, but decided to go in with his hockey partner, Schmertz, in the New York WFL operation. The Boston team's coach, Babe Parilli, and the players it had signed, became the New

York team. The New York franchise was shifted to Portland, Oregon.

Originally, John Rooney was set to purchase it and he hired Ralph Goldson, an assistant at Colorado, as his coach. He would have been the first black head coach in professional football and this got a lot of publicity. However, he became the first black head coach in professional football to lose his job when the deal with Rooney disappeared.

Bruce Gelker, who owns motels in southern California, had been trying to set up the Mexico City franchise for us. The red tape any American investors were required to cut through to establish a business in Mexico, even with Mexican investors, was so thick that we could see that we would have to discard that idea for the time being. Bruce was brought in to take over the Portland franchise and operate it. The price was $700,000. He sold it for a profit and has returned his interest to Mexico City.

As our first season approached we were having trouble locating financing in Oregon. We considered shifting the franchise to nearby Seattle, but could not secure the Washington University Stadium to use until the new domed stadium is finished there, and sponsors of the new stadium were committed to obtaining an NFL franchise.

Asked $18,000,000 for an NFL franchise, Tampa interests considered throwing it back and throwing in with us, which would have been a bombshell, but it didn't work out. At the 11th hour, we were negotiating with Dallas interests for the Portland franchise. But it is not impossible Portland will support a pro football team and our opportunity might have been their only one.

On a trip to Chicago, I landed in the same hotel at which Frank Sinatra and his friend, the former vice president Spiro Agnew, were staying. Rumors spread swiftly that they were interested in purchasing a franchise from me,

259

possibly the Anaheim franchise. Frankly, I did not discourage these news reports, but I never supported them. I felt it did not hurt to have persons of such prominence and wealth associated with my new venture, but it was only a coincidence that we wound up in the same hotel. They never approached me.

For awhile it appeared the former USC football player John Wayne, better known as a movie star, of course, would become the owner in Anaheim, where the team would have been called the "Dukes," but he bowed out. Tommy Prothro was a possibility as a coach in Anaheim or a member of a syndicate which would finance a franchise in his home town of Memphis, but the former UCLA and Ram coach chose instead to take the coaching job at San Diego in the NFL.

I sold my franchise to a corporation, in which I am a minority stockholder, who in turn sold it to a Philadelphia group headed by Jack Kelly, Jr., a former Olympian, son of a former Olympic rowing gold-medalist and brother of the movie star who became Princess Grace of Monaco. The purchase price was set at $690,000. The franchise will operate in Kennedy Stadium, in competition with the Eagles, another flop in Philly, which has been waiting for winners.

Many NFL franchises have been failures on the field and are vulnerable to competition. Schmertz and Baldwin had trouble finding a decent place to play in New York because Yankee Stadium was not yet renovated. They settled on Downing Stadium on Randalls Island, which is small and unsatisfactory. But when the big ballpark is ready, the big town may be ripe. The Giants have been floundering.

Nick Mileti sold majority interest in his Chicago club to Tom Origer for $400,000. A successful businessman, Origer promptly named his team the Chicago Fire, which is about as imaginative as you can get. He will share Soldier Field with the Bears, who have been booed a lot lately.

Bassett planned to operate at the Canadian National Exhibition Grounds in Toronto, which was one of the few small stadiums we lined up, but it was adequate and a new stadium was promised him there. When he signed three stars from the two-time Super Bowl champion Miami Dolphins—Larry Csonka, Jim Kiick and Paul Warfield—interest among Canadian fans ran high.

However, representatives of the Canadian government, seeking to protect the Canadian Football League from competition, introduced a bill designed to keep the World Football League away. We had a fighting chance to stay, but as time for our first season drew near, we ran out of time to fight. Bassett shifted his franchise to Memphis, selling a lot of it to local businessmen.

Like many other cities, Memphis had been kept on the NFL track by assurances that it was in line for an NFL franchise. But you can only keep a hungry guy going by dangling a carrot just out of reach for so long before he loses his appetite. When in 1974 Tampa was awarded an NFL franchise and Seattle seemed set for another, Memphis interests grew realistic and reversed their previous stand.

No doubt the signing of the three Dolphins, plus several other established NFL stars, made us appear real in the eyes of many who had doubted us and added a great deal to our attraction. In any event, the Toronto Northmen became the Memphis Southmen and moved into a massive stadium and an area starved for professional football.

Thus, the remaining five founding fathers of the WFL all had located their franchises.

We brought in others. Those who bought in first got the best price. I spoke to four groups from Detroit and settled on the most promising one for $350,000. The group includes the city's black mayor-elect and is primarily black, some of them movers and shakers from the city's Motown record industry. The Wheels became the first major league sports franchise with predominantly black ownership. Louis Lee is the president.

Bill Putnam, former president of the Philadelphia Flyers and the Atlanta Flames of the NHL, came in with the Birmingham Americans for $500,000. His top partner is a lady, Carol Stallworth. (The Detroit ownership includes ladies, and a gal, Dusty Rhodes, is assistant general manager of our New York Stars. Obviously, we are in the forefront of women's lib, offering equal opportunities for all.) The Birmingham team will play at Legion Field, home of the University of Alabama. It seats 72,000 fans and I expect the team to be a big success.

A Florida syndicate led by Fran Monaco, who owns medical laboratories, purchased a franchise for Jacksonville for $500,000, which became the base price for the remaining investors. His team was nicknamed the Sharks and will operate out of the 70,000-seat Gator Bowl.

Joe Wheeler bought in for $500,000 for a franchise for the Washington, D.C. area. He could not obtain permission to play in RFK Stadium, which the NFL Redskins use. Then, he planned to play in Annapolis, midway between Baltimore and Washington, but use of the Naval Academy facilities could not be cleared. He took his team to Norfolk and nicknamed it the Virginia Ambassadors. But he had only a 32,000-seat stadium for use there and when he could not clear lighting for night games, he gave up.

His franchise was sold for $1.6 million to a group in Orlando headed by Rommie Loudd, the former UCLA football star. In Rommie, we have another black owner. Above and beyond his group's contracted purchase price, it had to pay $800,000 to Jacksonville's Monaco for the right to enter his territory.

However, since Wheeler had paid but a small part of his contracted fee up front, the league gets half the purchase price and half the territorial fee. The league gets it, not the founding fathers. The way I worked it out, the league gets a little more than $1 million as its share of these interlocked deals, which will help the league get onto firm financial ground.

Two of my tennis partners had wound up with the other two of our franchises.

Larry Hatfield, who made his money in data processing in Mississippi, moved to Orange County and invested in trucking, put in $750,000 to take over the southern California franchise, which will operate out of the home of the California Angels, Anaheim Stadium. It was nicknamed the Sun, another of those singular nicknames inspired by the Chicago Fire. The Portland Storm and the Philadelphia Bell are others. I don't know if this is good or bad, but it is original. A fellow member of the Balboa Bay Tennis Club, Larry wanted to operate independently with the Sun, so he bought out one partner with cash, and another, his trucking business partner, by turning over his share of the trucking business to him.

Another sporting rival and personal friend, Danny Rogers, settled our Hawaiian franchise in Honolulu for us. He found financial sponsors there, although the primary sponsor is Sam Battistone, the 34-year-old son of the founder of the 375-outlet Sambo's Restaurants chain, which grossed $140 million last year. He resigned as president of Sambo's to form Invest West Sports in his home town of Santa Barbara.

Counseled by such sharp sports operators as Bill Bertka and Shelly Saltman, Battistone operates sports camps, has a big piece of the International Track Association, a big piece of the new New Orleans team in the NBA, a small piece of the Hawaii Leis in World Team Tennis, and paid $550,000 to purchase 50 percent of the Hawaiians in our new World Football League.

The Hawaiians have had to operate in the 25,000-seat Hula Bowl until the new 50,000-seat Halawa Stadium is completed. It ran into delays when the lady witch doctor there refused at first to bless it because of the deaths that had occurred during construction. Such construction is always dangerous, but workers refused to return until a high priest persuaded the lady to put her blessing to the project, thus canceling the curse. Well, it's not the first time I've been cursed.

We suffered many reversals, but that was to be expected. The most disappointing one was the loss of Toronto. This was compensated for somewhat by gaining Memphis, which we thought we had lost. We'd like to have both.

I don't think we were treated fairly in Toronto. Americans are operating a major league baseball team in Montreal. Canadians wanted to operate our major league football team in Toronto. The Bassetts are considered one of Canada's finest families. Canada is supposed to be a country of free enterprise, like ours. But efforts to stifle competition have driven considerable talent out of the country. That representatives of the government should seek to legislate competition out of the country was shocking.

Canadians were deprived of an attractive team and a place in an exciting new professional league. Had we had time to fight, we might have won, and I believe we will be back. I expect us to be in Toronto in 1975. I expect us to be in Vancouver, too. Some members of our league want a merger with the Canadian league. I do not, but we could consider it.

I expect us also to be in Mexico City by 1975 and maybe in

264

Tokyo and major cities in other countries eventually. I am certain violent, colorful American football will flourish in Mexico and Japan and it is only a matter of overcoming the obstacles to setting up shop in these foreign countries. It takes time.

We lost out in Seattle, Tampa, and Phoenix, among others, largely because of NFL interest in these towns. We would have liked to have had these towns. I think now some of them may wish they had gone with us. Phoenix, which waited for an NFL franchise rather than seek one in the WFL, wound up without pro football. Tampa paid the awesome price of $18 million for its NFL franchise and I know many there wish now they had invested half as much into putting twice as good a team in the WFL. We are happy to have Honolulu, Birmingham, Memphis and Jacksonville, among other cities I knew the NFL coveted.

There are now four pro football franchises in Florida and that may be too many. However, each city involved has a lot to offer individually and we will just have to wait to see if they all survive. We are starting off in small stadiums in Detroit and New York, but if the Wheels can hang on in the 20,000-seat stadium on the campus of Eastern Michigan University, and if the Stars can hang on in the 20,0000-seat stadium on Randall's Island, I feel the future is promising in both communities.

A lot depends on how our new organizations operate. As I have pointed out, you can organize a new league and find sponsors for franchises, but you cannot guarantee that they will operate efficiently and effectively. They may promise they will put in the time and money and energy to be successful, they may promise patience until their franchises can be established, but they may not produce under pressure.

However, if we do not have some of the multi-millionaires the old American Football League had behind it when it got

265

going, it appears we were fortunate to find sportsmen of sufficient personal wealth to put our program over the top. I think outsiders were surprised at what our owners were willing to put into our operation. They have cooperated at every turn so far.

Some of the general managers and· coaches our owners signed were well-known, others were not, but within the fraternity of football all are respected. The past was forgotten. John Bassett, Jr., signed as his general manager, Leo Cahill, a man whom John's father, John Bassett, Sr., had fired from his Canadian Football League team. But Cahill is considered a football man of considerable class. John McVay became the coach. I doubt they imagined when they signed they'd wind up in Tennessee, but things move fast in this business.

Howard Baldwin signed Babe Parilli, the ex-pro star, to coach his club in Boston and the Babe wound up working for Bob Schmertz in New York. Jack Pardee, the former Los Angeles and Washington pro star, signed to be general manager and coach of the club in the Washington area and wound up in charge of the team in Orlando. Well, this is the way it goes.

The Canadian League also provided the general manager and coach in Birmingham, Jack Gotta, and the coach in Chicago, Jim Spavital.

Many former NFL stars joined up. Ron Waller, who coached San Diego last season, became coach and general manager in Philadelphia. Tom Fears, who coached two teams in the NFL, became coach and ex-Ohio State star Curly Morrison the manager in Anaheim. Ex-San Diego standout Ron Mix became manager in Portland.

Many former head coaches and assistant coaches on the top professional or college levels moved in. Dick Coury became coach in Portland, Mike Giddings in Honolulu, Jim Garrett in Houston, Bud Asher in Jacksonville, Dan Boisture in Detroit. Former Michigan State star Sonny Grandelius became the manager in Michigan.

Most of these teams set up their own scouting systems, but to help we hired former NFL players Henry Lee Parker and Mike Mercer to set up our player personnel and scouting system and such former NFL stars as Dick Bass and Marlin McKeever to assist them in player procurement.

We obtained a scouting report on college talent. We were accused of buying it. Well, we might have, but we did not have to. One was given to us. Cloak and dagger stuff. There we were in the bushes, picking them off, one by one. But we do not intend to sign undergraduates. We do not want to make enemies in college football, which forms a farm system for pros.

If your opposition underestimates you, as it always seems to do in such situations, you can sneak up on them and catch them napping. We sent letters to NFL players asking them their contract situations and interest in us and so forth. We sent these to them in care of their clubs. These letters were treated as fan letters, as we thought they would be. Secretaries simply forwarded them to the players. They did our work for us. It was shockingly simple.

Of course, many agents and players approached us or our teams directly. In some cases, they indicated to us they were available when they were not. We had no intention of trying to get around valid contracts to sign players. We did not want to be involved in any more court cases than necessary. But in most cases, avenues of approach to attractive players were opened up to us.

We wanted the cream of the collegiate crop if we could get it, but we preferred to put our top dollar into proven pros and were prepared to wait for these players for a year or two until their contracts expired. We knew we would have to get by with a number of pro rejects for awhile, but felt we would get the fans on our side if they knew we were going to get stars soon. And we assume we will uncover a lot of overlooked talent along the way.

We were prepared in mid-January when we held our formal announcement press conference at the Marriott Hotel in Los Angeles and then later in the month when we held our first draft meeting at New York's Marriott Essex House. By lottery, Memphis got the first pick and he was David Jaynes, Kansas' all-American quarterback. We didn't get him, but we did get Danny White, another all-American quarterback out of Arizona State, signed by Memphis. We also got Notre Dame's defensive backfield star Mike Townsend, signed by Jacksonville, and UCLA running backs Jim McAllister and Kermit Johnson and USC offensive blocker Booker Brown, all signed by the Southern California Sun.

The latter first opened the floodgates. Although it was not revealed, McAllister and Johnson each received $100,000 a year for three years and Brown $50,000 a year for three years, a total package of three-quarters-of-a-million-dollars put together by our Anaheim operation. Mike Trope of World Sports Management represented the players and reported that they did much better than anything they could have done with NFL teams. They were attractive stars, coveted throughout the NFL, and by joining us, they first caused us to be taken seriously.

We have considered a draft system in which each team will have territorial rights to particular powers in college football, which might be a big boost in building interest. For example, our Southern California franchise may have first rights to graduating USC players. And possibly UCLA players, too. Our Birmingham franchise might have priority on Alabama talent, and possibly Auburn talent, too. Our Toronto team didn't want the University of Toronto. It took Notre Dame. Now that it is in Memphis, it may prefer University of Tennessee talent. We will have to make a final decision as to whether this system will work.

As much as possible, we want to accommodate players on the places they prefer to play. This is something we can offer players that the NFL does not. We will work out deals between ourselves so the teams that can sign players will get the rights to them. We are trying to sign players to long-term contracts, but these will contain an option clause with arbitration rights so they are not submitting to slavery. We want to avoid bidding wars that might get out of hand, but we have proven we are prepared to pay a fair price for talent. We have returned a choice to the players and are prepared to bid competitively for the ones we want.

We worked it out so each of our teams could construct preferred lists of prime pros it hoped to sign. But if they could not sign these players and others could, rights would be passed on. The NFL Players' Association was about to strike. The players are dissatisfied with their situation in the NFL and have put a great many demands on the owners, who were reluctant to meet them. We didn't encourage an NFL strike, but when it came it did not reduce me to tears. If we can give top pros more of what they want, we should get our share.

I doubt that few believed we would. Despite the history of the ABA and WHA, most observers guessed that we would sign few players of importance. The NFL was so big it obstructed the vision. It is incredible, but many NFL executives, writers, and broadcasters seemed shocked when good players got good offers from us and we got their signatures on the dotted line. What do they think the players are playing for, fun? If you can get more money or better working conditions from another firm, you make a move. There is nothng sacred about the NFL, nothing immoral about the WFL.

Perhaps inspired by the bonanza Ben Hatskin created for

the WHA when he landed Bobby Hull with league help, John Bassett brought me the proposition that netted three stars from the NFL championship Dolphins in Miami. An agent for Larry Csonka, Jim Kiick, and Paul Warfield—Ed Keating of Mark McCormack's office—had approached him with a proposition. Bassett wanted to pursue it, but he wanted league help. He got it. We envisioned it as an investment in the future of our league. Like the Hull deal, it was closed swiftly.

We agreed to pay half of the $1 million front money promised them on a three year, three-million-dollar contract to be divided among the three of them as they wished. Our $500,000 was to come from contributions of $42,500 from each of our teams. The owners agreed that it was worth it to them. It was.

In signing, Csonka pointed out that he had found it impossible to have a real friendship with Miami owner Joe Robbie. He said he felt he should operate as a businessman because that's the way Robbie did. The three players had been fined during holdouts, they'd had to battle to buy decent tickets to their own games, they'd been paraded like trophies at parties. They did not even want to talk personally to Robbie when he telephoned during their negotiations with the WFL. They refused to worship at the shrine of the NFL.

The floodgates were opened wide with the announcement that three of the top players in pro football had jumped to the new league. Agents and players started to stream through to talk terms with our teams. The return from our investment in the three Dolphins came with the arrival of many other NFL stars into the WFL fold.

We tried for a Bobby Hull bonanza. We offered O. J. Simpson a $2-million deal for five years, $1 million up front and $200,000 in annual salary. He could have played for the team of his choice, presumably Southern California, where he lives, and that team would have had half the cost of his contract shared by the league as an investment in the league's future. He chose to remain in Buffalo where he will make half as much money. But we got a lot of great talent.

Another great running back, Calvin Hill of Dallas, made the move to Hawaii. A great tight end, Ted Kwalick of the San Francisco 49ers, made the move to Hawaii, too. A good defensive back, Richmond Flowers of the New York Giants, succumbed to the lure of the Islands. Well, maybe it was more than hula skirts and soft breezes. As I understand it, Kwalick collects $500,000 over three years, plus a $100,000 condominium and other fringe benefits. He was making $75,000 a year. Hill was making $65,000 a year. He gets $500,000 for three years.

Quarterbacks are the key to any football team and attracting top ones was important for us. We swiftly landed three of the best when Oakland's Kenny Stabler signed with Birmingham, Oakland's Daryle Lamonica signed with Southern California, and Craig Morton of Dallas inked with Houston. As this is written as I understand it Stabler will get $1,000,000 for five years, Lamonica $500,000 for three years and Morton $150,000 a year.

Such veteran performers as Virgil Carter, George Mira, Randy Johnson, John Stofa, Greg Barton, John Huarte, Gary Collins, George Sauer, Ron Jessie, Bill Bergey, Jim Seymour, Warren McVie, Paul Seymour, Paul Robinson, Hoyle Granger, John Elliott, and Gail Cogdill also have made the move to the WFL at this writing and more are arriving every day. Most may not be available until 1975, some until 1976, but we can wait. Some will be with us in 1974 and we will be getting off the ground in good shape.

A lot of people may have laughed when a few fat fellows turned up in tryout camps conducted by our clubs, but we

271

were looking for a sleeper or two while waiting for the stars to show up. We are not far from putting formidable teams on the field. If the history of the other rebel leagues hold up, it will not be long before our new league has clubs that can compete with the best of the old league.

NFL clubs are complaining that their stars who have signed with us will have divided loyalties for a season or two, but I prefer to respect the integrity of these players. I feel sure they will give their best to the teams which are paying them, no matter what league they are in. If the NFL is so insulted that their stars chose better offers and prefers to release them, we are prepared to put them on the payroll immediately. Court rulings so far suggest only that we cannot employ these players promotionally in the present as long as they are marked only for future delivery. We will respect this. We will lodge an antitrust suit or test the NFL option-year clause in court only if the establishment interferes with us unfairly.

We have signed some great stars who asked that the announcements of their defection not be made until season's end and we are respecting this. In any event, throughout our first season every team has been able to point with pride to the certain improvement these defecting NFL stars will bring to the team's second season. This is quite a selling point.

We have begun an operation which will have a $36 million budget in its first year. We may pay $15 million, $20 million or more for players. Air travel alone will cost $2.5 million. Stadium rentals may run $1.8 million. We are providing major jobs for approximately 450 players, 50 or 60 coaches, and countless executives, scouts, and staff personnel. Ours is a major business venture.

As I write this, our first season has started as a smashing success. The early attendance was too good to be true. We drew crowds of just over 55,000 and just under 65,000 in Philadelphia, just under 60,000 and just over 40,000 in Jacksonville and over 60,000 in Birmingham. I always am optimistic, but I was stunned. And suspicious. So it came as no shock to me when our owners in Philadelphia admitted that its announced attendance of 120,000 to its first two games included around 100,000 admitted in at less than full price, and some at no cost at all, and those in Jacksonville confessed about half its 100,000 total for its first two games were in on reduced rates or free passes.

As I have said before, you can't completely control the operations of your owners. But I have always said and, after these revelations I repeated emphatically, I want only true paid attendance reported. You cannot fool the press and public and I know better than to try, even if others do not. This situation hurt me and it hurt our league, especially because it hurt the credibility of our league. The worst part of it was that doubts sprang up about absolutely honest reports of good attendance elsewhere in our league.

The fact is that just getting as many people as we did into our ballparks at the start of our season in midsummer was remarkable, regardless of what they paid or did not pay, and paid attendance is encouraging in most towns. I now believe we will be a smashing success in some cities. We will not succeed in others. We have some soft spots. But, as you know by now, I expect these. You anticipate problems. And you solve them. That's the way I work. Attendance in New York and Honolulu should pick up sharply when we get into the good ballparks lined up there. Detroit and Portland pose problems, as do one or two other franchises. We will lick these or we will move into other towns. We will either shift franchises or start new franchises in attractive cities soon.

As I see it, I stand to profit by more than a million dollars from the formation of my league. I don't see anything sinister

273

in this. You enter business to make money. This is big business and I expect to make big money. I hope to have a lot of fun, too, and finish with a sense of accomplishment. Whatever money I make, I will split with my partner. It is a fair return for what we are putting into it. I do not know how long I will stay in it. I am sure something else will come along to pull me away before long. The lure of politics is one thing which pulls at me. But I plan to stay in the World Football League longer than I have in my other ventures. This is a larger venture, and I am more deeply invested in it and committed to it than I was with the others.

I will serve as commissioner and this time I am prepared to do all the hand-holding necessary. It will work, and I will make it work. I feel sure it will be a big success, and I look forward to all the ups and downs on the way to the top. We will take some backward steps, I am sure, but more forward steps. We will have problems for which I will have to provide solutions. One way or another, I will work them out. It is enormously exciting. Well, that's what life is, as I see it—making the most of yourself, making a good life for yourself and your family, finding exciting things to do, taking up challenges, taking chances, working hard, having fun, living to the limit.

CHAPTER 15

As Others See It

DENNIS MURPHY
[BEFORE WORLD TEAM TENNIS BEGAN ITS SEASON]

"After the basketball and hockey leagues, guys were coming out of the woodwork to suggest sports leagues to us. Someone suggested another roller derby league. Someone suggested another soccer league. Someone suggested rugby. Rugby might have a chance on an international level. It has a lot of football in it, and it's rough and exciting. Someone suggested lacrosse. It's a good game. A lot like hockey and basketball put together. Rough and fast. If it was known here. . . . But it's not. They are trying an indoor league back east. Someone suggested volleyball. There's definitely a chance there. Table tennis, too. Tiddlywinks? Truthfully, someone did. I guess they were kidding. I guess. We're going into the table tennis, I think. Since the Red China thing, it's gaining popularity. A lot of people play the game. The pros play a sensational style of game. A team-table tennis league or tour will work.

"Right now, the one I'm into is team tennis. I'm not in-

275

volved in Gary's World Football League. He asked me in. But by then I was too tied up with my team-tennis league and my L.A. Sharks in the World Hockey Association. That was before I got tied up as president of the WHA. By then I had my team-tennis league set to go with George MacCall as commissioner. I asked Gary into the team-tennis league, but by then he was tied up in the football. I think Don Regan talked him out of the tennis. He didn't think it would work. I think it will be the best of all the leagues. You have low overhead. We figure if we can average 3,000 paying customers a match we can make money. I think this will be the first league to make money the first year.

"Fred Barmen came to me with the idea of putting together a tennis tour for the gal pros. His daughter, Sherry, plays tennis and is a good friend of Billie Jean King, who was campaigning for a better break for the gals. Virginia Slims came into it as a sponsor for them and has helped them a lot. I was asked if I'd be willing to help them put on tournaments. I didn't like it. I saw too many problems. It just didn't ring a bell with me. I didn't go for it. Then I thought, why not teams with both men and women? The Davis Cup is the biggest thing in tennis with men's teams competing from country to country. Why not mixed teams competing from city to city? You get an identification with your team, your players. You'd only need a few top players. You wouldn't need a big building. You could play indoors or outdoors almost anywhere.

"I got together with Larry King and Jordon Kaiser, who own the Chicago franchise in the WHA, and we talked about it and we agreed it was a good thing. They went along with me on it. We charged $50,000 a franchise. We're each taking one. With sixteen franchises, the other thirteen brought in about $650,000. It'll be divided three or three and a half ways. Fred Barmen will be in for a cut or a founder's fee or a royalty or something. I figure to make $200,000 or so off the top. I made some money out of the hockey. It's time I started to make some money out of these leagues. That's what we go into it for. That's what all the planning and traveling and talking and sweating is for. And the fun of it. It's fun. It's exciting. To conceive a league and get it going and see it be real, that's exciting, pal.

"I took San Diego, but we're moving it to Honolulu. I've sold two-thirds of it. Kaiser took Chicago. The Kings took Philadelphia. John Bassett took Toronto. We have other franchises in New York, Boston, Pittsburgh, Baltimore, Miami, Chicago, Detroit, Cleveland, Houston, Denver, Minneapolis, Los Angeles, and San Francisco-Oakland. Jerry Fine is serving as president of the Los Angeles franchise, the Strings. We had a draft and drafted the top players, and we've been signing our share. I don't think we'll get Arthur Ashe or Stan Smith until our second year. Rod Laver was the first player picked and he may play for San Diego or Honolulu. We have got some good ones. John Newcombe will play for Houston. Billie Jean King, of course, will play for Philadelphia. So will Fred Stolle. Tony Roche and Françoise Durr will play for Denver. Ken Rosewall and Evonne Goolagong will play for Pittsburgh. Jimmy Connors will play for Baltimore, Tom Okker for Toronto, Cliff Drysdale for Miami, Rosie Casals for Detroit, Manlolo Santana for New York, John Alexander for Los Angeles, Roy Emerson for San Francisco-Oakland.

"We'll play some men's and women's singles and mixed doubles. The women's matches will count as much as the men's. The games will count, not the sets. We'll have cumulative scoring. If your man and woman win 6–4 sets, you're ahead 12–8. We've revised the scoring of games so we'll have short sets. We want to hold each match under three hours. Billie Jean King is determined to get the people hollering.

She says tennis has been held back by people sitting on their hands, then politely clapping a good point. She wants to get the people involved. I don't know how the players will like it, but she wants to stir up some excitement. I think it will be exciting.

"We're not in competition with anyone in tennis. We're adding to tennis. We've been fought at first by some of the several groups that control tennis. We expected that. They're always fighting among each other. We plan to play about four months a year—May through September. The International Lawn Tennis Association has resisted us, but there's no way we can be stopped. They felt we'd interfere with some of their European tournaments. They're trying to bar some of our players. Our franchise holders are prepared to offer alternative tournaments to our players. We're working it out. Jack Kramer's Association of Tennis Professionals said there was no way his players would be permitted to sign with us. But they're not slaves, and they're signing. Lamar Hunt's World Championship Tennis tour players are signing with us. The United States Lawn Tennis Association is ready to sanction us. We will contribute to their development fund. These things can be worked out.

"We'll probably pay our players about $30,000 a season on the average. That's reasonable. They'll still have eight months a year or so to cash in on the major tournaments. A Newcombe may make $75,000 or so. A second player $25,000. Three others $20,000. That puts the payroll at about $160,000 a team. With travel and all, the overall budget may run $250,000 a season. Each team will play twenty-two home matches. Let's take a low figure of 3,000 persons per match. Let's take a low figure of $5 a ticket on the average. That's $330,000 gross. There's no way we can miss.

"Gary and Don were too conservative on this. It's one time they were wrong. I'm taking care of them. They're representing us legally. I don't know about their football. There you're talking about at least a $3 million overhead each season. There you need crowds of 30,000 or more just to break even. There you're bucking the most powerfully established league in the business. In a sense, we're going our separate ways. Mike O'Hara, who was with us in the ABA from the beginning, is now deep into his Pro Track Tour. That's another tough nut to crack. You're dealing with a lot of numbers. The athletes are expensive, and you need a lot of them. You need 8,000 fans or more per meet just to break even. I've got the best bet going for me, I think. By the time this comes out, we'll all know if I was right or wrong. Who the hell knows in this crazy business."

MIKE O'HARA

"When we started the ABA, 90 percent of the people said we'd never get off the ground, including some very smart people. But it's alive today even though we made a million mistakes. None of us really knew how to do a professional sports thing, but we learned. The WHA has got off to a stronger start because of that learning. Seeing the WHA come together got me so excited I bought a franchise—I went into one with Gary Davidson. We paid $25,000 for it and kept it six months. That franchise is now the Quebec Nordiques, one of the stronger ones in the league, and they paid $250,000 for it. I got part of that, and got something out of the ABA.

"So, I've made money in professional sports twice in a row. When we came out with the pro track, the International Track Association, only about half the people said we'd never get off the ground. I guess they figured the guy's done it twice in a row. Well, I didn't really do the other two, but I was part of those efforts. This one I've done. It's my baby. And it got off the ground. We lost money our first season, but we expected that. Now, we've made money in our second season. Our average attendance jumped from 7,500 fans a meet to over 12,000. Our first year we had 16 meets, but they were all indoors. Our second year we've had 14 meets, but three of them were outdoors and two of them, in Japan, drew close to 60,000 fans. Next year we'll go outdoors more. We've spent more money than we thought, so we need a higher average attendance to make money, but we made a little our second season and we're only about halfway to our potential. We're getting some commercial sponsorship, too, which helps.

"We got some great athletes the first season, many more than people thought we'd get—super performers like Jim Ryun, Kip Keino, Bob Seagren, Lee Evans, Brian Oldfield, Randy Matson. We got more this second season, like Steve Smith in the pole vault, Rod Milburn in the hurdles, Dave Wottle and Chris Fischer in the half-mile and Ben Jipcho in the mile. That gives us Seagren versus Smith, a natural, to go with Oldfield-Matson, Wottle-Fischer Ryun-Keino-Jipcho, and so forth. You have to have at least two top men for competition in each event. As you get more, you get depth of competition. We got two great sprinters in John Carlos and Wyomia Tyus. We dressed up our meets a lot. We set them up so we could spotlight the stars at their peak moments, rather than have their performances lost in the shuffle of a three-ring circus. We used gimmicks, like the big shotputter Oldfield racing against gals, and Bob Hayes running against other pro football players and a lot of the news media ridiculed us for this, but it was entertainment and our most asked-for events.

"We're in our infancy, but we're growing up fast. This is one sport where a professional operation was badly needed. There weren't major leagues going like there are in baseball, basketball, hockey, and football. There was only amateur track. The Olympics are enormous, sure, but they come along only once every four years. And you can't eat gold medals. I suppose a lot of the athletes were paid under the table, but what were they paid? How did they feel about it? We've given the top competitors guarantees in order to get going. And we give them a chance to win prize money for performances. They're respectable.

"Before, great track performers had no place to go when they'd had it with the amateur scene. A man grows up; he's got to make a living. Now we're beginning to get the great young guy, too, who doesn't want the amateur hassle, who wants to be paid for practicing his profession. A lot of promoters talked about pro track before. We made it a reality.

"Dennis is all right. His tennis has a good shot. Gary and Don are all right. Their new football league has a shot. It seems that there is a lot of room for a lot of expansion in professional sports."

JOHNNY DEE

"Why not another basketball league? The NBA is solid. The ABA is established now. I was frustrated in attempts to buy ABA franchises in Dallas and Memphis. So I plan to start my own league—the World Basketball League. There are plenty of ballplayers around. We'll operate economically. We'll have eight-player teams. How many times do you see the ninth or tenth or eleventh player on court in the NBA or ABA, anyway? It's a waste. We won't disqualify players for fouls. Why foul out your stars? Instead of playing 48-minute games, we'll play 100-point games. Kids don't grow up playing basketball by keeping time—they play to a certain score.

"We won't have six guys getting together and forming a league by rounding up other guys and splitting the franchise fees. We'll find a strong leader, a commissioner, to invite bids and investigate and award franchises. We'll go mostly into cities where they do not have major-league professional basketball. We're considering Honolulu, Miami, Cincinnati, St. Louis, Pittsburgh, Fort Wayne, Syracuse, Long Beach, Minneapolis–St. Paul, Baltimore, New Orleans, and Dallas, which used to have teams; Mexico City, Montreal, Mobile, Montgomery, Hartford, Wichita, Rochester, Jacksonville, and other cities which have not had teams, as well as Oakland, New York, Chicago, and Los Angeles, which have teams. There are a lot of cities that can support big-league basketball."

SEAN DOWNEY

"New major leagues have developed in other sports and it's time for one in our national pastime, baseball. My World Baseball League will have a far broader concept than the existing league. We'll have 32 teams in four divisions which will operate on an intercontinental basis with clubs in this country, South America and Asia. Baseball is world-wide now. It is played and is popular in many countries. Cities such as Tokyo and Mexico City are sure to support a world-wide league. We're selling franchises at $150,000 each and already have sold one to an individual in Mexico City, as well as others in Tampa, Memphis, Birmingham, Jersey City, and Columbus, Ohio. We'll have a team in our nation's capital, Washington, D.C. I won't name our franchise-holders now, but they will announce themselves at press conferences in their respective cities at the appropriate time.

"I do not expect any trouble signing good players. We will attract them with the same sort of salaries that have brought players into the new football, basketball, and hockey leagues. And we feel sure the courts will permit players to make moves when their current contracts expire. We do not believe baseball players can be bound for life any more than football players can. More than 70 established players have been in touch with us already, including six members of the world champion Oakland A's. They are definitely interested. Players like Reggie Jackson, Pete Rose, and Johnny Bench could command the same sort of salaries from us as Bobby Hull and Larry Csonka commanded from their new leagues. We'd like a progressive man such as Dick Williams as commissioner.

"Baseball as presently played and structured is a bore. We will introduce innovations which will breathe new life into the game. We will have designated hitters. And not just one a game. And designated runners. And three-ball walks. We'll double the value of a steal of home late in a game. We're going to help the American public fall in love with the game all over again and, as the song says, it will be better the second time around. I'm also considering a team-boxing league. I have big plans on many fronts."

TONY RAZZANO

"The World Football League hasn't cornered the rights to a new pro football league. My Universal Football League is going to go into operation next year. One of the two is going to have to drop by the wayside, and we don't intend for it to be us. We haven't said much because we're business people. We're not promoters who put out emotional talk. I've been organizing out of my offices in Dayton, but we're going to have a summit meeting with our key people in New York City and there may be some announcements after this. We're putting this together very methodically. Right now, we're not interested in making a lot of smoke. We want fire—the real thing. We'll have $3 million franchises in cities such as Toronto, Mexico City, Anaheim, Birmingham, Tampa, Seattle, Phoenix, Chicago and New York. We will have at least ten teams on the field next year. Maybe twelve. Maybe fourteen. Money is no problem. We're alive and kicking."

MAX MUHLEMAN

"My first impressions of Gary Davidson were not good. I was skeptical of his ability and doubted his methods. After I got to know him, I came to respect him as much as any man I've ever met. He respects sports and he respects business and he has come to the conclusion that they can be combined to the profit and enjoyment of a great many people. He wasn't bound by old ideas. He took a fresh approach. He has amazingly accurate vision. He can see how things will develop. He has good judgment and makes good decisions. Some people are all on the surface. Gary runs deep and there's a lot you don't see until you get close to him. He'd make a marvelous senator or governor. He'd get things done. He's ambitious, but he's honest. He's above board.

"The name of the game in business is to make a profit. Gary gets his, but so does Don Regan, so do I, so does everyone connected with his ventures, including the players and coaches. Maybe you lose money at first, but if you operate intelligently and keep going you come out ahead in the end. We wouldn't if people didn't want to buy what we're selling.

We can't force games down throats. We put out an attractive product. Successful men are behind us. Major companies are sponsoring us. Managing our properties in the World Hockey Association was one thing, and it went well, but conducting the commercial end of the World Football League is another thing which will go even better. Hockey has a following. Almost everyone follows football.

"Gary picked a big winner this time and my company picked a winner when I put in with Gary."

DON REGAN

"Naturally, when you come up with a good thing everyone wants to get into the act. I don't know if the other pro football league will get off the ground, but then a lot of people doubted we'd get off the ground. We have a lot of things going. We've had a lot of things suggested to us. We're considered specialists in sports leagues now. No one else has established leagues from scratch. A lot of guys come through our doors with brainstorms. I'm sure Dennis gets them, too. Everyone wants to get their baby born. A guy came through here with an idea for a golf league. One would work if the pro tour they have now didn't pay so well. You couldn't lure pro golfers away from that gold mine. Dennis has his team-tennis league. I wish him well with it. I'm not sure people will pay to see Rod Laver play twice a week for ten weeks in one town. And when they don't have a Laver? Well, we'll see. Murph is sold on it. He's an enthusiast.

"Stuffy Singer came in wanting to start a handball league. O.K. Good sport. But better to play than to watch. Maybe people would pay to watch the best, but how many seats could you rig around a handball court? Volleyball has been

285

suggested. I'm interested in that. That was my game. And it's a great game. Great to play, great to watch. It's beginning to grow in popularity.

"A group of show business executives has put together the International Volleyball Association and I'm going in on it. David Wolper of Wolper Productions is president and Marty Starger and Barry Diller of ABC, David Gerber of Columbia, Gerald Leider of Warner Brothers and Berry Gordy of Motown will hold franchises along with myself, Mike O'Hara, and others. We expect to have twelve franchises in action by 1975, and New York, Los Angeles, Chicago, Toronto and Vancouver are among those set.

"I may locate my franchise in Cincinnati. Wilt Chamberlain, the only nationally known volleyball player so far, will head up the L.A. package. Chuck Nelson, a former Olympian and five-time all-American, will be league administrator. We plan to play summers and expect to have NBA and ABA basketball players, who are suited for this sport, on our teams. We will have at least one woman on court at all times. The gals really play this game and making it a mixed sport adds another dimension of appeal. I think it will work.

"Soccer hasn't caught on in this country yet, but I think the new league of a couple of years ago in this country quit too soon, just as it was catching on. The league has been kept going in some cities on a reduced level. We're putting together a league of teams representing countries overseas to play overseas. I feel sure it will work, and it could be the base for a league here.

"We have not discarded our world concept for our World Football League. It just takes longer to get in operation in other countries than it does in your own country. I'm almost certain we'll have a team in Toronto and Mexico City in our second season. And I feel sure we will put together a league of teams which will play in Japan, Germany, England, and other countries one season soon, teams which will have their own league, but will play some games against teams in this league and participate in championship playoffs. The possibilities are exciting, and we have people overseas pursuing it. I have a certain amount of wanderlust. I like to travel. I look forward to it.

"Gary and I are regarded as young, but the fact is we're fast approaching middle age. We've been making a lot of money. Dollars aren't as important to us now as accomplishments. We want to do what we want to do before it's too late. We have a lot of confidence in ourselves now. Maybe we're cocky. When we went into the ABA, we had nothing to lose. We didn't know a good thing from a bad thing. When we went into the WHA, we had a lot to gain. We knew a good thing when we saw it by then. We knew how to operate to make the most of something. Now we have approached the football league from a base of success, but we have so much sunk into it and the costs are so much greater than the risks are we could lose everything we have if we fail. It's still fun, but it's not a lark anymore. It's serious stuff. Don doesn't want to see Don and Gary go down the tube, especially Don.

"We're taking on the big boys now. The NFL owners have much more money than the NHL owners. And they're an enlightened opposition. Presumably, if they are not idiots, they have learned lessons from the NHL's mistakes. I suspect some of them have had heart failure as it has sunk in that we are for real. We have big stadiums in big cities for the most part. We have a good television contract for a starter. All right, it's not network, but compare it to what the AFL, ABA, or WHA had its first season. Or what the ABA has today after seven seasons. Or the WHA after two. Once we establish ourselves, the networks will want us. The NFL won't be able to stop them, or risk antitrust action. And when we get our world

287

concept going, we can go for international television via tele-star. There's the real potential. Soccer's World Cup in 1968 was the biggest single program in the history of television sports.

"We knew we had to go fast. The NFL has accelerated its efforts to tie up the most attractive cities. If we waited longer, we'd have lost all of them. This way, we're getting some of them. We had to move fast, but we're off to a fast start. We've got a good thing going for us, and we're going to get it going. The NFL is not safe now, and now it must know it."

Pete Rozelle, NFL COMMISSIONER: [No comment]

Don Anderson: "A publicist could have stayed at USC the rest of his life and been happy. I hated to leave. But the WFL was too exciting to turn down. It's not only a matter of money. It's a matter of growing with a going concern. Gary Davidson excites your imagination. He does things the sup-posed experts say he can't do. He made the WHA work, and he'll make the WFL work. Initial interest has been incred-ible. I think I can say we're definitely off and running on the right track."

John Bassett: "What do I think of Gary Davidson? I think he's a handsome, hustling, ambitious, opportunistic son-of-a-bitch, and I love him dearly and admire him im-mensely and would go to work for him anytime."

Bill Putnam: "I've been associated with the establishment with the Philadelphia and Atlanta expansion franchises in the NHL. The opportunity to buy the Birmingham franchise in the WFL may have taken me outside the establishment, but it was too good a gamble to pass up. Gary Davidson is a young man who makes leagues work. He has made two work so far, and I see no reason why he can't make a third work."

Tom Origer, CHICAGO WFL OWNER: "I read Cooper Rollow's story in the Chicago *Tribune* and called Gary Davidson immediately and told him I was coming to California. The major-league football market is proven. You haven't been able to buy a Bear ticket for the last fifteen years, and they haven't won many games in recent years. Chicago needs a second team.

"I'm a self-made man. I was a bus driver who didn't have a dime. Building a business is as easy as shooting ducks off a log. I have built successful businesses in contruction. I have good people running my business interests for me, and all I do is play handball and basketball and spend time with my kids. I need something to do.

"I always wanted to own a football team, but I'll run it like a business. It's football, and it's Chicago. I may call 'em the Bootleggers. I'll think of a catchy name."

[He named them the Chicago Fire.]

Larry Hatfield, ANAHEIM WFL OWNER: "Gary came to me three months ago and suggested I invest in the southern California franchise. He knew of my reputation as a guy who can take something from scratch, organize it, administer it, and make it work. I met him at the Balboa Bay Tennis Club, where we fool around with basketball and tennis.

"I made my money in data processing in Mississippi. I moved to Orange County and got into other enterprises. I didn't know if I wanted to gamble on this thing, but Gary is a persuasive salesman. I was introduced at the press conference announcing the formation of the league as the owner of the team in Anaheim, and I began to get excited about it.

"Pro football is enormously attractive to the public. We

have an attractive territory with a fine stadium. I have a general manager and a coach of the highest level. I've signed the first important players in the league. All we need now is a name."

[He had a contest, which produced such prospects as No-Names, Godzillas, Orangutans, Eurekas, Orange-Peelers, Barracudas, Vipers, and Alcoholics. He settled on the Southern California Sun. That's singular: The Southern California Sun.]

Curly Morrison, MANAGER OF THE SUN: "Friends of mine kept asking me if we were really going to get this thing off the ground. I told them I was selling my house in Laurel Canyon and moving to Orange County. My wife and I saw something on the TV news about the new league some time back. I'd been out of football awhile and wanted to get back in. I told her if this thing is going to go, I want in on the ground floor and the heck with trying to buy the Ram season seats. As general manager I ought to be able to get seats for my new team, shouldn't I? But we didn't even have a ticket manager. However, we were flooded with requests for season seats. Well, maybe not flooded. But we got wet. We're going to have the best team in the league. How? I don't know yet, but we'll pull it off."

[Six weeks before the season started, the Sun has sold 12,000 season tickets. All the good ones were gone.]

Tom Fears, COACH OF THE SUN: "We'll get players everywhere we can. We'll even look under rocks. I coached the New Orleans expansion team in the NFL. After that experience I don't know why I've been itching to get back into football, but I have been. You pay twenty times as much money for a franchise in the NFL as you do in the WFL. Make that forty times. And you can't get one-fortieth the talent. We signed the first big names in our league—UCLA running backs Jim McAllister and Kermit Johnson and USC blocking lineman Booker Brown. I didn't get anyone as good as those guys all the time I was in New Orleans. Here, you start even with your rivals and have a chance to build something."

Jack Gotta, COACH OF THE BIRMINGHAM WFL TEAM: "I'd reached my peak as a coach in the Canadian League, winning the Grey Cup with Ottawa in 1972 and 1973. I'm only forty-two and still young enough to accept a challenge. I'm from the U.S., but I have played and coached in Canada. This gives me the opportunity to come home. I guess they came after me and others like me because we were the best guys outside the establishment. But we're going to get establishment guys, too. We're going to give the establishment something to think about."

Tex Schramm, MANAGER OF THE DALLAS COWBOYS: "It didn't take us long to find out how the WFL would operate. It has been the history of our civilization that people can be bought. We've had some pretty good examples of it in some of our highest places. The WFL conducted its draft with a scouting report which was bought from someone who had access to it. Either it was an outright purchase or obtained with the promise of a position in the future."

Gil Brandt, DALLAS NFL SCOUT: "It's what you call industrial espionage. It's disappointing that we have people who will prostitute themselves for a few dollars."

Don Klosterman, MANAGER OF THE LOS ANGELES RAMS: "I do not believe as many players will jump the NFL for the WFL as jumped to the AFL. I was with the AFL. We had substantial money people as owners, like Bud Adams, Lamar Hunt, Barron Hilton, Sonny Werblin. The players had faith in these people. But the first couple of years we were still lucky to get by. Today the pension fund is so good in the NFL it will be hard for a player to leave it. And a football player always wants to prove that he's the best. And we're the best."

Bob Woolf: "I represented a lot of athletes. I'm also sympathetic with team situations. I want everyone to make a profit. After all, the team owners put up the money. And I think the WFL owners are underestimating what they'll lose. They're thinking of a half-million to a million dollars a year for a couple of years. I think they could lose one and a half to two million a year for years. And these guys are not as well funded as many of the original AFL owners. However, the WFL is the greatest thing that could have happened for the players. It sets up a rapport for discussion in our negotiations."

Manny Fernandez, MIAMI DOLPHINS: "The NFL has us over a barrel. Most players would love to see the new league get off the ground. There is probably room for such a league. Pro football is the most popular sport with the biggest TV money, and its players are the least paid. The new league finally gives them a little bit of wedge. You've got to make the money while you can. People might wonder about my loyalty to the ball club, but what about the club's loyalty to the players? If you're not able to produce here, you're down the road. That's as far as loyalty goes."

Larry Csonka, MIAMI DOLPHINS: "The World Football League offered Jim Kiick, Paul Warfield, and myself more than we anticipated, even more than we asked for originally, more than we could have gotten from Miami. We agreed to go as a package because we thought it would bring the best deal and that is exactly the way it worked out. We would have been foolish to pass up the sort of future security our contracts provide us and our families. Loyalty is not a key issue. We had no choice which team we'd play for when we were drafted. We could be traded at any time. We have given the Dolphins our best and we will continue to do so until our contract runs out. We'd love to go out with a third straight Super Bowl victory. And then we will give our best to our new team in our new league. Money was a big consideration, but not the only one. We were not all happy with the organization in Miami. I don't want to talk about it, but we're looking for happiness, too."

Daryle Lamonica, OAKLAND RAIDERS: "I no longer was happy with the Oakland Raiders. The new league gave me a choice. The southern California team offered me a much better contract than I had been getting. I had a choice and it was pretty clear-cut."

Ken Stabler, OAKLAND RAIDERS: "Money didn't make me make my move. I was born in the south and raised in the south and played college football in the south and the Birmingham bid gave me the opportunity to return to Alabama. Also if I can do for the WFL what Joe Namath did for the AFL, I will feel that I really have accomplished something for football."

Joe Namath, NEW YORK JETS: "If I find I am able to play football this season, I will play out my option with the Jets. And then I'll decide on where I go from there. It's flattering to hear I helped get the AFL off the ground and to have it suggested I could do as much for the WFL. It's flattering to hear I may be offered a lot of money. It would be something to think about."

Jim McAllister, NEWLY SIGNED WFL PLAYER: "Southern California is my home. I've played with Kermit Johnson since we were in the fourth grade. We wanted to stay together. A new league will make a deal where you can play in your home area or wherever you want to play. The money was right. It was there now. It might not have been there later. Why should we have waited to see what the NFL would do for us?"

Mike Trope of World Sports Management, REPRESENTATIVES FOR MCALLISTER, JOHNSON, AND BROWN: "After a careful analysis of the figures being paid NFL rookies and veterans, we found that what the WFL offered was unbeatable. We spoke with no less than seven NFL clubs. We felt the players were at their peak value. Our job is to get the best deal we can for our clients, and in this case we felt this was the best deal. We are not partial to the WFL. We are partial to the idea of a second league which gives players bargaining power."

Rich Roberts, LONG BEACH *Independent-Press-Telegram:* "I think the NFL has reached the point where it needed competition. It is too fat, too smug with its product, too satisfied that it has become the national pastime which can do no wrong. The Rams were one of the few teams in the NFL last season which played interesting and exciting football. Most teams depended on field goals, and their games were dull. The college games I saw on television were more wide-open and entertaining. I had occasion to see a city championship playoff game and was surprised how much faster I had to write to keep up with the action.

"I think the WFL can be a boon to pro football fans if it restores balance between offense and defense. I am, however, afraid of gimmicky rules which will go too far. I think the WFL can be a boon to pro football players by providing them bargaining power and a choice of places to play. I worry, however, that salaries will shoot up to the point where the players will be spoiled and operating a team will become difficult economically. I look forward to seeing some WFL games, but worry about overexposure of football on TV, which could kill interest.

"It's one of those wait-and-see situations. It will be interesting."

Robert Markus, CHICAGO *Tribune:* "The question everyone is asking is: Will the new WFL get off the ground? My answer is: Of course it will. The real question: How high will it fly?"

Rich Koster, ST. LOUIS *Globe-Democrat:* "Davidson could manage an upset. He's done it before."

John Hall, LOS ANGELES *Times:* "Are we having fun or are we having fun. It's exciting. More jobs, more room, more action for all. Beautiful. Let's have a new league every week. But the Sharks of the WHA have just been sold to their third absentee group in less than two years. The silver linings have their clouds. The AHA helped hike basketball salaries out of sight. The WHA is even shakier. We wish the WFL well and pull for them and all the new people. But it's a funny thing about dream machines. Many quickly dissolve into nightmares."

Bill Verigan, NEW YORK *Daily News:* "Those wonderful folks who launched a war by founding the World Hockey Association have struck again."

295

Bud Furillo, LOS ANGELES *Herald-Examiner:* "I'll tell you all you need to know about Gary Davidson. He never finishes a sentence. He's in too much of a hurry. His league will work because he will make it work. He's moving too fast for anyone to catch up to him."

Melvin Durslag, LOS ANGELES *Herald-Examiner:* "There is no objection in the least to a new league starting if it can serve some constructive purpose. Is it able to offer first-class entertainment without running up the price of tickets, without undue burden on creditors? AFL owners saw their investments explode in value. That's all that's needed to dilate the pupils of those hungry for a rapid buck. Their tongues hang out a foot. They start to pant. Like a pride of lions, they smell a kill."

Wells Twombly, SAN FRANCISCO *Examiner:* "Other than the desire to romance a beautiful woman or go drifting off into the sunset in a yacht with purple sails, there probably isn't a stronger instinct in the minds of most men than owning one's own sports team. Gary Davidson manufactures franchises like hamburgers. He's the Colonel Sanders of sports. He has created a need for things where none existed. He is 39 and looks 29, proving that sin doesn't necessarily show in the face. This is a great American Sportsman in the truest sense."

Gary Davidson: "I am a sportsman. I am also a businessman. I make a business of sports. The leagues I create would not remain in business if there was not a place for them. They create jobs for players and other people in the profession. They raise their standards of living. They provide entertainment for the public. If I make money along the way, what's wrong with that?"

GARY DAVIDSON is commissioner of the World Football League. He lives in Laguna Beach, California, with his wife, Barbara, and their two daughters and two sons.

BILL LIBBY is the author of over forty books, many of them on the subject of sports. He lives in Westminster, California, with his wife, Sharon, and their two daughters.